Dangerous Adolescents, Model Adolescents

Shaping the Role and
Promise of Education

Perspectives in
Law & Psychology

Sponsored by the American Psychology-Law Society / Division 41 of the American Psychological Association

Series Editor: Ronald Roesch, *Simon Fraser University, Burnaby, British Columbia, Canada*

Editorial Board: Mary Durham, Jane Goodman-Delahunty, Thomas Grisso, Stephen D. Hart, Marsha Liss, Edward P. Mulvey, James R. P. Ogloff, Norman G. Poythress, Jr., Don Read, and Regina Schuller

Dangerous Adolescents, Model Adolescents

Shaping the Role and Promise of Education

Roger J. R. Levesque

University of Arizona
Tucson, Arizona

KLUWER ACADEMIC / PLENUM PUBLISHERS
NEW YORK, BOSTON, DORDRECHT, LONDON, MOSCOW

Library of Congress Cataloging-in-Publication Data

Levesque, Roger J. R.
    Dangerous adolescents, model adolescents: shaping the role and promise of education/
    by Roger J.R. Levesque.
        p.   ; cm.—(Perspectives in law & psychology; v. 13)
    Includes bibliographical references and index.
    ISBN 0-306-46767-4
        1. Education, Secondary—Social aspects—United States.   2. Teenagers—
    Education—Social aspects—United States.   3. Problem children—Education—Social
    aspects—United States.   4. Educational law and legislation—United
    States.   I. Title.   II.   Perspectives in law & psychology; v. 13.

LC191. 4 L46 2002
370.11'5—dc21

                                                                                    2002023011

ISBN 0-306-46767-4

©2002 Kluwer Academic / Plenum Publishers
233 Spring Street, New York, New York 10013

http://www.wkap.nl/

10 9 8 7 6 5 4 3 2 1

A C.I.P. record for this book is available from the Library of Congress

For my brother
Gilles Lucien Levesque, 1960–2001

Preface

Teachers make a difference. As someone who grew up in one of the poorest and rural areas of a poor state and ended up attending elite graduate and professional schools, I have much to credit my public school teachers. My teachers sure struggled much to teach an amazingly wide variety of students from different backgrounds, abilities, and hopes. Given that reality, which undoubtedly repeats itself across the United States and globe, one would think that I should be quite hesitant to criticize a system that produces countless grateful students and productive citizens. I agree.

The pages that follow surely can be perceived as yet another attack on already much maligned schools that do produce impressive outcomes despite their limited resources, increased obligations, and the sustained barrage of attacks from competing interest groups. Some may even view the text as an affront to the inalienable rights of parents to raise their children as they see fit. Others surely could understand the analysis as another assault on our decentralized legal and school systems that should retain the right to balance the needs of communities, parents, schools, and students. I clearly did not intend, and do not see the ultimate result, as yet another diatribe on the manner teachers, parents and communities treat students.

I embarked on this project to understand what kind of environment today's adolescents need and what teachers, parents, and communities can do to address those needs. I also embarked on this project to determine how adolescents and their environments best can be supported to effect the outcomes and ideals our society formally promises but does not always deliver. As a result, I have been struck by the possible role law and basic social science can play in efforts to create responsive schools, families, communities, and most often ignored, adolescents. I also have been intrigued by the tendency to polarize the rights and obligations of parents, schools, communities, and students. An honest look at the actual rights and obligations that serve as fodder for the polarization reveals much less support for absolutes than it does for shared interests, goals, expectations, and needs. Likewise, an honest look at social science evidence reveals that no single person nor single institution can be charged with the responsibility of promoting positive adolescent development. The analysis that follows simply offers what we know about schools' responses to adolescents' developmental needs and explores the contours of what laws can allow and, hopefully, can foster. In addressing those issues, the text certainly leaves room for further analyses, especially some that would envision concrete steps for reform and more concrete ways to address polarizing tendencies. This text has a more modest goal: to examine and envision what can be done to address adolescents' needs and propose that we actually can better address those needs while remaining faithful to the rights of others.

My hunch is that those who read the following most likely will feel the same way I do: grateful for the education that they have received and hopeful that others can dream and achieve their own goals. My hope is that we can take that gratitude and hope as the starting point to engage with the research, analyses and proposals offered here and try to imagine how schools can help deliver the promises that our liberal, democratic, civil society reminds us we must constantly evaluate, develop, and seek to achieve.

ROGER J. R. LEVESQUE

Acknowledgments

The final product of this project benefitted much from the editorial guidance provided by Ronald Roesch, editor of the *Perspectives in Law and Psychology* series. I did not expect that he actually would be the one to edit the text and take such an active role in sheparding the manuscript through the development process. The end result certainly benefitted tremendously from his broad understanding of psychology and law and from his perceptive suggestions for revisions. As I am approaching other projects, I now realize even more deeply how Professor Roesch not only helped strengthen this text but also spurred directions for future works. I expect to be in his debt for a long time.

The initial conception of this project benefitted much from the guidance and support of Bruce Sales. His response to my initial conception of this book led me to rethink an entire portion of the manuscript. That rethinking ultimately led me to add an entire chapter and produce what I see as the book's most important contribution—the need to link our social science understanding of moral development, developmental criminology, and optimal functioning with laws and policies that shape adolescents' schooling. Given the result of Professor Sales' early response to this project, I remain quite grateful to him and still amazed that I have been fortunate enough to join his program at the University of Arizona.

Much occurred during the initial conception and final revisions of this book, and many events clearly impacted its content. My family grew by one. Helen, my wife, and I were blessed with our third child, Thomas. Thomas has brought great joy and a wonderful sense of craziness to us and his brothers, Henry and Marc. That joy and feeling that the world is ours to conquer certainly fueled much of my optimism. That sense of optimism came to a quick halt the day Professor Roesch and reviewers accepted the text for their series. Although I was delighted to have the book accepted, it was on that very day that I learned that one of my older brothers was involved in a life-threatening accident. My brother died less than three days later. The horror, shock, and devastation felt by so many, and the continued need to live our lives without my brother's physical and emotional presence, did much to confirm that people can and do make a difference. When people have passed away, there seems to be a tendency to bestow them with high praise and high regard for the manner they lived their lives as spouses, parents, children, siblings, friends, colleagues, and even as strangers. I would like to claim an exception, for few I know could live up to my brother. Others may like to claim exceptions too. In fact, I suspect that many would want to claim exceptions for people they know, which leads me to conclude that there is much more hope in this world than we tend to imagine. For that feeling of hope and the many things my brother has done and continues to do for me, I would like to acknowledge and thank him from all my heart. His untimely and tragic departure has left a lot of pain, but I thank God every day for having sent him to me and his family.

Contents

II. CHALLENGES FACING ADOLESCENTS' EDUCATION

CHAPTER 3. DANGEROUS ADOLESCENTS   65

Adolescent Offenders and their Offenses   66
    Nature of Offenses Deemed Worth Addressing   67
    Characteristics of Adolescent Offenders   69
The Place of Schools in Addressing Adolescents' Offending   73
    Control Measures   73
    Curricular Responses   77
    Community Influences   78
Dangerous Adolescents, Education and the Law   81
    Constitutional Parameters   81
    Legislative Mandates   88
    State Mandates   100
    Preliminary Conclusion   106
Conclusion   108

CHAPTER 4. MODEL ADOLESCENTS   111

Model Adolescent Social Development   112
    Nature of Social Values Deemed Worth Developing   113
    Characteristics of Adolescents' Social Development
        and Model Social Orientations   115
    Preliminary Conclusion   123
The Place of Schools in Fostering Model Social
        Development   124
    Curricular Responses   124
    Schools' Moral Climates   130
    Preliminary Conclusion   134
Model Social Development and the Law   135
    Federal Constitutional Parameters   136
    Federal Legislative Mandates   143
    State Constitutional Mandates   144
    State Legislative Mandates   146
    Preliminary Conclusion   149
Conclusion   149

CHAPTER 5. THRIVING ADOLESCENTS   153

Adolescent Mental Health: Its Dysfunctions and Promotion   155
    Mental Health Dysfunctions   156

III. FOSTERING ADOLESCENTS

I

Developing Law to Educate Adolescents

1

Education's Role in Fostering Adolescents

Society pays close attention to adolescents' actions. Much of the modern history of adolescence involves attempts to control and limit this age group's freedoms deemed potentially disruptive to society. So fervent is the scrutiny and concern for controlling adolescents that their actions frequently serve to index society's general health and civility. As a result, when both society and adolescents face challenges and encounter disruptions, the public responds with a sense of crisis. The crises are deemed particularly potent when the disruptions occur in public places, especially in schools that essentially exist to control and direct adolescents into responsible citizenship. In those instances, both adolescents and society are deemed at risk.

Recent murderous rampages by students, armed with guns and ammunitions more befitting soldiers on battlegrounds than students on playgrounds, illustrate how adolescents serve as barometers of societal health and civility. The events shocked and horrified a public that otherwise had become inured to reports of violent crime. Many sought answers as to why students would pose such a public threat. Speculations about the root causes offered a variety of sources: inadequate home life, over-burdened teachers, inattentive school officials, corrupting media, easy access to weapons, declining moral standards, sex discrimination, victimization, racism, inadequate penal systems, etc. (e.g., Jenson & Howard, 1999; Sousa, 1999). All explanations linked to a perceived deterioration in the manner adolescents now treat one another in an increasingly troubled and challenging society.

3

Although the young killers exemplified a distressed society unable to foster adolescents, they also served to confirm the essence of a resistant, defiant, and precarious adolescent subculture. Evidence of adolescents' alleged resistance to authority takes many forms, so much so that even normal adolescents are perceived as defiant and hedonistic. Their speech is viewed as uncivil; and their modes of dress—such as boys' long hair, earrings, and baggy pants—often are seen as vulgar or at least as expressing too much autonomy and self-expression (Myhra, 1999). Their interests continue to be viewed as narcissistic and lacking in commitment to the welfare of others or society (Cohen & Cohen, 1996). Their interactions with others are perceived as harsh and marked by rampant bullying and harassing (Stein, 1999). Adolescents' romantic relationships are deemed inconsiderate, and actually violent at so many levels that they themselves do not even recognize the violence (Higginson, 1999). Their music is viewed as so coarse, insensitive and immoral that it incites them to violence (Strasburger, 1997). Even their aspirations are maligned as they allegedly make adolescents drifting dreamers with unrealistic goals (Schneider & Stevenson, 1999). Although available evidence does not seem to match popular perceptions that adolescents, as a group, are in crisis any more than other age groups, society continues to fear that adolescents are in a state of moral decline, and that the family, school, and church have lost their power to shape the coming generation responsibly.

SCHOOLING'S SPECIAL ROLES AND FAILURES IN FOSTERING ADOLESCENTS

Society had responded to the plight of adolescents. One of the most common features of the American political landscape includes charges levied to all major social institutions to take better care of adolescents. The family, child welfare systems, juvenile justice systems, schools, religious organizations, and even the media and other big businesses are exhorted to reconsider how they treat adolescents. All institutions are currently being challenged, revived, dismantled, or reformed to shore up adolescents' proper social development. For example, welfare reform increasingly aims to address adolescent pregnancy (Levesque, 2000a); and the reform's promise to increase the number of working parents creates important challenges to fill non-school hours for adolescents whose parents will work rather than directly care for them (Quinn, 1999). Health reform's emerging focus on managed care also impacts adolescents; the renewed focus on prevention and healthy development directly aims at service provision for adolescents (Santelli et al., 1998). Juvenile justice reforms increasingly treat adolescents more like adults and seek to abolish the traditional rehabilitative features of the juvenile court, a dramatic move that responds to new perceptions of crime and criminal behavior as well as to changing views of adolescents' needs and capabilities (Feld, 1999). Even though the limited data we have seem to suggest that the intended effects of juvenile justice reforms are not being realized, the (mis)perceptions of adolescents transfer to other social institutions. The get tough approach for the sake of enhancing proper development even finds expression in educational mandates, as reflected in efforts to eliminate social promotion, introduce zero-tolerance policies, mainstream exceptional children and provide more power to parents to direct their children's education (Adelman & Taylor, 2000). Even religious institutions reconsider the place and needs of adolescents, a recognition that becomes increasingly obvious as religious organizations become central to efforts to provide services to adolescents in need (Cnaan, Wineburg, & Boddie, 1999) and religion becomes viewed as highly linked to adolescents' health (Wallace & Forman, 1998). No institution remains immune from efforts to respond differently to adolescents' needs and perceptions of what adolescents may need.

Although many institutions are being challenged to respond to the needs of adolescents and society, only public schools must accept and transform all adolescents so that they become productive citizens capable of contributing to a democratic, civil society. Although facing the difficult challenge no other institution bears, schools have not been the site of public support. Instead of support, sociopolitical responses to school failure repeatedly result in weak public confidence and constant attacks. Schools have been wracked by polarizing political conflict over their educational missions; undermined by taxpayer revolts; weakened by teacher-bashing and by massive resource and racial inequalities; and continuously subjected to rhetoric that places schools at the center of culture wars (Hunter, 1991). Students themselves do not like school much either (Steinberg, 1999); most students report being bored about one-third the time they are in school (Larson, 2000) and nearly half report being bored most of the time (Scales, 1999). Likewise, schools play an important (but not necessarily determinative) role in promoting adolescents' distress (Schulenberg, Maggs, & Hurrelmann, 1997; Elliott, Hamburg, & Williams, 1998). Given these failures, it is not surprising to find a sagging confidence in public schools and a profound sense of despair that characterizes popular discussions of adolescents and their education (Loveless, 1997).

Public schooling certainly has not been a stranger to conflict, but the impact of social conflict on schooling now appears unusually excessive. Since its beginning as an effort to inculcate a common (Protestant,

Anglo American) culture through compulsory, common schools, public education has been at the center of repeating cycles of struggles over cultural turf, community boundaries, and efforts to create cohesion and unity out of diversity and self-absorption (Levesque, 1998a). Yet, it is only within the last decade that the challenges have been so great to question seriously the very notion and existence of public schooling. Commentators now note that the compact between the public and public education is close to null and void, so much so that leading commentators consider public schools essentially dead (Liberman, 1993) or, if not dead, at least irretrievably about to be transformed (Minow, 1999). The increasing abandonment is particularly momentous given that the commitment to public schools decreases as the civil rights movement aggressively expands to address new mandates regarding race, gender, disability, economics, sexuality, violence and multicultural issues. As society burdens public schools and recognizes their fundamental place in ensuring more people's rights, desertion increases and challenges the very nature of schools deemed the bedrock of democratic life. In fact, the increased regulation needed to foster democratic schooling urges commentators with a wide variety of expertise and from a broad spectrum of political ideologies to conclude that society must move beyond public schools as a means to educate adolescents (Perkinson, 1995). Even those committed to public schooling argue that it is necessary to save public education from public schools (Arons, 1997) and that a system of non-public schools best meets public school values (Sugarman, 1991). As a result, one of the most popular approaches to privatizing public education—providing parents with vouchers and control to enroll students in schools of their choice—permits the sole legal requirement for education provided by alternative schools to be the simple confirmation of students' attendance (Keller, 1998).

Although commentators offer different futures for schools, differing views frequently agree on fundamental points. Schools ostensibly have lost their ability to foster adolescents. While no single body of data can document the state of American education and it remains important to recognize many schools' successes, all major evaluations point to consistent failure. Most notably, the National Assessment of Education Progress, which provides the "nation's report card," reveals that even dramatic reform efforts have been far from successful. Nearly one-third of the nation's high school seniors fail basic geography questions, almost two-thirds fail basic history questions, and where there has been the most improvement, mathematics, only 16% of seniors meet the requirements set by the National Educational Goals Panel (Macchiarola, Lipsky, & Gartner, 1996). Further, commentators typically agree that adolescents themselves are in need of reform so that they could be more caring and responsible adolescents. For example, numerous reports reveal the subtle and ignored forms of maltreatment adolescent victims suffer at the hands of peers and how even victims engage in high levels of offending, much of which occurs in schools (Levesque, 1998b). Both areas of agreement distill to the fundamental point that schools' alarming failure roots in their inability to inculcate values and provide the skills necessary for adolescents to be productive and responsible members of society.

Despite pervasive agreement among commentators that schools fail both adolescents and society, reform proposals paradoxically fail to focus on adolescents and their place in society. A close look at current discourse about educational policy making and educational reform reveals that it has virtually nothing to do with adolescents. Recent efforts to impose national educational standards are grounded on the need to address the nation's economic vulnerability, not adolescents' individual needs (cf., Heise, 1994). Likewise, arguments about school choice essentially involve issues of parental choice to determine their children's entry into and exit from particular schools, not children's own choices (Ravitch & Viteritti, 1996). Concerns about student expression and adolescents' need for information really deal with school official control of curriculum, not students' demands and legitimate needs (cf., Verchick, 1991). Reforms to address school violence deal with societal fears of guns, gangs and violent adolescents, not necessarily the everyday fears and needs of students (Hyman & Snook, 1999). Cutting-edge policy approaches that guide the development of further educational reform and seek to include all relevant stakeholders actually fail to include students and opt to include their representatives—parents (Evans, 1992; Parker, 1996). Even commentaries that urge a more aggressive turn to human rights law in order to recognize adolescents' fundamental right to education in hopes of enacting more effective reform essentially ignore the adolescents they ostensibly aim to assist (cf., Levesque, 1998c). Although these mandates also include important forces that temper reforms so that they actually do consider the needs of adolescents, the mandates do clearly point to concerns that frequently override adolescents' own needs and interests. The needs and rights of adolescents in school settings remain pervasively subordinate to other concerns. Current discourse about education does not offer much hope to those interested in adolescents' own educational rights and the development of policies that address adolescents' peculiar needs.

Despite persistent failures of school reform, few commentators on law and education have sought to offer a different paradigm that actually would include a concern for adolescents' own interests, needs, and rights. In fact, discussions lump adolescents with children and fail to consider adolescents' peculiar needs and place in society. Nevertheless, existing models actually do explore adolescents' rights to the extent that they treat adolescents as children. The dominant model that pervades discussions of children's educational rights rests on the fear that championing the rights of those to be educated will unacceptably abandon students to their rights (Hafen, 1993) and lead to useless litigation that will be costly and damaging to perceptions of public schools and to the reputations of school officials best suited to control students (Pedersen, 1998). That fear often leads commentators to support more authoritarian measures in homes and in schools (Dupre, 1996) and to argue that indulging children's rights leads to violence and "open season on teachers" (Johnston, 1999, n. 24). Commentators who address the educational rights of children, though, increasingly champion the notion of family choice and pay more attention to community needs than to children's own interests (Salomone, 2000). Those who do champion children's own educational rights challenge the illegitimacy of abandoning children to their parents' control, even to the extent that they view the parental right to place children in parochial schools as unlawful (Dwyer, 1999). Even these latter commentators who include adolescents in the rights they champion, though, seemingly abandon adolescents. Those who advocate this approach fail to enumerate the nature of schooling that would take adolescents' rights more seriously since it remains unclear how public schools, as evidenced by the numerous criticisms highlighted earlier, actually do (and can do) a better job at fostering adolescents. Given the violence, moral malaise, and low academic achievement levels that afflict many public schools, reinventing private schools in the image of public ones remains as problematic as efforts to reinvent public schools in the image of private schools controlled by private rather than public interests.

Much like legal commentators who discuss the legitimacy of children's educational rights, experts who concern themselves with adolescent life or with formal schooling's place in fostering healthy social and psychological development also seemingly fail to champion the rights of adolescents. They fail to do so to the extent that they do not offer alternative paradigms and do not delineate the type of legal system that could sustain alternative approaches to adolescents' schooling. Instead, policy makers continue to turn to schools to eradicate or alleviate whatever new and larger social problems confronting society (Cuban, 1990). Leading reformers increasingly call upon public education systems to do more than teach and to confront issues that were unheard of in the recent past, with the most prominent proposals championing the need of schools to become—massive child-care systems (Finn-Stevenson & Zigler, 1999), disease and mental health provision systems (Dryfoos, 1995; Kronenfeld,

2000), and even systems that provide families with legal assistance to navigate social service systems (Goodmark, 1997). As commentators call on schools to do more in service provision, they place less effort on describing the types of schools that would be needed to foster adolescents. Clear and important exceptions to the trend exist. Several now highlight a need to harness the legal system to reform the nature of schooling to address, for example, sexual harassment and the rights of adolescents to protection from violence (Levesque, 2000a; Stein, 1999). Yet, bridging existing social science evidence with the law to offer comprehensive, systemic legal reform in light of our understanding of the place of adolescents in law and society remains to be done.

The gap in legal analyses and reform proposals is significant. The needs and social crises schools face do more than account for school failures. They reflect the vital societal role schools must play in efforts to maintain basic social institutions and ensure individual fulfillment. Ever since society regulated schooling, it has recognized and sought to foster schools' role in personal and social life. The Supreme Court, for example, has recognized the essential nature of education, viewing education as central to "maintaining our basic institutions" and "the fabric of our society" (*Plyler v. Doe*, 1982, p. 221) and as a "principal instrument in awakening the child to cultural values, in preparing him for later professional training, and in helping him to adjust normally to his environment" (*Brown v. Board of Education*, 1954, p. 493). Unsurprisingly, exigent crises lead to even more powerful proclamations of schools' role in building democratic societies, healthy economies, and upright citizens (Loveless, 1997). Yet, the beliefs confirm the seriousness of education's contemporary predicament more than they help address adolescents' needs.

The continued failure to respond appropriately to adolescents' needs suggests that, if changes in public institutions impacting adolescents are actually to benefit adolescents, reforms must do more than overhaul current systems. Reforms must consider adolescents' peculiar needs, rights and place in society. Yet, as we have seen, adolescents' rights and how they impact efforts to address their needs remain pervasively ignored, excluded from public consciousness, and neglected in commentators' discourse.

A NEW DIRECTION FOR SCHOOLS AND LAW REFORM

The failure to develop a model of adolescents' needs and rights to complement suggestions for reforms in the massive restructuring of public services and schooling's place in modern society suggests at least one fundamental proposition. Successful reform requires a more refined and comprehensive image of adolescence, both individually and collectively. Although in several ways not immune from the political biases that impact reform, the social sciences already offer broad guidelines that may be used to effect more competent adolescent development, more civil relationships, and more concern for society. The social sciences also understand how society can create environments conducive to learning and preparation for living in a democratic society. The legal system has yet to harness these insights to enhance the socialization of adolescents. This text delineates the extent to which laws and policies may accommodate adolescents' needs and foster social systems so that schools may move toward recognizing adolescents' own rights and needs.

Chapter 2 provides further introductory materials to complete Part I's analysis of the law's historical and contemporary place in educating adolescents. The chapter details the role of law in the development of formal, public schooling in the United States. The analysis first charts modes of education in colonial times and their transformation with the advent of common schools—a system of schools that aimed to provide moral training, discipline, patriotism, mutual understanding, formal equality, and cultural assimilation. The review reveals the need to consider social, political, economic, and familial forces that impact perceptions of adolescents to understand school reform and its effectiveness. The historical analysis then continues to describe fundamental themes emerging from the progressive era to the cosmopolitan period, ranging from the early 1900s to the 1980s. The review reveals a general societal effort to control adolescents' educational choices, homogenize adolescents' experiences, and to absorb diversity while still trying to respect cultural differences, ensure parental rights and foster adolescent autonomy. The discussion further reveals how the legal system, as exemplified by Supreme Court jurisprudence, essentially repeats what have become the contradictory goals of education. The Court balances bipolar conceptualizations of educational purposes: either the cultural necessity of preserving community values or the adolescents' necessity of freedom to ensure the development of a self-actualized adult who will participate meaningfully in democratic processes. The Court's view of education's dual roles opens an important window of opportunity for those interested in school reform and rethinking the balancing that constitutes adolescents' rights.

Part II bridges research on adolescents' experiences and place in law with the need to rethink the dual roles currently bestowed on education: education's need to inculcate values to ensure community preservation and simultaneous need to preserve adolescents' own capacities for individuality important for democratic societies. Thus, this part examines particularly controversial educational reforms that highlight the extent to which society must inculcate values and how educational institutions might do so to reflect adolescents' changing place in society. Again, the legal rationale for the discussion derives from the manner the law allows (and sometimes requires) school officials and parents to place more focus on adolescents' control of their own rights and the extent to which social science findings confirm adolescents' increasing need to control their own lives.

For heuristic purposes, the analysis necessarily disaggregates components of adolescents' social and psychological development. Discussion focuses on research from three different fields that rarely intersect—fields of research dealing with problem adolescents, model adolescents and optimally thriving adolescents. The reality, of course, is that these components of adolescent development remain intricately intertwined. As we will see, when programs of research do examine different components of adolescent development, they often find links. Thus, adolescents who exhibit the most positive healthy development engage in many risk activities deemed delinquent; in fact, a certain *low* level of delinquency seems critical to healthy emotional and prosocial development (Shedler & Block, 1990). The categories and areas of emphasis, then, will serve to highlight critical points and themes that actually do span all aspects of adolescent development and suggestions for proper societal responses.

Chapter 3 is the first of three chapters devoted to examining adolescents' educational rights in the context of how adolescents' public lives require reforming the provision of education. The chapter examines trends in social science findings relating to delinquency, violence, and violence reduction efforts. Given the massive amount of research in this area, the discussion focuses on the peculiarities of adolescents' violent and delinquent behavior and the roles schools play in the creation and alleviation of such behavior. The analysis then examines school-related legal responses to adolescent offending and victimization. Those two discussions reveal an increasing disjuncture between legal conceptions of adolescents' rights and what can be done to address violence and delinquency more effectively.

Chapter 4 examines schools' efforts to foster responsible public behavior, how schools increasingly must respond to legal mandates that permit yet limit the extent to which schools may indoctrinate adolescents so that they become more prosocial citizens. The chapter evaluates numerous laws and legal principles that regulate the manner schools encounter issues of morality across the curriculum. Like the previous chapter's discussion of how laws may comport with empirical findings, this analysis is prefaced by a social science review of adolescents' moral development. The review examines both the peculiarities of adolescent moral development and the roles schools play in fostering or stifling the development of moral and prosocial adolescents. The social science and legal analyses urge re-evaluation and reform of legal mandates.

Chapter 5 details the current failure to address adolescents' mental health needs and the necessity to address those needs in order to foster less violent and more model behavior. This chapter addresses the nature, extent, and opportunities to enhance existing links and the need to consider the role of mental health in school reforms. The analysis first examines the nature of adolescents' mental health dysfunction and adolescents' positive mental health. The discussion then focuses on the peculiarities of adolescent development that challenge efforts to foster positive mental health, a discussion that serves as a springboard to discuss the role of schools in shaping mental health outcomes across adolescent development. As with previous chapters, the social science analyses provide the necessary background for a legal analysis of current and emerging efforts to address adolescents' mental health issues in school settings and the roles schools can play in fostering healthy mental health.

Part III responds to the failure of schools to enhance adolescent development through enacting legal reform. This part consists of Chapter 6, which charts ways the legal system could better foster healthy adolescent development. The proposals complement the previous chapters' suggestions that the legal system must consider adolescents' diverse needs and aim to foster adolescents' abilities to exercise responsible self-determination. The analysis supports, and responds to potential criticisms of, an increased need to restructure—through law—the moral foundations of education. The conclusion emphasizes how current approaches to adolescents' needs and popular views of adolescents' roles in the most fundamental social problems confronting society—violence, racism, sexism, poverty, disability, discrimination, etc.—ironically ensure that the problems will continue. The conclusion places the text's central concern—the development of adolescents' educational rights grounded in a social science analysis—as a necessary part of efforts to provide adolescents, and everyone else, with greater opportunities to flourish in our democratic society.

2

Law and the Development of Public Education

American history reveals the law's powerful role in directing adolescents' education. The law has long served to specify what could be taught, how it should be taught, and even ensure that adolescents are taught. Given the law's centralizing role, formative developments in law and social influences on those laws necessarily serve as initial discussion points for understanding current educational trends and for imagining future efforts. Although links between the law's historical role and future reforms remain uncharted, the discussion need not go unguided. As we will see, numerous commentaries already chronicle well key historical moments in the development of public schools. These discernable periods have left critical imprints on the nature of public schooling and the social forces that sustain it. The periods span from the 1600s to the 1980s—from colonial times, to the construction of the modern common school system, to the progressive era and up to the cosmopolitan period. Although historians understand well those periods, many of which have been the subject of important controversies and commentaries, the role of law in those periods remains less documented, with the notable exception that many commentators do mention that law played a necessary role in the establishment of public schools, both in its design and implementation.

The pervasive lack of detailed analysis coupling historical and legal developments provides the impetus for the analyses that follow. The law impacted public schooling much more than by the obvious manner it mandated school attendance and required the establishment of schools. Legal systems influenced schooling by exerting powerful leverage on formal and informal institutions that would help shape images of adolescents and society that fostered school reform. This leverage means that we must examine when why, how, and for whom society (and the many social institutions constituting it) constructed a system of formal education. A close examination of the dominant (and some diverging) currents in each historical era contributing to the construction of formal education necessarily reveals the manner society, through its public schools and the law, construes its collective obligations to adolescents and what it expects from adolescents themselves.

A central theme that emerges from the historical record reveals that society constantly seeks to preserve itself, and through that need, exhibits a desire to save and control adolescents so that they will ensure social stability. As we will see, that need would lead to the emergence of formal schooling and the founding of "common schools," those aimed at inculcating common values and skills into the next generation. The same need now urges a recent move away from public, common schools and explains why common schools still retain their essential validity. Indeed, many of the historical and present challenges facing public schools stem from efforts to establish common schools for all and efforts to determine the place of adolescents in society. The law gains importance in those efforts to the extent it can encourage, reflect, and delimit the contours of those challenges and determinations.

The analysis that follows emphasizes the law's role in schooling and institutions impacting schooling. In fact, the discussion of the law's role in the prevailing rationale for schooling—the preservation and sometimes reconstruction of society—serves as a foundation for the remaining chapters. The analysis suggests that educational reform must move beyond focusing on academic skills alone and must respond to adolescents' place in society. Educational reform must both reform the nature of schooling itself and embark on concomitant improvements in the legal system's responses to adolescents' familial and communal experiences. Although constituting an ambitious agenda, urging consideration of the law's multiple forces and roles remains a far from radical approach to understanding and fostering educational reform. The historical record reveals well how the law's already expansive reach continues to expand. As it has in precolonial times, the law influences education through pressure exerted on the control and development of adolescents by variously regulating the institutions—mainly family, work and church—that serve to enculturate adolescents. The law now also influences education through new socializing institutions—child welfare and juvenile justice systems—developed to "educate" adolescents, respond to new images of adolescent development, and forge a new place for adolescents in schools and society. Despite the development and significance of non-school institutions in the education of adolescents (and the reshaping of those institutions and their relationships to schools), public schools have become the dominant center of response to modern society's demands. Schools have become the site of societal responses to social crises, most notably a rise in family breakdown, racial tensions, youth violence and victimization, religious dissension, economic deprivation, disease epidemics, and conflicting views of adolescents' place in society and the law. This chapter details how schools have assumed this powerful socializing role in adolescent development and the manner law and social forces shape that role.

THE COLONIAL PERIOD

Antecedents to today's educational system trace as far back as colonization. Colonization of the United States began with the 1630s' migration by those dissatisfied with conditions in Europe, those who sought various new opportunities, and those who had no choice but to migrate to the colonies. Many different motives underlaid the establishment of the colonies. Although the search for profit played a key role in urging exploration, historical records, though, reveal different motives for those who would actually settle. The Puritans of New England left the fullest record, and the reason they did so reveals their intentions. The Puritans documented their efforts because they hoped to set an example for the Old World by establishing a model Christian commonwealth (McClellan, 1999). To serve as an example, they migrated to establish religious utopias based on their interpretation of the Bible and sought refuge from persecution for their religious faith (Button & Provenzo, 1983). Concern that their children would drift away from faith and culture would lead colonists, including those who were not Puritans, to mold several basic institutions that would exert control over their children and, through that control, educate them into their proper place in society.

COLONIAL EDUCATIONAL INSTITUTIONS

Methods of obtaining educations essentially were the same methods used to socialize children into adulthood. Becoming an adult entailed an ongoing process rather than a discrete sequence of sharing common experiences of a distinctive legal status. No common age-graded experiences predetermined when a child would leave home, become apprenticed, obtain gainful employment, or get married (Bledstein, 1976). The heterogeneity was significant for at least three reasons. First, the diversity and absence of age differentiation in social gatherings meant that this part of the life course was too undifferentiated to constitute a formal and sociolegally recognized period of adolescence (Kett, 1977). As we will see, the "discovery" of the period of adolescence actually would come approximately 250 years later. Second, how the notion of adolescence essentially did not exist in colonial times reflects the absence of the need to formally educate adolescents. Colonists lacked formal, widely accepted institutions devoted solely to the education of children. Third, the available conceptual vocabulary to distinguish children from adults reflects colonial Americans' educational opportunities. Although the adolescent stage of life connoted neither a uniform set of experiences nor a fixed age span, colonists used the category of "youth" to describe individuals whose ages spanned from 10 up to 30, a time frame so large that colonists' term lumped together young children, apprentices, farmhands, servants, and slaves (Kett, 1977). This broad category of youth reveals that colonial efforts to educate adolescents needed to address immense diversity in individual development and place in society; these diverse experiences and needs fostered different educational "systems." The more educational systems needed to address common needs, the greater role law played to help address those needs and even foster more common experiences.

Although seemingly limited and informal, several institutions offered educational opportunities. Families served as the center of education, and education had a religious purpose. Thus, the most devout families used a range of occasions to instruct their children. So that children would be raised in faith and be credits to their families and communities, they were taught to read and sometimes to write so that they could be disciplined and drilled in the church catechism (McClellan, 1999). Despite variation in the extent to which families from different social and economic backgrounds and individuals within certain families benefitted from education, historians generally report that families responded to the educational inclinations of society and taught children basic educational skills, including reading levels necessary for religious activity (Cremin, 1970).

Families also educated other peoples' children. After families of origin had provided a grounding for education, it was not uncommon for these families to apprentice their children to other families. In addition to obtaining educational opportunities from families, youth gained educational experiences from apprenticeships. Although these family-type arrangements could be informal, they typically provided that masters go beyond the basic training of the child for a vocation and provide basic education in religion and civil law (Seybolt, 1969). Likewise, in some instances, the agreements called for masters to teach the skills of reading, writing, and arithmetic. Apprenticeships also served as the dominant manner children without families received educations. Colonists placed out orphaned, wayward, destitute, or dependent children to work with other families' production of their needed goods; or integrated them into their own families; or involved them in the family economy of their masters (Hawes, 1991). In addition to apprenticeships, indentured servitude was an important means of educating youth, particularly those who migrated without families. This form of education was very prominent in the South, where the training mirrored the commanding socializing force of the patriarchal household in New England (Galenson, 1981). Importantly, education did not necessarily mean learning to write or read; education meant that adolescents would understand and behave in certain, approved ways. Ways of learning were educational in the broadest sense of the term.

Youth received educations not necessarily because of their own desires and aspirations. Colonists often used education in the form of work, particularly apprenticeships and servitude, as a form of punishment for youths' unruly and immoral behavior (Brenmer, 1970). As noted earlier, children became adults by working with, acquiring the skills of, and by functioning as adults. The extensive focus on labor, however, reveals more than the primary manner individuals became adults. The use of labor to educate indicates well the communal, rather than the exclusively nuclear familial, character of child rearing in colonial times. Even when young people left their own parents' homes, they lived with their master's household or with other families. The focus on family-based labor and education also reveals attempts to exert control over youth. Colonists molded institutions to operate as families that provided stability, demanded accountability and sought to instill civility.

The above two educational institutions—work and family—played key roles in socializing and educating youth; but these institutions were complemented and reinforced by religious institutions. The colonial period reveals the church's tremendous impact on everyday life. The church played an overt, forceful, pervasive and significant role in efforts to control and educate youth in family and community life (Smith & Hindus, 1975). Church leaders and other community members actively oversaw child rearing, so much so that the colonists viewed child rearing as a communal endeavor in which religious, community, and private responsibilities overlapped (Sutton, 1988). As a result, families and masters were supervised both by caring and curious neighbors as well as civil and religious authorities. In addition to impacting families, churches played a key role in educational efforts. Education and religion were entwined, so much so that religion ultimately served to justify the founding of schools and public school systems.

In addition to apprenticeship, familial, and the church's efforts to educate youth, the colonies directed and supported schools. As with the previously examined means of offering educational opportunities, schools and their support varied tremendously. Colonial schools ranged from community schools supported by public funds meant to provide education for all to a more manorial system aimed to educate the elite deemed worthy of education (Cremin, 1970). Variation derived from four interrelated sources: the cultures transported from the Old World, the geographical location of the colony, the dominant modes of production, and the significance of religion. Variations in the nature and support for schools derived from the manner different groups of colonists transplanted and modified their cultures and institutions to deal with new conditions and the reasons for migration. These above sources of variation find clear expression in comparisons of Northern and Southern colonies.

The different colony's new environment and modes of production related closely to variations in schooling. Sustenance farming meant that individuals would gather together in small towns in the North. The emergence of small towns allowed people to live in close proximity, which, in turn, allowed for the inception of centralized schools in community settings. In addition to small towns, religion inspired educational opportunity in the North; and education reinforced family structure (Cohen, 1974). The commercial, agrarian orientation of the South meant more dispersed communities. As a result of dispersion, the southern regions did not develop formal schools but instead focused on educating youth through families, churches, and communities (Urban & Wagoner, 1996). The South's wide distribution of the population meant that schooling was more individualistic and generally unavailable for all but those who could maintain tutors on the plantation. The dominance of class-oriented education in the South helped ensure that it lacked the more religious fervor of the North and the family structure to encourage education. As a result, indentured servants, indigent and orphaned children who migrated to the South received little education compared to their Northern counterparts. The South had little incentive to educate them; and the system of chattel slavery even ensured that education would not be provided to many for fear that education would incite rebellion. Most southern colonists tended to accept the prevailing precept that education was essentially a private matter, a nuclear family's concern (Urban & Wagoner, 1996). Thus, New England colonies provide the major exception to the general rule that education mainly occurred at the private level—in private schools, dame schools (a person's home), or classic one-room schoolhouses with one teacher who had contracted with parents. Even in the North, though, education still was organized locally, not compulsory, and not universally free. Formal educational opportunities reflected the diversity of community needs, and those needs helped justify formal schooling or its lack of it.

LAW'S ROLE IN EDUCATING COLONIAL YOUTH

The divergences in education may have been wide, but the law still played a powerful and centralizing role in all educational efforts. The laws of the late 1600s and early 1700s exerted considerable oversight over the schools, limited the power of schools, and provided important justifications for schooling. Colonial governmental organizations oversaw schooling even before the colonies became states with constitutions. Massachusetts' famous "Old Deluder Satan Law" provides an often-cited example (Dillon, 1879, pp. 106–107). Passed in 1671, the statute required townships with over 50 households to teach children to write and read to counter Satan's effort to keep men from knowledge of the Scripture needed to escape the powers of temptation. The Middle Atlantic and Southern colonies were more pluralistic; religious pluralism was evident in the diverse sects that became part of the region. The diversity meant that each religious group designed its own educational system to reflect its religious beliefs. It would take many years for other colonies to follow suit and enact broad laws regulating schooling. When they did, however, they too emphasized the moral education of youth. Thus, in 1723, Maryland passed an act to provide for the "liberal and pious education of the youth of this province" (Dillon, 1879, p. 112).

It is not surprising that colonists justified educational efforts in terms of the need to inculcate traditional religious ideals. Legislatures frequently were motivated by the consideration that ignorant people would easily fall victim to evil forces that would drain them of their religious and moral values. Although the intense focus on education for religious purposes—saving youth—has been seen as limited to the Northern colonies that first provided for public schooling, other educational mandates reveal the significance of religious beliefs and need to inculcate moral values in the other colonies as well. Laws reveal that religion served in statutes not only to justify schooling but also to justify the control of those who taught in schools and in churches. Teachers pervasively came from the ranks of ministers; and schools of higher education were founded to produce ministers of religion (Lubick, 1999). As early as 1619, the Council of Virginia ordered a "college to be erected in Virginia for the conversion of infidels" (Dillon, 1879; p. 110). Even in states that were undeveloped in terms of legislating schooling revealed the importance of religion and concern for the inculcation of values by controlling those who would teach. In 1712, South Carolina passed a prescription regarding who could teach in Charleston schools, and that statute reveals concerns about the advancement of religion. The statute provided that the master "be of the religion of the Church of England, and conform to the same, and ... to chastise and instruct youth in the principles of the Christian religion, as professed in the Church of England" (p. 114). The focus would endure. When the colonies did become states, education was significant enough to warrant statements in their constitutions. Those statements again conspicuously reflected the need for a religious ideological system. Those who would teach, for example, were required to exhibit piety and good character, and colonists defined piety as religious orthodoxy (Cremin, 1970). Thus, Massachusetts' constitution, ratified in 1789, called for the "support and maintenance of public Protestant teachers of piety, religion, and morality" (Nolan, 1998, p. 130). New Hampshire's constitution, framed in 1784, provided support for "public protestant teachers of piety, religion, and morality" in the belief that "morality and piety, rightly grounded in evangelical principles, will give the best and greatest security to government" (Id.). These statutes illustrate the moral sentiment that governed the educational environment it helped create.

Although seemingly simple, the laws reveal several key points. The laws reflect communal concern with educating children and the need to address children's inclination toward sin through teaching the doctrines and principles of Christianity. The laws also reveal the state's responsibility in guiding the development of education as a condition of saving individuals, a prerequisite to ensuring the development of society. Given that responsibility, the state took it upon itself to control the content and conduct of education, establish supervision of education, use public funds to support education, require education for all students, and develop such massive regulation without input from the local community and parents. In the North, which would lead the effort toward more common schools for all, these mandates reflected the pervasive belief that salvation of the human soul was the major function of the body. Man was created to prepare the soul for eternal life; and intense study of the Scriptures increased the chances of salvation. These regulations reflected well the need to control and inculcate youth.

The moral sentiment prevailing educational endeavors is important to emphasize. It reflects adults' control over children and the need to model civil behavior. The effort to control reflects a dominant theme of the institutions that regulated the lives of youth. The authority was present in formal and informal environments that educated youth: homes, work, church, and community. Although numerous, these educational settings and surrounding social environments had much in common. They operated within statutes that limited adult power to inculcate youth. Although the power was limited, adults commanded the respect and attention of children in some form of domestic relationship: Either it was a parent-child relationship or one in which other adults stood *in loco parentis*, in the place of parents. Regardless of the adult in charge, educational settings exerted considerable power to control and educate youth.

The broadest power over children's lives undoubtedly constituted the authority granted parents by the legal system. Reviews view parental authority over children as nearly absolute. As with today, the patriarchal family served as a primary means to govern youth. To the colonists, the family was hierarchical and patriarchal (Grossberg, 1985). All but death or maiming were within the parental prerogative to correct and control their children. In 1646, Massachusetts passed an important "stubborn child" law, a statute that made a child's stubbornness a capital offense (Teitelbaum & Harris, 1977). The law, which several of the other colonies quickly adopted, applied only to "stubborn or rebellious son[s], of sufficient years and understanding (*viz.*) sixteen years of age" (Sutton, 1988, p. 10). By applying to what we clearly would consider adolescents, the legislation sought to enforce traditional authoritarian relationships, to assure rigid conformity of thought and action in future generations, and to sustain the community's allocation of responsibilities among appropriate spheres in the social order—all of which would limit broader social conflict and maintain established authority (Teitelbaum & Harris, 1977; Sutton, 1988).

Importantly, families did not escape direct regulation in the manner they raised their children, and those limitations related to educational mandates. Legal systems mandated families to provide educational opportunities, an important form of regulation that contradicts the general view that parents had control over their children up to the point that parents were deemed sovereign. Laws that limited parental sovereignty took many forms. If parents were judged incompetent or inattentive to their children's (and their community's) welfare, laws provided public officials with the power to intercede in family matters. Public inspectors could visit homes to insure children's proper care and education. Communities could send children in need of care to others, as revealed in apprenticeship laws and indentured servitude laws (Urban & Wagoner, 1996). Some laws also explicitly stated that parents had an obligation to educate their children. In 1642, Massachusetts law compelled heads of households to ensure that their children learned to read and understand the principles of religion and the capital laws of the country (Dillon, 1876; p. 105). Other New England colonies passed similar laws. These laws were considerably important as they underscored the community's intrusive role in education. Those derelict in their duty could be fined, have their children placed as apprentices, or could be subject to criminal penalties from legal authorities (Wall, 1990).

The governmental willingness to support parental power—even to the point that parents could put to death children over 16 who cursed or smote them—was not evidenced as so extreme in other relationships. However, the transfer of parental power through the legal doctrine of *in loco parentis* ensured that those who did serve as authority figures could be quite severe in their control of children. Teachers apparently exerted considerable control over their charges, but they probably had the least power compared to other authority figures. Documents from the period provide no examples of litigation involving the extreme discipline of colonial students (Bybee & Gee, 1982). The nature of educational institutions provided extra-legal methods that operated to limit their prerogatives, such as their reliance on the parents and community for food and shelter and the wide variety of students who could restrain teachers by the potential of their retaliation (Bybee & Gee, 1982). Apprentices and indentured servants, though, generally were in positions that favored their masters. For example, for disrespect or physical retaliation, an apprentice could be whipped publicly and imprisoned (Seybolt, 1969). The power granted masters was deemed necessary since adolescents were often sent to them as a form of punishment for unruly and immoral behavior (Bremner, 1970). On the other hand, when youth were in situations where others had more power over them, youth actually were bestowed considerable rights. Thus, laws required masters to go beyond the basic training of the child for a vocation to the provision of a basic education in religion and civil law (Seybolt, 1969). Colonies enacted statutes that enjoined guardians to educate those in their charge. In 1643, for example, the Virginia Assembly's statute provided that guardians "educate and instruct them according to their best endeavors in Christian religion and in the rudiments of learning" (Urban & Wagoner, 1996, p. 28). Although other colonies would enact similar statutes, the extent to which these statutes were followed remains unknown. The statutes do reveal, though, the extent to which communities acknowledged the significance of education and sought a public role in ensuring education. The colonial experience reveals the significant power adults wielded over those who served them.

As much as the above laws affirm adults' immense power over adolescents, they also delimit the boundaries of that power. The legislation sought to enforce traditional authoritarian relationships, to assure rigid conformity of thought and action in future generations, and to sustain the community's allocation of responsibilities among appropriate spheres in the social order—all of which would limit broader social conflict and maintain established authority (Teitelbaum & Harris, 1977). Although seemingly focusing on control, it is important to note a change in the nature of that control. Rather than having parents enjoy sovereignty over their children and masters over their charges, the law entrusted control to the state. The state provided the outer limits of adult's rights, obligations, and responsibilities toward youth—all to ensure that youth would take their proper place in society.

The period beginning with colonialism and ending with the revolution reveals education's important functions. Regardless of its form, education served to control adolescents. This control reveals how education responds to assumptions about the nature of adolescents and seeks to build the type of education appropriate for them and society. The formal role of schools in the pre-Revolutionary period must be acknowledged, but it remained subordinate. Schools were subordinate to more powerful educational agencies—the family, the community, and the church, all of which sought to save and control adolescents.

Despite the dominant ideology of hierarchic and patriarchic control found in key institutions, the environment produced by this focus actually did not control youth as much as may have been hoped. Although adults expected deference and the prevailing ideology of child-rearing fostered the control of youth, youth still managed to escape control. Despite the tight network of formal institutions committed to moral education and the extraordinary public scrutiny of family life, many were able to escape scrutiny. Several historians now note that some families were able to evade official scrutiny and allow their children to live instead by much less demanding cultural dictates (Gildrie, 1994; Greven, 1977). Likewise, considerable evidence reveals how adolescents actively resisted whenever possible. Many report how the experience of youth involved more "patterns of disorderliness and violence" rather than the romanticized picture of stability, control, and order (Kett, 1977, pp. 60–61). Characterizations of adolescents of the late 1700s and early 1800s continue to describe them as restless, and society began to view young people as a new social problem. It was this lack of control, and the perceived need to foster greater social reform, that would contribute greatly to the founding of the common school movement.

THE POST-REVOLUTIONARY "COMMON SCHOOL" PERIOD

American revolutionaries essentially ignored education's potential role in building and preserving a more perfect union of states. Revolutionaries pervasively limited their major effort to establishing independence from England. In terms of experiences in the colonies, revolutionary leaders generally sought to preserve the status quo and not change the nature of their fellow citizens. The forces that led to the revolution, though, necessarily contributed to changing theories of schooling, transformations in community and family life, and even the dramatic "invention" of adolescence. The legal system again reflected and fostered important changes. Although this era continues to be viewed as one when public schools were community and state matters, growth in the states that joined the union involved a consistent effort to support and establish common, public school systems.

SOCIAL TRANSFORMATIONS IN ADOLESCENT LIFE

A key notion to emerge after the Revolution was a deliberate cultural nationalism. The Revolution emphasized the worth of governments based upon the principles of classical republican ideology of responsible citizenship. Jefferson was perhaps the only major theorist to have put forth his ideas on education during the revolution; and his proposals to create a system of common, public schools were pervasively rejected until the 1830s when more support for the scope and impact of his proposal was seen as a necessary response to rapid social changes (Button & Provenzo, 1983). Even Jefferson, though, had not advocated too radical changes. His efforts ignored large segments of the population (especially women and Blacks) and aimed to educate elite leaders (Perkinson, 1995). Eventually, Jefferson was joined by Benjamin Rush and Noah Webster who all advocated what would become "common schools" (Butts, 1978; Madsen, 1974). These reformers envisioned schools that would transmit the principles of the new republicanism and serve as the medium through which governments could empower a virtuous citizenry to establish a new national social order.

The works of Jefferson, Rush and Webster reveal a consistent emphasis on properly educating individuals so that they can assume the responsibilities of citizenship. Education in responsible citizenship meant learning the virtues of liberty, just laws, morality, hard work, and patriotism. Although those responsibilities were often described as participation in democratic governmental institutions, preparing individuals for that form of participation ensured that education had other corollary mandates. Education was given the task of generating a free and virtuous society, of preparing youth for commercial opportunity, of forming a national character, and shaping homogeneity out of diversity. These tasks constitute the core of the common school movement's key goals all aimed at creating and sustaining a national order.

The needs of the young nation were not enough to counter resistance to common schooling. Resistance came in several forms. Few shared deep anxieties about national cohesion enough to relinquish their control over the education of their children. Free and compulsory universal education necessarily meant higher taxes. Common schooling also meant a move away form local autonomy over educational mandates, a move away from the traditional belief that strong communities of concerned adults would find the appropriate means to perpetuate society's values and to produce citizens of faith and virtue. Likewise, the founders' federal conservatism recognized that, although knowledge was the best guardian of liberty, education did not belong in federal hands but instead in those of states (Pulliam & Van Patten, 1999). Thus, the Tenth Amendment to the Constitution defaulted to the states the power to create, maintain, and govern schools. These concerns were significant enough to prohibit efforts to develop more common schools—those dedicated to developing more broadly held social values—through the end of the 18th century. Even those important reasons for resistance, though, could not counter the fears and needs that would arise from enormous social changes that followed the Revolution.

Profound demographic, social, and economic changes of the late 1700s and early 1800s provided significant opportunities for school reform. Those rapid changes essentially involved the transformation of America from a rural, agricultural society into an urban, industrial society (Wiebe, 1967). Although the structural changes emerged from the predominantly household-based manufacturing of consumer goods to more mass production that differed among regions of the country, industrialization transformed the economy which in turn revolutionized family life. Traditional sources of social order—stable hierarchical social structures, patterns of cultural and political deference, webs of extended kinships, and tight-knit communities—weakened as images of control and orderly change gave way to visions of opportunity, movement, and freedom. As explored below, these changes greatly influenced family structure, family dynamics, images of families, and ideologies of child development. In addition to contributing to the formal recognition of an adolescent period, the changes also reaffirmed the image of adolescents as individuals who must be controlled and protected from the harsh realities of life so they could take their proper role in society. That image of adolescent life has been considerably powerful. The image, and its supporting forces and rationales, both allowed for and impacted the development of schooling and, more broadly, reflects the essence of the traditional—and now reigning—model of adolescent life.

Changes in the very structure and composition of families contributed immensely to the traditional model of adolescent life that now serves as the dominant model of how society should approach the adolescent period and the education of youth. Prior to industrialization, families essentially produced what they needed to consume. That mode of production joined people within working households. The result was that families were rather extended; families consisted of parents, children, other relatives as well as apprentices and perhaps journeymen (Demos, 1986). In response to industrialization, families lost their productive capacity and became, instead, units of consumption (Grossberg, 1985). As a result, family patterns changed; intergenerational influences waned and families declined in size.

Changes in family structures and economic production also affected family dynamics that, in turn, contributed to a different need for children and need for families. Changes weakened patriarchal authority and allowed for new images of nurturing mothers to compete with traditional images of parentage, and new images of childhood emerged to reflect and reinforce the gentler image of parenting. This transformation was made possible by the advent of smaller families that allowed them to disconnect family life from community life. In the community, the metaphor of the marketplace increasingly characterized interactions. That vision viewed adults as individuals who prized liberty and individuality, as individuals perceived as autonomous and unconnected (Grossberg, 1985). As the community was envisioned as an arena of choice, the family was perceived as the opposite. Families increasingly were differentiated from the community and viewed as social units that were enduring and connected; unlike the community, the family prized hierarchy and dependency over equality and autonomy. Families served to prepare their young for a life in the open, restless, and mobile society that would not necessarily nourish them as adults.

In separating community and family life, explicit roles emerged to guide adults and children within families. Caring husbands were supposed to provide economically for their families and caring women were expected to provide sanctuary for their beleaguered husbands and for the spiritual and physical nourishment of their children (Mintz & Kellogg, 1988). Caring parents were those who placed children at the center of family life. The value of families became inextricably intertwined with the production and socialization of emotionally and physically healthy children. Children served to justify both the husband's remunerative efforts in the marketplace and the wife's non-remunerative efforts in the home. Children became so integral to families that families without children were not characterized as families (Schneider, 1968).

These changes signaled a transformed family life. Rather than being like the community, the family was imaged as a safe haven from the harsh realities of communities. However, the family was still one marked by parental control over children. Society structured family life so that children were under the charge of parents obligated to maintain and educate children and help society produce healthy adults. The focus on adult control reflected a sense of urgency in efforts to educate and shape children's values before they could move beyond the protective environment of the home community into a world of strange people, restless activity, and alluring evils.

It is important to note that the image of parental and societal obligations was omnipresent, even though not all groups in American society universally experienced the actual socialization process. Class and ethnicity, which were interrelated, affected the ages of leaving home and duration of familial residence, length of schooling, and age of entry into the workforce (Clement, 1997; Graff, 1985; Zelizer, 1985). Despite these diverse experiences, reform was spurred by the vision of middle-class childhood—an image of children who were not expected to participate in the formal productive process (Kliebard, 1985; Woodhouse, 1992). The result was that children became viewed as valuable property and a vulnerable class in need of protection, a class inclined toward neither good nor evil, but essentially malleable (Kett, 1977). Thus, even though several children did not easily fit into its projection, the image of family life's role in child development became settled with changes in economic production, family structure and parental roles.

The ideals of domesticity meant that adolescents and families who did not fit into mid-19th century, middle-class conceptions were viewed as problematic. Middle-class adults sought to differentiate the middle-class adolescents from their more dangerous working-class and middle-class counterparts. Numerous examples highlight efforts to differentiate, which ironically would lead to efforts to make the other classes more like the middle class, efforts that would find expression in the development of social institutions discussed below. A most notable characteristic of this era involved new attention to gender differentiation, with much concern focused on the need to protect middle-class daughters from precocious sexuality (Farrell, 1999)—a concern that would eventually spread to other classes. Also subjected to much middle-class adult concern were the gangs of lower-class and working class youth who became more visible in urban street life; these groups were seen as dangerous because of their focus on physical prowess, rowdy and potentially violent behavior. Concern also was placed on dramatic increases in immigrants from Europe who brought with them languages, religions, political heritages, and cultures different from the Anglo-Protestant Americans who had preceded them (Hofstadter, 1955). These differences helped solidify the image of middle-class life, even though it is unclear that even the middle-class lived up to its own image.

The image of middle-class life gains particular significance in that it guided responses to societal changes, massive immigration and growing industrialization and urbanization. All of these changes created undesirable conditions perceived as threats to the foundation of middle-class society (Fasick, 1994). Industrialization encouraged migration and fostered population changes that weakened the informal systems of social control based on families, churches and family-based labor; those changes in systems of control produced cultural conflict and threatened traditional value systems of the middle-class. These features of early 19th century America increased the potential for youth's autonomy and independence and rendered problematic their social control and integration. The changes in family, community, and work life meant that the traditional methods of informal social control no longer proved as effective. The impulse toward freedom, then, was complemented with a move toward moral rigidity. The growing absence of external, institutional restraints required the development of strong internal controls. As a result, social changes insisted on rigid self-restraint, rigorous moral purity, upright personal conduct, and a precise cultural conformity. Although the range of religious doctrines widened in these years, a distinctly evangelical temperament pervaded society, as exemplified by moral crusades to control children's development.

The contrast between middle-class and the more dangerous lower- and working-class fostered a new image of child development. As we have seen, even though several youth did not fit into prevailing images of what children were like or what children did, all were viewed as malleable and valuable. These two features were critical and needed to support the dramatic social reconstruction of childhood and the education of youth. The notion of malleability was used as a means to secure help for children, especially those of poor immigrant families, and for society itself (Fasick, 1994). Children were seen as humanity's redeemers and this role was reflected in the prevailing notion that children would mature and determine society's future. Given the urgency, society could no longer afford the variegated patterns and informal methods to engage in intensive training of the young. The solution envisioned by adult reformers was to construct more regulated, age-segregated environments during the perilous years of growing up—schools. Reformers, then, were worried not solely about the character of their own children but also about the character and education of other people's children, especially the children of America's rapidly growing immigrant population. Schools were meant for more than the achievement of personal salvation, they would preserve harmony and order. The tendency to place personal moral conduct at the core of social hopes for social stability and political liberty gave schooling a new significance. Good citizenship and the good society meant a concern with the morality of the individual citizen held the best hope for the preservation of freedom, the protection of order, and the growth of (middle-class) prosperity.

The reform movement that lead to the establishment of the common schools, the *child-saving movement*, reigned during later 1800s to the early 1900s. The movement led to the establishment of several governmentally controlled institutions and regulations (such as child labor laws, juvenile justice systems, and child welfare laws), but it would be schools that would constitute the broadest, systematic attempt to deal with the perceived threat of lower classes and the somewhat contradictory perceptions of all children as priceless innocents. That movement involved an amalgam of middle-class reformers, professionals and philanthropists, but particularly middle-class Protestant women of Anglo-Saxon descent. These activists championed the need to recognize the special, vulnerable position of children in families and society and sought greater control of both children and the lower classes which were deemed in need of assistance to raise their children into productive citizens. These reforms renewed community interest in children's lives and fostered the recognition that communities inextricably connected to family life; communities were allowed to control families through laws that never had been so potentially intrusive. Importantly, rather than simply co-opting family life, these reforms were seen as complementing and reinforcing the important roles of families or simply acting in their stead when they had failed.

These shifts were so prominent that it was within that period that a truly fundamental change in the sociolegal image of childhood occurred—the more formal invention of adolescence. By the early 1900s, the term "adolescence" was popularized, most notably by Stanley Hall (Hall, 1904). Hall and other experts viewed childhood as consisting of a series of developmental stages that differentiated children deemed immature and vulnerable from the more mature and less malleable adult. Couched between childhood and adulthood was the period of adolescence, which was now conceived as a natural and universal developmental stage. This development in the formal invention of adolescence resulted from the same forces that had spurred the child-saving efforts. The child-saving metastructure enforced age-segregation, prolonged dependency, and promulgated rules that governed the social lives of youth (Macleod, 1998). The focus on mutability, vulnerability and inherent worth contributed to views of adolescence that constituted a period not close to adulthood but rather as a part of childhood. The develop-ments reflected the centrality of and cultural emphasis on childhood that must be allowed to progress through developmental tasks to achieve full physical, psychological and moral maturity (Empey, 1979). Adolescence was conceived as a stage that routinely produced crises, which if left unat-tended and unregulated could generate more crisis and social turmoil as well. For example, vulnerable girls who engaged in precocious sexual activity jeopardized their futures as well as those of their children and the future of all generations (Farrell, 1999). The focus on potential crisis and need for direction produced a concept of adolescence that would serve to justify the prolonged social and economic dependency of youth, and rationalize the differentiation, separation, and segregation of adolescents from adults, until the adolescents were mature enough to be deemed adults. This broad-gauged standardization of youthful experiences into age-segregated activities removed adolescents from the remainder of adult society and created what is now viewed as a distinct adolescent sub-culture, a physically, emotionally, and socially demarkable period in human development (Demos, 1986).

The role schools played in the emergence of what we now recognize as modern adolescence reveals the power of the common school move-ment. That immense power took many forms, as revealed by revisionist accounts of common schools' new roles in defining the morality and social values taught to adolescents as future adults of a common society. Katz (1968) proposes that the common school movement primarily aimed to train workers for new factories, educate immigrants into acceptance of values supportive of ruling elites, and provide order and stability among the expanding population of cities. Kaestle (1983) argues that the common school also aimed to ensure that the United States would not become a multicultural society. Tyack and Hansot (1982) emphasize how white Anglo-Saxon Protestant men headed the movement, established curric-ula, set pedagogical precedent, and publicly debated what values were to be taught; they conclude that women and non-white persons were sys-tematically excluded from holding positions of power and from defining the contours of public debates. Spring (1997) views the teacher's role as to teach children not to transgress laws, thereby replacing the police. That concept of teacher as police made the common schools the central institu-tion for the control and maintenance of social order. Walkerdine (1985) reveals how women, viewed as natural caretakers, were viewed as crucial to the development of republican citizens for the nation. According to this view, women were viewed as naturally suited to inculcate moral virtues in the young; women were expected to teach children to "self-regulate" and internalize self-control through a pedagogy of maternal care. These accounts of common schooling highlight how numerous economic, political, and moral interests converged not only on schools but on the social reproduction of the next generation.

Given the role schools needed to play in adolescent life and society, the focus on the "common" nature of schooling constituted an important political move. The focus allowed the movement to keep political controversy out of schools. Although that may have been a critical part of the reason for the effort to find common interests, concerns, and needs, the aversion to controversy was much more than a political concession. The focus on commonalities was fundamentally political in terms of its view of how people should run their lives and the state's role in socializing adolescents. It stemmed from early conceptions of common education. As we have seen, education was a didactic more than participatory exercise. Educators (parents, ministers, masters, teachers, and schools) expounded common truths, such as moral imperatives common to all religions (at least to all Christians), rather than engage children intellectually and develop their cognitive abilities (Pyle, 1997). The common schools, then, were the first public, universal attempt to preach and actually instil majoritarian values to all children in America.

LEGAL REFORMS AND NEW IMAGES OF ADOLESCENCE

The new images of childhood and rapid social transformations led to profound changes in the legal regulation of adolescent life and schooling. As the social reforms of the early 1900s extended children's attributes to the post-pubescent period the laws governing infants were similarly extended. In essence, adolescents became children under adult control and choice, and subject to adults' paternal attention (Levesque, 1994). Although the early 1900s witnessed a great deal of compulsory legislation for youth, the legislation which would have the broadest impact would be compulsory education. Compulsory education derived from America's middle-class establishment's view that a common-school could foster appropriate American values in children. As we have seen, common school reformers believed that education could be used to reduce tensions between social classes, eliminate crime and poverty, stabilize the political system, and form patriotic citizens. Education became viewed as an assimilative force that could Americanize the diverse, expanding, and "disrupting" population of immigrants in America's industrializing cities.

As with previous periods, religion again played a decisive role, so much so that common schooling often is viewed as a means to assure the dominance of Protestant Anglo-American culture (McClellan, 1999). Justifications for government-sponsored education continued to be based on traditional religious codes of moral life. Champions of the common school appealed to religion and the importance of moral values to justify government's duties. Horace Mann, a powerful figure in American educational reform, provides a notable example as he cited to the power of divine providence, the will of God, the rights of the child, and the importance of performing "domestic, social, civil, and moral duties" to argue "the absolute right of every human being that comes into the world to an education; and which, of course, proves the correlative duty of every government to see that the means of that education are provided for all" (Mann, 1847, cited in Bremner, 1970, p. 456). At the turn of the century, then, religious orientations remained strong but had become muted by other moral principles that derived from the European Enlightenment that impacted more than the declarations of independence and constitutional government. Although far from abrupt, the changes proved strong enough to challenge conspicuously religious orientations and justifications for education. This section examines how the law responded to the diverse needs for a single, common school.

Because of cultural pluralism, the establishment of the common school necessarily involved appeals to the symbols that resonated throughout society as a whole. Those who would champion the common school realized that diversity fostered by immigration and urbanization made defenses for state education rooted in Protestant theology less palatable to the general citizenry. Reformers promoted instruction that stressed the development of the republican traits of good citizenship. Although those justifications previously had been present, neutralizing the distinctive characteristic of the religious systems of moral understandings meant that ideals of good citizenship and commitment to the common good became more important. Rather than placing emphasis on skills or general knowledge, common school reformers placed far more emphasis on character, discipline, virtue, and good habits (Kaestle, 1983). Statutes illustrate well the extent to which the common schoolers aimed for specific virtues and sought to divorce education from particular religions. Statutes contained directives that were virtues related to religion but arguably common to all religions and necessary for civic participation. These virtues included moderation, truthfulness, frugality, patriotism, temperance, promptness, and industry. Massachusetts, for example passed a law that required teachers to "impress on the minds of the children ... the principles of morality and justice, and a sacred regard for truth; love of country, humanity and universal benevolence; sobriety, industry and frugality; chastity, moderation and temperance; and all other virtues which ornament human society" (Flanders, 1925, p. 159). Likewise, Washington, in 1897, mandated that "It shall be the duty of all teachers to endeavor to impress onto the minds of pupils the principles of morality, truth, justice, temperance, humanity and patriotism; to teach them to avoid idleness, profanity and falsehood; to instruct them in the principle of free government, and to train them up to the true comprehension of the rights, duties, and dignity of American citizenship" (p. 160).

In addition to a focus on civic responsibility, the new statutes also forbade sectarian influence within the public school, even to the extent that statutes forbade the use of sectarian instructional materials in the classroom. In 1875, for example, Arkansas forbade teachers employed by common schools to "permit sectarian books to be used as a reading or textbook in the school under his care" (Flanders, 1925, p. 153). In 1895, New Hampshire found that "no books shall be introduced into the public schools calculated to favor any particular religious sect or political party" (p. 153). In 1879, California would adopt a constitutional mandate prohibiting "any sectarian or denominational doctrine be taught or instruction thereon be permitted, directly or indirectly, in any of the common schools of this state" (p. 152). These codes reveal well the shift away from a strictly religious basis of education to a greater focus on civic republicanism that nevertheless still sought to promote moral values.

Concern for the control of adolescents and the need to foster adolescent development took several decades to reach the point at which society was ready to transfer the education of children from private undertakings to a society-wide system of education. The frequency of reference to education's link with moral and civic virtues suggests that the belief in common schooling became an article of political faith by the end of 19th-century America. North Dakota exemplified the states that adopted preambles delineating the political and moral purposes of schooling in their constitutions:

> A high degree of intelligence, patriotism, integrity and morality on the part of every voter in a government by the people being necessary in order to insure the continuance of that government and the prosperity and happiness of the people, the legislative assembly shall make provisions for the establishment and maintenance of a system of public schools which shall be open to all children of the State of North Dakota and free from sectarian control. The legislative requirement shall be irrevocable without the consent of the United States and the people of North Dakota. (Thorpe, 1909)

The provision does much more than emphasize links between morals, civic virtues and well-functioning society. The last clause established that the common school had become an "irrevocable" and thus inalienable guarantee of the republican form of government.

By the early 1900s, states did more than provide free education, they took steps to ensure that children attend them through the successful

accomplishment of compulsory education laws. By 1910, all but a hand-
ful of Southern states had passed compulsory education laws (Tyack,
James, & Benovot, 1987). Again, the dominant rationale involves appeals
to the need to prepare children for citizenship and for the benefit of society. Even at this point, though, much of the rhetoric and reports championing the need for compulsory education champion the rights of children,
even though the dominant rationale for that right rests on the need to
educate children for society's benefit (Nolan, 1998). Despite arguments
that children had basic rights to be educated, state statutes did not reflect
educational rights in those terms; students were to be educated in schools
designed to advance the potential person status of children by developing
competencies for productive societal membership.

Although the focus clearly meant to secure the development of productive societal members, the role of parents remained critical. Schools
were championed as a means to assist parents in the upbringing of their
children. In assisting parents, however, the transfer of children from work
to educational settings clearly involved a projection of middle-class childhood and middle-class needs onto individuals and families from other
social spheres. Several view schooling as the manner to deploy youth
within the economic sphere and serve as an important way to instill the
culture's authority structure and to ease adolescents' passage into the
world of work (Callahan, 1962; Lapsley, Enright, & Serline, 1985; Troen,
1985). This development signaled a severe limitation in parental power
that did not fit the mold of middle-class family life. Reformers viewed
schools as ideal environments to inculcate individuals into middle-class
values. Common schools served as a tool for a moral crusade to instill
democratic values, and to transform the masses into productive citizens
imbued with virtues of industry, temperance and frugality (Katz, 1968).
Parents' roles in the transformation were critical, but it was the image of
what parents should do—prepare their children for responsible citizenship—that dominated the reform.

School reform allowed the state to abrogate parental prerogatives
and grant its power of *loco parentis,* the state power to act in the place of
parents, to its ideological apparatus, the schools. As societal changes
removed children's economic value derived from child labor, schools
became children's major work setting. Schools replaced the powerful
role work had played in socializing individuals into adulthood and
community life. Rather than encouraging incorporation into adult and
community institutions, the state enforced the segregation of youth. The
development in compulsory schooling, coupled by the necessary child
labor legislation, rapidly changed the everyday experiences of youth. The
legislation effectively and systematically excluded youth from adult roles,

deprived them of adult status, and prolonged their dependency well into their teenage years. With that exclusion came the ability to control and mold children, to protect them from exploitation, and to oversee their parents (Rothman, 1980). Thus, by the 19th century's end, both educational and familial values markedly shifted from overt coercion and authoritarianism as a means of social control to participatory democracy and a "pedagogy of love" (Walkerdine, 1985, p. 206).

Schools provided the ideal site for deploying a shift from authoritarian control to internalized self-regulation as a means of social control and ensuring civility. To develop self-regulation, schools focused on the significance of individual character to achieve social morality, the importance of the family in building character, the significance of schooling to avail oneself of economic opportunity, and the need to unify America into an American Protestant culture. Despite the common school's attachment to democratic principles, the educational experiences of many were marked by discrimination and lack of control over the nature and extent to which they even could receive primary and secondary educations (Clement, 1997). Education sought to maintain the status quo through individual self-governance, acceptance, and perpetuation of the dominant cultural values. As a result, Blacks, Native Americans, the poor and women to a large extent had educational experiences that followed models of colonialism. Despite considerable focus on control and the need to regulate potentially dangerous and disruptive youth and their families, the movement still offered limited opportunities for many. Whether schools acted as structures of opportunity or of regulation and social control continues to be a subject of debate. Regardless of debates, schools clearly had inculcating functions aimed to develop citizens capable of sustaining dominant social structures.

It is important to note that other institutions were reformed and complemented school reform efforts. The juvenile justice system illustrates well how reforms swept through and developed institutions to serve children, families, and society. The formal beginning of the current juvenile justice system, at least its basic ideology of reform, actually had emerged in the early 1800s. The 1820s witnessed the establishment of the first publicly funded and legally chartered custodial institutions for juvenile offenders—the Houses of Refuge and Houses of Reformation (Sutton, 1988). These houses reflected many of the same elements of the common school movement that sought to bring adolescents under the formal control of public authority. By allowing for the removal of children considered directly or potentially delinquent, the houses provided a new means of control and containment that allowed the removal of children of urban immigrants and lower classes whose families did not provide adequate moral direction (Rothman, 1980). By saving children, activists literally intended the houses as sanctuaries and havens that sheltered youth, much as the ideal families were supposed to do. Indeed, the houses were molded after the family, which granted the houses of refuge and reform all the discretionary authority of the family, with the additional legitimation of formal law. Juvenile institutions would retain the houses' fundamental goals—to achieve a better imitation of ideal family life, and through that achievement the rehabilitation and prevention of problematic behavior.

The above efforts, which culminated in the modern juvenile court system—a separate system designed for the special needs of youth—replicated other efforts to impose middle-class views of child-rearing. The system mirrored, reinforced, and extended previous efforts in three important ways. First and as we have seen above, the basic ideology for reform allowed for intervention in immigrant and poor families derived from images of middle-class childhood. Second, the removal of youth from the criminal justice system reflected the previous effort to socially differentiate children from adults, and emphasized benevolent assistance to children as a means to control their behavior and the child-rearing patterns of their parents and communities. Third, the new system *legally* allowed public officials to intervene in the family and determined what actions officials should take. The development of the houses of refuge and reform, and the ensuing juvenile court system, reflected the creation of a strong, centralized state government that formally regulated social problems previously addressed informally and locally. Indeed, by 1928, all but two states had a juvenile court system (Platt, 1977). Reformers had sought and achieved legislative sanctions to pursue their goals, and those sanctions would allow for the legal redefinition of juvenile deviance and solidify the creation of the period of adolescence.

Following the Revolution, then, American society embarked on molding new institutions to serve social needs by transforming children. Although different institutions emerged, schooling became a primary means of reforming a diverse culture through its children. The effort to establish common schools, though, was hampered by contradictions and resistance. The contradictions were fundamental. The leaders of the movement saw education as serving Americans by helping them find their identities and realizing their full potential not only as individuals but also as citizens. At the same time, the movement's leaders felt the obligation to sustain political stability by properly shaping the attitudes and values of the younger generation. Likewise, the movement pervasively sought to foster religious values yet sought to control religious freedoms; schools sought to help parents, yet schools abridged the rights of parents.

Schools intended to preserve freedom and individualism; yet, they also meant to limit and control new class lines, broaden ethnic diversity, and accelerated geographic mobility. Schools would provide for the personal development and education of the individual and at the same time maintain political order and stability among members of the society. Given the contradictory purpose of common schools, it becomes surprising that so many were established, let alone financially supported and deemed compulsory.

The common school movement ended with important reforms. The common school movement dramatically restructured children's daily associations and exerted powerful adult control. Likewise, both children and adults were regulated by the state; common schools were administered by the state and local government. In addition, a new focus on preserving society, rather than simply saving youth for themselves, became a key goal. The common school movement established standardized state systems of education designed to achieve specific public policies. The common school also had the purpose of achieving public goals, such as remedying social, political, and economic problems. Schools existed for the public; schools were an instrument of government policy that could be used to control and solve economic, social, and political concerns.

THE PROGRESSIVE PERIOD

With compulsory education instituted in a society-wide basis and provided at state expense, educational issues regarding the states' roles in schooling took a different turn. Concern no longer centered on whether state governments should control education. Instead, concern centered on matters involving the control over the type of education that should take place in public schools and who should control the education that takes place within schools: federal bureaucracies, state governments, local community leaders, businesses, professional elites, teachers, parents, religious organizations, or students themselves. These issues were addressed and partially resolved by the Progressive era. Partly because the era has been marked by numerous agendas and massive social reforms (Berube, 1994), resolution of who or what should control educations required and supported by the state pervasively remains ignored in discussions of the progressive period. Instead, the era is best known for its other notable achievements and massive social reform efforts involving the extension of the individual-rights emphasis in education, concern for equality and efficiency, concern for adapting society to fit the needs of diversity, and the beginning of the Supreme Court's guidance of laws regulating educational reform. Without doubt, the latter reforms and achievements were ground breaking, but the manner the reforms addressed (or ignored) the fundamental question of who controls the content of education left the progress precarious. To a large degree, the significant developments typically associated with the progressive era actually pale in comparison to the significance of the manner reformers resolved issues of control that ultimately would alter the nature of modern education.

SOCIAL AND PEDAGOGICAL REFORMS

As with previous educational reforms, several social processes sustained the rise of the progressive movement. The industrialization and urbanization that began the nineteenth century continued to develop and contribute to numerous economic and social problems. Three changes particularly impacted adolescents' educational experiences. First, capitalist systems were viewed as exploiters of adolescents' labor, even though the increasingly sophisticated technological culture had the effect of making the services of the young increasingly superfluous and decreased the need for their labor. Second, new waves of immigrants arrived and challenged dominant cultures. The immigrants brought new customs and religions as they migrated from largely unfamiliar countries of southern and eastern Europe. Third, the failure of industrialization, in the form of the Great Depression, set in motion a chain reaction that caused citizens to contemplate steps to redress the imbalances of economic power. In addition to important changes in laws regulating industry (Davis, 1967), the Depression also resulted in increased efforts to address the needs of the poor in crisis, particularly their children. Although the needs of the poor would lead to several reforms, their apparent needs would enormously impact schooling and dominate its reform.

The economic and social problems influenced greatly the development of new images of children and the responsibilities of schools to respond to those images. Rather than focus on the needs of parents or society, leading progressives argued that schools had the responsibility to meet children's own basic needs. Under this approach, the state justified involvement in child development on the grounds that intervention helped fulfill children's rights and needs. Eminent reformers urged that everyone had a right to demand an education which met their own needs, and that for its own sake the state was obligated to supply this demand. Progressivists still drew arguments from the complex mixture of cultural systems evident in the common-school era, such as the need to provide schooling to secure economic reforms and preserve social harmony. But, their proposals diverged from previous reforms in the manner progressives tended to place a clear focus on individual freedom and need to foster self-determination, a focus that would draw considerable criticism.

The focus on individual freedom is most evident in the approach to the environments school reformers exhorted teachers and other school officials to create. The common schooler's approach to education was more a didactic than a participatory exercise. Teachers in 19th century America were viewed as those who expounded truths rather than guides who intellectually engaged children. Since the 19th century view conceived adults as expounding what was right, children did not have to discover such truths under a teacher's subtle guidance. The approach reflected Mann's approach to developing the common schools and attempts to preach majoritarian values, as discussed earlier in this chapter. Unlike champions of the common school, progressives promoted another approach. Most illustrative of their approach is Dewey's (1899/1990) challenge that schools should be a participatory rather than a didactic experience. Although Dewey placed great emphasis on the child's own development and discovery, he also envisioned teachers as offering room for them to develop. This is a critical point: Dewey's focus on teachers' roles generally are lost upon educators who emphasize the child-centeredness of his approach (Prawat, 2000). Through participatory environments, Dewey proposed, children would learn the lessons of democracy. Only by helping each child develop their own potential could communities achieve their own maximum potential (Dewey, 1899/1990). Under this approach, teachers followed the child's personal interests, yet they attempted to shape the direction of those interests so that children's pursuit of their natural inclinations still conformed with social needs and requirements. Aligning school experiences with real-life occupational and democratic experiences of the surrounding society would make schools a vehicle for the improvement of society. In his classic text, *Democracy and Education*, Dewey (1916, p. 87) noted the significance education holds for democracy:

> The devotion of democracy to education is a familiar fact. The superficial explanation is that a government resting upon popular suffrage cannot be successful unless those who elect and who obey their governors are educated. Since a democratic society repudiates the principle of external authority, it must find a substitute in voluntary disposition and interest: these can be created only by education. But there is a deeper explanation. A democracy is more than a form of government; it is primarily a mode of associated living, of conjoint, communicated experience.

Although child-centered, teaching took children from where they were to where the educators wanted them to be; schooling developed individual children's social capabilities so that they could participate in democratic life. Despite commitment to individual freedom, then, progressives championed schools as sites critical for incubating the democratic way of life.

The focus on participation and preparing students for democratic life would lead the progressive movement to impact two important curricular reform efforts that emerged during the early part of the 1900s: character education and the "mental hygiene" movement. The mental hygiene movement was motivated by an optimism and unbridled faith in science, particularly the science of the conception of personality (Cohen, 1983). Mental hygienists saw personality as malleable and saw the problems facing the nation as those of the individual personality that could be controlled. Given the ability to mold the early development of personality, education reforms guided by the mental hygiene movement aimed to emphasize child-centered pedagogies that could address personality issues through scientifically controlled behavior. Character education focused on Americanization and social efficiency. Like the mental hygiene movement, character education aimed to shape children's conduct according to values identified by supposedly value-neutral scientific methods (Beane, 1990). Unlike previous attempts to instill character and moral traits, progressives hoped to cultivate in students both a quality of open-mindedness and a general ability to make moral judgements. Their view of ethical behavior was that of a disinterested expert who brought both a spirit of inquiry and competence to solving problems. Reversing the emphasis of earlier moral educators, progressive educators expressed little interest in the specific moral habits of individuals (such as drinking or sexual activity) as long as moral behaviors did not impede the ability to be productive citizens (McClellan, 1999). Character, then, involved contributing to the creation of a more humane and democratic society; character education would mean civic mindedness. By emphasizing the need to judge actions by their social consequences, the progressives provided a new, purely secular standard by which to make moral decisions. Progressives would be known for their emphasis on embodying the social values of efficiency and productivity through one's industrious nature and conduct (Berube, 1994).

Regardless of leading progressives' motivations, their focus on character and mental hygiene reflected a move away from the consensus achieved by different religious groups about nonsectarian public schools. The productive system of modern society placed a premium on specialization, technical expertise, and the ability to interact smoothly in impersonal structures. Success depended less on character in the traditional sense than on skill, efficiency, and social competence. Schools responded by increasing their academic offerings, providing apprenticing, and offering vocational counseling. To acquire these skills, students remained in school for longer periods of time and were more influenced by schools. To offer these programs, schools had to move away from the traditional focus on moral education and train students for skills demanded by a distinctively modern society.

Unlike previous periods, the progressive period contended with another transformation: the increasing role of leisure. Technological advances and economic changes created new opportunities for pleasure and recreation. Most notably, mass media brought messages of personal freedom to more adolescents and the automobile revolutionized courtship (Bailey, 1988). Schools would need to respond to leisure demands which before had occurred within the context of homes and under the control of parents, churches, and communities. The new freedoms of the era took place away from the scrutiny of the home and community.

Dealing with these new freedoms and responding to changes in economic production would lead the progressive movement to become known for its expansion of schools as the new agency for social control and assuring the domination of Anglo-American culture. Rather than achieving pedagogical reform to achieve social justice, the movement has been interpreted as doing the opposite (Spring, 1997). The pedagogical alterations sought by Dewey and the progressives's concern with child-centered teaching and more democratic relations between students and teachers would only have a limited impact on educational experiences of the era. This is not to say that they would not influence education in the eras that would follow and impact what some see as the medicalization of education in the schools assumed therapeutic function formerly borne by parents, families, and other social agencies (Cohen, 1999). Despite that apparent impact, many revisionists view the movement as yet another means to instill middle-class virtues. Instead of the virtues derived from religion, the movement would evidence virtues through participation in industrialized society, a new view of virtue that has lead many revision-ists to charge that progressives were much less progressive than they claimed and that progressives actually pandered to business and corpo-rate interests of industrialization (Berube, 1994).

Although the progressive's success in influencing the style of school-ing may be debatable, few debate how the progressives revolutionized the administrative control of schools (Urban & Waggoner, 1996). Reflecting the era's faith in science and efficiency, the progressive agenda included reorganizing schools under "scientific" principles and adminis-tering them through school superintendents. These efforts would lead to massive changes in the control of schools. To foster and sustain progres-sive ideals, reformers focused on school organization and management and would take the control of the nature of education away from local leaders and bestow power to a new class of professionals trained as administrators.

The move toward the professionalization of administrators involved many critical reforms. The first most notable change involved an effort to centralize decision making by reducing the size of school boards. This effort, though not without opposition, swept away the localized approach to education. The board functioned as a corporate board of directors. It would set overall policy and monitor its implementation while refraining from interfering in day-to-day operations. Several rationales served to help reduce the size of school boards: smaller boards were deemed to be more efficient; they would remove schools from political conflicts; and they would be run by experts trained in the science of teaching (Tyack, James, & Benavot, 1987). Although the neutral authority of science was used to argue that school systems could remain above politics and that experts could best decide what most benefitted children and society, the reduction of school boards also meant that they became more representative of the progressive reformers' social class. While centralization advocates proposed that the board members would set policies that would benefit all, skeptics argued that the boards would be less attuned to the practices of the constituents, particularly their religious traditions (Urban & Waggoner, 1996). Critics of the reform movement also argued that the public schools were becoming less and less schools of the public. Reformers transposed models of efficiency from the business world to justify fundamental alterations in the administration of schooling.

In addition to efficiency in management of schooling, efficiency became a critical part of the pedagogical process. This second aspect of the most notable transformation brought by progressivism involved the manner progressive reforms actually reversed the accomplishments of the common school period. The common school curriculum emphasized the common moral elements thought important for all citizens. By the 1920's, though, American public schools had a diversified and largely uncommon curriculum. The transformation emerged from a change in the purpose of education. The common curriculum, based on the view that schools served as training grounds for the development of a common moral community and citizenship based on a polity of equals, had sought to develop all individuals into good citizens with proper American values. Progressive reform sought to develop other values that reflected a largely economic purpose for education and sought differentiation. The dominance of values that would serve economic interests reflected an attempt to accommodate the differentiated economic roles that students would play in their lives. The effort was justified by the notion that the system provided equal opportunity for all students to develop to the fullest of their abilities. The shift away from education for moral, civic virtue to economic betterment was a fundamental shift. Schools recognized students as the material for capitalist production. The differentiation of schooling into academic, vocational, and commercial emphases led to the development of guidance programs and standardized tests to place students into "proper" curricular tracks (Button & Provenzo, 1983). Schools were to use science to distinguish between students; science would permit tracking while not violating the rhetorical commitment to democracy, equal opportunity, and common education.

Questions of efficiency and scientific measurement shaped educational curricula and debates. Although Protestant values still imbedded cultural ideologies, the growth of the social sciences allowed for the introduction of new forms of social control. The social sciences offered new tools to measure efficiency and virtue. Most notable during this period is the development of the IQ test which provided a view of intelligence that allowed for a focus on meritocracy (Spring, 1997). Tests would allow for equality and self-determination, as they would place success and failure squarely on the individual rather than political or economic influence. Social inequalities that set students up to fail, or the possible cultural bias of standardized tests, were issues successfully countered by the neutral, scientific means of measuring students.

The focus on science and the periods' unbridled faith in science help account for much of the progressive movement's eventual failures. Most notably, faith in science helps account for the movement's apparent failure to acknowledge blind spots towards problems of poverty and race. Although progressives laudably sought to help the immigrant poor, for example, their approach had a nativist element. Progressives sought assimilation and encouraged immigrants to shed their cultural and ethnic trappings. Progressive education—in the form of fostering self-determination and effective participation in society—failed to adapt to a growing constituency and instead gained its greatest success in elite private schools (Berube, 1994). Progressivism largely failed to help the poor and minorities achieve educationally; they also failed to ensure that they could remain in schools rather than leave to join the workforce mainly to help their families (Berube, 1994). Efforts to address these failures would mark the beginning of the era that would follow.

LEGAL RESPONSES TO SOCIAL TRANSFORMATIONS

Legal responses reflect a move away from simply championing the need to have schools and move toward considering what should be the content of education deemed compulsory. Prior to this period, the federal government had dedicated its role to fostering state development. In the late 1700s, for example, Congress had divided the Northwest Territory so as to reserve land to support schools within each township (Pulliam & Van Patten, 1999). In the late 1800s, the federal government had established the Department of Education, whose future would vary in terms of its role as collecting information about schools and advising schools about federal programs and laws (Pulliam & Van Patten, 1999). During the early 1900s, Congress continued its largely supportive role. The progressive period, though, would mark the beginning of a more aggressive federal role. Unlike prior periods, the federal courts, rather than Congress, would begin to dictate the substance of education served in public schools and the extent to which private schools could play a role in educating students.

Despite the progressive belief that the Supreme Court avoids dictating the types of morals teachers should teach, the earliest Court decisions dealt directly with the power of states to inculcate certain values and ways of life through public schools. The cases involved the extent to which the state could control curricular matters and the roles of parents in educational endeavors. In addition, the challenges would involve the state's power to coerce children to attend common schools and be inculcated into particular values. The Court would solve the problem in three ways. First, it sought to ensure that the public schools were indeed common schools and that the schools were available for those who desired to attend. Second, it provided parents with the right to opt their children out of common schools. Third, even though parents could opt their children out of public schools or programs, the state still could reasonably control the nature of children's educations to ensure that children were prepared for societal membership. Although leaving much power to parents, then, the Supreme Court left state officials with considerable power to determine the nature of education.

The ground breaking case, *Meyer v. Nebraska* (1923), concerned a challenge to a state law that forbade the instruction of young children in a foreign language. Although the case directly involved the rights of teachers to teach and practice their profession, the case is better known for the Court's announcement that parents had a right to "establish a home and bring up children" (p. 399) and that the state had impermissibly interfered with the rights of parents to control the education of their children (p. 401). The Court, however, decided the case on a narrow ground—that the state interfered with the teacher's professional calling. The Court recognized as valid "the desire of the legislature to foster a homogenous people with American ideals" and did not contest its "power to prescribe a curriculum" or even demand that instruction be in English. The Court left large discretion to the state to Americanize America through schooling.

The second case, *Pierce v. Society of Sisters* (1925), struck down a state law that had declared it a misdemeanor for a parent or guardian to send a child between the ages of eight and sixteen to school other than the public school in the district where the child resided. The Court reaffirmed and recognized the rights of parents as it ruled that the statute "unreasonably interferes with the liberty of parents ... to direct the upbringing and education of children under their control" (pp. 534–535). In an oft-quoted statement in support of parental rights, the *Pierce* Court found that "the child is not the mere creature of the State; those who nurture him and direct his destiny have the right, coupled with a high duty, to recognize and prepare him for future obligations" (p. 535).

The cases established the powerful rights of parents to control their children's educational experiences. Although the cases continue to be cited to affirm parental rights, they also recognized the rights of the state and affirmed that children also belong to the state. Often ignored are other passages where the Court emphasizes the state's interest in regulating education and its inculcative functions. The Court acknowledged the "power of the State reasonably to regulate all schools" and to require that "certain studies plainly essential to good citizenship must be taught, and nothing be taught which is essentially inimical to the public welfare" (p. 534).

The power of the state to inculcate democratic values became even more pronounced in important developments in student's own rights. The major case involved the Court's specific recognition of students' right to protection from governmental intrusion into students' right to engage in speech and to protection from government-compelled speech. In *West Va. State Brd. of Ed. v. Barnette* (1943) the Court used unusually powerful language to find "that no official, high or petty, can prescribe what shall be orthodox in politics, nationalism, religion, or other matters of opinion or force citizens to confess by word or act their faith therein" (p. 642). The opinion sweepingly rejected educations based on principles other than democratic values. *Barnette* was a marked departure from the *Myer* and *Pierce* decisions that had defended the majority's right to use schools to foster a homogenous people.

The decisive rejection of schools that would foster undemocratic values was further reflected by an even more controversial case, *Brown v. Board of Education* (1954). In *Brown*, the Supreme Court recognized that schools are a "principal instrument in awakening the child to cultural values, in preparing him for later professional training, and in helping him to adjust normally to his environment" (p. 493). Given the central role of schools, the Court continued to find that communities could not segregate minority children and deprive them of equal educational opportunities. Through this decision, the Supreme Court held that all laws concerning or permitting school segregation were in conflict with the Fourteenth Amendment and ordered involuntary segregation to cease within a "reasonable time." Although the decision met with considerable opposition, it nevertheless placed the legal system in the middle of educational reform as the Supreme Court arrogated to itself the role of arbiter of educational mandates.

In addition to federal mandates, it is important to emphasize how the progressive movement altered much of the legal framework governing public schools (Tyack, James, & Benavot, 1987). Consolidation of school districts was a key goal of educational reformers. States granted new charters to cities, abolished old ward school boards and concentrated power in smaller central school boards. Legislatures also fostered rural school consolidation and prompted differentiation of schooling especially at the secondary level. The laws also specified certification of teachers and professional categories in administration. These transformations were championed, sustained, and obtained by administrative progressives. The reforms ultimately resulted in a massive expansion of public authority under state control. More than ever before, the state became the major arena to design broad social policies and centralize authority in changing social institutions. As we have seen, courts pervasively upheld states' broad educational authority.

The period denoted as progressive resulted in important efforts. It was during this period that educational issues appeared, for the first time, before the Supreme Court. That appearance is significant. Litigation at the federal level reveals a new role for the Supreme Court and the beginning of the nationalization of education. Nationalization confirmed the legitimacy of broad governmental involvement beyond local levels of jurisdiction. In addition to these structural changes, the period would provide important pedagogical orientations that continue to impact reform efforts that seek to teach all students and recognize their individual places and roles in society.

THE COSMOPOLITAN ERA

Historians of the cosmopolitan period of education typically set its range from the end of the 1950s through the 1980s. Like previous periods, the cosmopolitan era involved massive expansion, controversy, and change in adolescents' educational experiences. The educational enterprise of the cosmopolitan period magnified prior concerns with the meanings of democracy as society responded to advances in technology, more fluid social orders, economic crises, international tensions and challenges to moral life. These changes fostered an early move toward more liberal approaches to education, particularly in terms of adolescents' rights, civil rights, and social-economic rights. By the end of the period, however, the changes contributed to retrenchment toward a generally more conservative approach to education, one which would focus on reducing adolescents' control over their education, challenging civil and economic reforms, and contesting the very notion of public schools.

SOCIAL AND POLITICAL TRANSFORMATIONS AND EDUCATIONAL REFORMS

Compared to its surrounding decades, the 1950s were notable for their relative calmness. Calmness emerged after the demise of McCarthyism—a series of charges against and search for alleged communists in various governmental agencies, media, and universities. Although the "threat" of domestic communism diminished substantially with the decline of McCarthyism, the end of the '50s would mark two exceptions to the decade's tranquility. First, the second half of the decade witnessed an increased fear of international communism, an apprehension sparked by the Soviet Union's successful launch of Sputnik, the first space satellite. Sputnik would lead Americans to design policies that would harness scientific and technological capabilities and contribute to massive educational reform. The other exception to the otherwise tranquil '50s was the increasingly forceful civil rights movement that had gained momentum with *Brown v. Board of Education* (1954). Thus, Sputnik would have a tremendous and immediate impact on schooling while *Brown* would serve as a catalyst for substantial changes in social relations and policies outside of schools. Although known as a period of domestic tranquility, the 1950s actually would initiate changes in the central concerns of education, the civil rights movement, and international competition.

Although Sputnik spurred many broad changes in American life, it had three fundamental educational consequences. The first impact involved a new attention to academic studies. Sputnik and concern for fighting communism played a key role in shifting the public school systems' focus on intellectual development through the study of hard disciplines and cognitive skills, rather than a focus on the various forms of moral, civic, and social education emphasized by earlier generations. The second impact dealt with an impetus to provide federal financing for public education. As we have seen, the federal government already had played a role in funding education, but the successful Soviet launchings of satellites galvanized American politicians into action. Sputnik allowed advocates a more active federal role in schooling that tied federal aid to the national defense effort, which diminished conservative opposition. Although the federal aid was far from enormous, it would legitimize broad-based federal aid to education for the first time (Barksdale, 1981). The third impact resulted from the first two. To address opposition to focusing mainly on academic curricula and increasing the role of the federal government, reformers compromised to address the needs of other constituents, which resulted in a focus on guidance and counseling services, on sciences, and on student loans and fellowships for students prepared to attend college. As a result, one of the most notable reforms that would impact high school students would address vocational subjects and courses labeled "life skills" and "life adjustment"—umbrella approaches that quickly became an antonym for the standard academic curriculum. Although the particulars of life adjustment curriculum varied, their supporting rationale was the same as they sought to prepare the vast majority of students, approximately 60%, who were not served by either the vocational track or standard college preparatory studies (Urban & Waggoner, 1996). Most interestingly, and like the "child-saving" advocates before them, reformers argued that living in a democracy entitled students to the proposed forms of educations simply because they were American citizens and because adjustment studies were necessary for life in a "democratic society." Thus, although Sputnik contributed to an increasing focus on creating scientists and spawned a new role for the federal government, it spurred a curricular movement that judged subjects on the basis of their social utility and the extent to which they prepared individuals for different roles in modern society.

The 1960s brought a number of social and cultural upheavals. Many of the activities were experienced as wars. For example, the federal government dealt with a series of foreign crises, most notably the Vietnam War and Cold War. Equally importantly, the federal government pursued a "Great Society" agenda that included a "war on poverty" and responses to a violent civil rights movement. The social agendas of the 60s were marked by urban riots by minority citizens who reacted violently to their social and economic circumstances and by uprisings on many college campuses in protest of the Vietnam War. As a more dissident youth culture developed, the period became perceived as a time of genuine fracturing in relations between youth and their elders and the belief that American society was "Coming Apart" (O'Neill, 1971). Numerous analyses profiled the experiences of adolescents (e.g., Friedenberg 1962, 1965) and announced that modern social conditions were creating a crisis endangering healthy adolescent development. Critics singled out schools as harmful institutions that extended the adolescent period and created a minority group excluded from meaningful participation in society and political life. The argument was that schools, reflecting larger society, were at war with adolescents' attempt to develop meaningful responses to modern life.

Adolescents' place in modern life was affected by transformations in family life. The period is known for beginning the rapid changes in traditional family structures. To the extent that family life in the 1950s resonates as stable, the experience of the 60s is marked by challenges and instability, particularly as a result of the era's sexual revolution and challenges to marriage from the feminist movement (Farrell, 1999). Part of the transformation evolved from sharp distinctions raised between private and public realms. Sharply accentuating a trend that had begun with the Industrial Revolution, Americans in post war era thought of religion and morals as personal and private issues. The most notable revolution that would directly impact adolescents would involve increasing freedom in sexual behavior and control over reproductivity; all of which was confirmed by the liberalization of laws that allowed adolescents and adults greater individual control (Levesque, 2000a).

The social crises of the 1960s—efforts to end racial discrimination, waging of an unpopular war, deepening cultural pluralism, attempts to create meaningful places for adolescents, and a growing willingness to protect personal conduct from public forces—impacted schooling. The views of adolescents as social targets were coupled with civil libertarian critiques of schooling. The concern led to broad skepticism of all established authority which in schools resulted in concern that schools provide greater latitude for the young and limit the schools' roles in socialization, especially in moral and political values (e.g., Bereiter, 1973). Although proposals were often seen as extreme, they actually reflected public opinion which increasingly distrusted established institutions and feared the imposition of official values on private matters. Public education's focus on cognitive, rather than moral, education also responded to an increasing privatization of moral issues. The different norms and distinctions raised between private and public realms led schools to avoid moral questions that might be considered primarily personal. Americans in post war era thought of religion and morals as personal and private issues and assigned responsibility for them to home or church rather than the schools. The focus on the private was accentuated by new psychological theories that stressed the importance of early childhood in child development. Parents, likewise, were increasingly likely to challenge and scrutinize the moral education provided by schools.

The move to leave private issues outside of schools was complimented by the new approaches to social justice issues that increasingly were described as public concerns which should be addressed by schools. Efforts to expand the role of public institutions would take several important forms. Among the most influential developments would be a continuation of the minorities' struggle for equality that triggered a larger educational reform movement to eliminate poverty through education. The most celebrated Great Society initiatives funded innovative programs for the poor in the elementary schools and the Head Start program for preschooling for the poor (Berube, 1994). In addition to an equity reform movement geared to educating the poor, the 1960s would be notable for the revival of community control through participation. Again spurred by the Civil Rights Movement, a number of activists argued to expand the poor's participation in the political, social and institutional life. Rather than assuming that the poor did not want to participate, research had concluded that, when presented with opportunities for meaningful participation, the poor would become involved. For the first time, parental involvement became a policy issue. As we will see below, parents' involvement would have a long-range influence on American education, an influence arguably as forceful as other equity reform efforts. Although originally meant to make schools more democratic, parental involvement would raise the ultimate question of a democratic society, the participation of everyone in the political process, and the extent to which schools could remain common in the sense that they prepared students for living in one, democratic society (Ravitch, 1974). These reforms would ensure that schools remained at the center of efforts to address social issues.

Demonstrations that erupted on college and high school campuses in the late 1960s contributed to a revival of conservative educational policies of the decades that would follow. The escalation of demonstrations questioned many of the institutions and values of American life and convinced many that the United States was on the verge of radical social change and encouraged them to restore authority to society and the educational system. Nixon's election promised to solve the many social problems associated with student rebellion—civil rights, poverty, and the Vietnam conflict—with a return to basic education and the need to design education to prepare students for specific careers (Spring, 1997). More properly sorting students for the labor market became a key goal. Along with that goal came a rise in behavioral psychology that rejected concepts of democratic control of the classroom, with teacher-centered rather than student-centered methods (Cuban, 1984). Educators sought to avoid controversy and adopted programs designed to offend as few people as possible.

The 1980s, much of them characterized as the Reagan years, promised to change much of what had taken place in American life since the 1960s (Johnson, 1991). President Reagan's agenda sought to cut expenditures, trim federal bureaucracy, free the private sector from government regulations, and reduce taxes. These were a different direction than a focus on governments' more activist role in fostering equality and equity for racial and ethnic minority groups, the poor, and other underprivileged groups. That retreat from the general search for equality and civil rights accomplished with the active aid of the federal government also characterized educational policy. The equity movement that had dominated American education for nearly two decades ended with the new excellence movement that sought to educate the other end of the spectrum—the best and the brightest—in order to compete economically in the global marketplace.

The 1980's major reforms in education were identifiable in President Regan's 1980 campaign (Urban & Wagoner, 1996). The campaign highlighted three major goals. The first major goal sought to abolish the federal Department of Education. Although the Department remained intact, it did suffer severe cuts in federal funding that characterized Reagan's years in office. The second major goal involved returning prayer to a prominent place in public schools. Although the later part of the Reagan years were notable for an effort to encourage school prayer, they are better known for a return to a focus on traditional classroom discipline as the best vehicles for improving the moral and social development of youth (Goodlad, Soder, & Sirotnik, 1990). The last major goal involved tax credits for tuition paid by parents to private schools. This third effort, characterized as "school choice," practically meant a redistribution of the tax monies assigned to public education to students in private schools. Like the previous goals, the actual result was not achieved, but the attempt impacted an effort that continues as it responds to the failure of public schools argued to be unaccountable. In sum, then, the reforms reflected the overall domestic agenda of less intrusive federal government as it did succeed in reducing federal spending, raising public concern over moral education, and in sustaining a momentum for school choice plans.

Just as in previous eras, political changes fostered other reforms. One unintended reform was even more dramatic than the Reagan administration's advocated policies. The movement concerned itself with excellence. The excellence movement emerged from an apocalyptically titled report, *A Nation At Risk*, authored by the National Commission for Excellence in Education (1983). Although the report was sensationalized to engender public support for dramatic educational changes that had occurred after the launching of Sputnik in the late 1950s, the report did involve the image of the United States as economically threatened. The nation was at risk simply because of low work force productivity apparently stemmed from inadequate educational preparation for the dawn of an "information age" (p. xxi). The report resulted in a new effort to derive and impose national standards grounded on the need to address the nation's economic vulnerability, not the needs of youth. The focus on excellence decried what experts perceived as permissive, child-centered pedagogical strategies that they traced back to the 1960s (Ravitch, 1985). As an antidote to educational decline, these excellence supporters advocated a return to basic academic subjects and to traditional discipline policies in the schools. The report was not without its critics; many suggested that the crisis was related to demographic and economic shifts and the complexities of late 20th century life that challenged established curricular, instructional, and school organization patterns. However, the report, and the prevailing political winds, would have considerable impact on education and its reform.

A Nation at Risk (1983) began the latest reform movement in American education. The text reflected growing dissatisfaction with the quality of education and galvanized reform. By focusing on raising standards and the performance of public school children, the movement focused on helping the best and brightest compete in the global market. By championing systematic reform to counter the failures of public schools, their condemnation would lead many to advocate the alternative of private education and, ultimately, the privatization of American public education by corporations. The matrix of the excellence reform was economic in other ways as well. A key publication in the debate over privatization, *Politics, Markets and American Schools* (Chubb & Moe, 1991), argued a strong case for private school choice. Under that scheme, federal monies in the form of vouchers would permit students to attend any school they desired, including private schools; and the laws of the marketplace would ensure that both private and public schools would achieve maximum effectiveness as they competed for students. Privatization would also lead to the creation of "charter schools" which permit public school districts to be exempt from traditional regulations allowing for various degrees of privatization. These proposals would greatly influence current conceptions of the needed restructuring of schools' organization, management, and instruction offered to adolescents.

The Law's Move Toward Regulating and Dismantling Public Schools

Legal developments during the period encompassing the 1950s through 1980s were nothing short of massive and, from an historical perspective, radical. One of the most fundamental shifts involved increasing regard for adolescents' own rights. By the late 1960s, adolescents had acquired independent rights in juvenile justice systems (*In re Gault*, 1967) and schools (*Tinker v. Des Moines Independent Community School District*, 1969). Concern for abuses committed against adolescents and need to protect adolescents' individual rights even infiltrated the more private aspects of youths' lives—family relationships. In the late 1970s adolescents had acquired limited but nevertheless independent rights within their families, which allowed adolescents to exert control over their lives when parent-child relationships would fail to protect adolescents (*Bellotti v. Baird*, 1979). This new status was reflected by the Supreme Court's eventual recognition that minors were "persons" protected by the Constitution (*Tinker v. Des Moines Independent Community School District*, 1969, p. 511), a protection that inevitably led to an increase in adolescents' legal status.

The above developments generally equated adolescents with other oppressed groups. As such, they sought to broaden the due process rights of adolescents and curtail the traditional latitude institutions had enjoyed in enforcing codes of behavior. The schools were profoundly influenced by the legal challenges and changes. The courts did stop far short of providing students with the same rights as adults; but the recognized rights were intrusive enough to impact especially the manner educators addressed the behavior of students and the extent to which they would attempt to inculcate values. The rise of the students' rights movement often is associated with educators' move away from instilling values and fostering respect for authority and a move toward focusing on enforcing the legal minimum of proper behavior (McClellan, 1999). This minimalist view of educators' obligations casts a very negative view on adolescents' abilities to exercise rights while in school and contributes to the perception that developments in adolescents' rights largely account for schools' current failures.

The general response to the belief that students had increased rights led to the view that their rights removed discretion from schools and contributed to a decline in schools' effectiveness. The notion that students' rights were problematic was exacerbated by the major role assigned to schools. By the 60s, schools had become the means to address social crises. That role meant that schools were blamed for the apparent social pathology among adolescents in the modern era. Alarming rates of teen suicide, crime, drug use, and unwed pregnancy supported reformers' quick conclusion that schools' effort to encourage toleration and greater protection of adolescents' rights had failed to provide guidance to adolescents' ethical responsibilities to society (Greer & Kohl, 1995; Honig, 1985). Given these signs of failure, the 1980s would essentially be an era of retrenchment and move toward increasing schools' control over adolescents' freedoms.

The most notable development in the law's response to adolescents' educational experiences of the 1980s would be a visible retrenchment from efforts to foster adolescents' own individual rights. Although developments in adolescents' rights did not meet popular perceptions of their rights, the period would be known for a revival of the traditional view that adolescents are always in some form of custody and therefore generally subject to the control of adults (*Vernonia School District v. Acton*, 1995). As with previous developments, the legal changes would reflect other developments in the manner the legal system viewed adolescents. Most notably, the juvenile justice system and conceptions of adolescents' rights within their families would return to the more traditional paradigm of having parents control the rights of their children. Although juveniles would still have rights in the juvenile justice system, their rights to traditional rehabilitative measures would be reduced as a trend would emerge to simply transfer juveniles to adult courts (Levesque, 1996a). The rights of juveniles in families would also see a retrenchment as states would devise ways to reduce adolescents' access to services and resources outside their homes and a parental rights movement would arise that would focus on affirming parents' increased control over their children (Levesque, 2000a). The move away from further expanding the rights of adolescents would revive the traditional view of adolescents. Although the rights of adolescents in schools would see a visible retrenchment, the retrenchment would remain uneven. Four areas illustrate the trend in uneven progress and retrenchment.

School Official Power

Student ativism of this period tended to be confined to college and university campuses. Some high school unrest relating to the Vietnam War, though, did occur, as exemplified by a case that reached the Supreme Court in 1968—*Tinker v. Des Moines Independent Community School District* (1969). In that case, students challenged a school's prohibition against students' wearing black arm bands in protest of the Vietnam War. The Court found that students may not be confined to the expression of "officially approved" sentiments (p. 511). The case recognized the powerful influence of the progressive movement's attempts to develop student-centered schools that encourage students to participate in the learning process. The Court accepted a discursive and analytical approach to education where both teacher and student actively examine data (Gordon, 1984). Rather than being inculcative, the approach was meant to be reciprocal. The Court returned to one of its earlier decisions as it concluded that the First Amendment required a liberal education that may be antimajoritarian:

> Any departure from absolute regimentation may cause trouble. Any variation from the majority's opinion may inspire fear. Any word spoken, in class, in the lunchroom, or on the campus, that deviates from the views of another person

may start an argument or cause a disturbance. But our Constitution says we must take this risk, and our history says that it is this sort of hazardous freedom—this kind of openness—that is basis of our national strength and of the independence and vigor of Americans who grow up and live in this relatively permissible, often disputatious, society. (*West Virginia State Board of Education v. Barnette*, 1943, p. 508)

Although the Court's leading case of the late 1960's harkened back to the notion that democracy demanded respect for "hazardous" freedoms and that students had a right to those freedoms, the Court would retreat from the image of democracy and place the power to guide and direct democracy squarely on the schools. The cases that followed firmly swayed the control of school governance in the direction of school officials. In *Bethel School District v. Fraser* (1986), a 17-year-old senior delivered a sexually charged speech nominating a fellow student for elective office (p. 687). The Court affirmed that students' constitutional rights in public school settings are more narrowly defined than those of adults in other settings (p. 682). The limitation allowed school officials to curb forms of speech deemed threatening to others, disruptive and contrary to "shared values" (p. 683). Importantly, the Court reiterated its focus on community standards and the inculcative function of schools. Public education must inculcate "fundamental values necessary to the maintenance of a democratic political system" (p. 681). Included in these values are tolerance of diverse and unpopular political and religious views that must be balanced against the interests of society in teaching the bounds of "socially appropriate behavior" (p. 681).

The power of school authorities, acting as the inculcators of proper community values, was supported and developed further in *Hazelwood School District v. Kuhlmeier* (1988). Students alleged that their free speech rights had been violated when the principal deleted two objectionable articles from a school paper. One addressed issues of teen pregnancy and the other described the impact of parental divorce on students. The *Hazelwood* Court upheld the authority of school officials to control the content of school-sponsored speech based upon "legitimate pedagogical concerns" (p. 273). The *Hazelwood* majority emphasized the role of schools as the primary vehicles for transmitting cultural values and their discretion in refusing to sponsor student speech that might be perceived as advocating conduct otherwise inconsistent with "the shared values of a civilized social order" (p. 272).

The extent to which the state gained control over the curriculum was developed even more forcefully in cases that appeared only in the 1980s. The still leading case, *Board of Education v. Pico* (1982), established the "right to receive information and ideas" in the context of school libraries

(p. 867). In that case, a school board had removed a slew of books from its library and justified the removal on the basis that they were "anti-American, anti-Christian, anti-Semitic, and just plain filthy" (p. 857). The Court found that school boards could not remove books based on partisan politics. Although limiting the powers of school boards, their power actually remained considerably broad. Schools still had discretion to remove books based on educationally relevant criteria. The Court construed the school board's rights as "vitally important 'in the preparation of individuals for participation as citizens' and ... for 'inculcating fundamental values necessary to the maintenance of a democratic political system'" (p. 864). In curricular matters, the Court announced that school boards "might well defend their claim of absolute discretion" to transmit community values (p. 869).

Religion

The religion cases reveal the continuation of a long-term trend in removing religion from the classroom and from schools to the extent that school officials controlled the religious expression. In the early 1960s, for example, the Court had found prayer and Bible reading in public schools unconstitutional (*Engel v. Vitale*, 1962). The case noted the traditional source of legitimization but, more importantly, indicated the state's usurpation of authority over not only the structure of educational systems, but also the contents of instruction. But, by the end of the 1980s, however, the Supreme Court further elaborated upon what was permissible as it allowed for considerable religious freedom in public schools. The change took a decisive turn in *Lee v. Weisman* (1992). In that case, the Supreme Court considered a public high school student's challenge to a school policy that allowed principals to invite clergy to offer prayers at graduations. The Court held such invitations improper in that it was deemed attributable to the state which conflicted with student's right to freedom from religious coercion. The Court noted that students themselves could invite speakers. The focus on not stifling the religious rights of students would lead to important protections for adolescents in schools, as we will see in later chapters.

A similar transformation occurred in the use of public facilities and resources for religious groups. By the mid 1990s, the Court allowed religious groups to use public facilities. For example, in *Lamb's Chapel v. Center Moriches Union Free School District* (1993), the Court upheld the right of an outside religious group to use public school facilities after school hours to show a film series on the family from a religious perspective. Likewise, in *Rosenberger v. Rector and Visitors of University of Virginia*, (1995), the Court found that the denial of funds to a student-run newspaper with a Christian editorial viewpoint by a state university amounted to a viewpoint discrimination. The Court went even further in *Agostini v. Felton* (1997), which allowed public school teachers to provide remedial education in parochial schools. In that case, the Court focused on whether the aid was made available on a neutral basis to both religious and secular beneficiaries, and whether the beneficiaries made private choices as to the aid's religious/non-religious destination. The focus on choice is significant: so long as choice exists between religious and non-religious recipients, the decision to use those funds for religious purposes cannot be attributed to the state and thus does not amount to direct aid by the state.

Equal Opportunity

The third major development in the federal government and the Supreme Court's role in education involved addressing issues of equal opportunity. The most far reaching development concerned desegregation efforts. The activists' approach taken by efforts to integrate racial minorities into schools spread to other forms of exclusion. Several examples illustrate the trend, even though the different attempts attained different results and, most importantly, could actually be short-circuited by the rights of others.

Early efforts to ensure greater equal opportunity reveal how legal challenges to ensure adolescents' educational rights came in many guises. One of the most notable efforts to ensure equal opportunity involved the rights of the poor and minorities. In *San Antonio Independent School District v. Rodrigues* (1973), plaintiffs claimed that the Texas school system's reliance on local property taxes to finance public schools favored the wealthy and violated equal protection rights. The Supreme Court found that education, although important, was not a fundamental right guaranteed by the Constitution and that Texas' rationale—that its funding scheme permitted participation in and control of educational programs at the local level—provided a legitimate reason for continuing the allocation of funds. In *Plyler v. Doe* (1982) the plaintiffs, school-age children of Mexican children deemed "illegal aliens," challenged Texas education laws that withheld funds from local districts for the education of undocumented children. Although the Court reiterated that education is not a fundamental right, the Court noted education's importance in maintaining basic institutions and the impact of its deprivation on the life of a child to conclude that it was more than some governmental benefit indistinguishable from other forms of social welfare legislation. From this perspective, the Court held that the law violated equal protection mandates because the state could not demonstrate a substantial interest in denying undocumented children the free public education provided to other children (p. 230). In *Lau v. Nichols* (1974), the Supreme Court addressed the controversial rights associated with different culture's rights to education—bilingual education. The suit had been filed on behalf of Chinese American children in San Francisco who spoke little or no English. Their advocates argued that these children needed more than the usual instruction in English and that they require special attention that took into account their lack of facility in English. In recognizing the significance of education, the Court sanctioned bilingual education. As a result of *Lau*, several approaches to bilingual education would develop, some assimilationist and other aimed at retaining original cultures and languages.

Massive federal legislation also would aim to create opportunities that complimented and expanded the Court's findings. Most notably, the *1964 Civil Rights Act* contained several titles mandating enforcement of civil rights of black Americans. Among the Act's most important provisions were statements affecting segregation in education. The provision allowed federal funds to be withheld in districts that segregated their schools. Although the provision was virtually ignored during heated civil rights debates, it became rather significant as the flow of federal dollars to the states increased during the late 60s until now (Urban & Waggoner, 1996). The federal government would institute important anti-discrimination legislation and the Supreme Court would affirm that the legislation reached public schools. In *Aurelia Davis v. Monroe County Board of Education* (1999), for example, the Court affirmed that sexual harassment of students by students could constitute sexual harassment for the purposes of Title IX. Another significant act of educational legislation involved the rights of Americans with disabilities. The *Education for All Handicapped Children Act* (PL94-142), enacted in 1975, sought to assure that children with disabilities received the most appropriate, free public education available. As we will see in the next chapter, the Supreme Court would not only affirm the legitimacy of the act but even contribute to its expansion. This meant that more and more disabled students would be "mainstreamed"—placed in regular classrooms. The Court, in *Cedar Rapids Community School District v. Garret F.* (1999), would go even further and require school districts to provide highly specialized health care services and procedures. Without doubt, civil rights laws impacted and continue to impact students' educational rights and state's responsibilities.

Although the above developments provided students with equal opportunities, the rights remained limited. The limits are demonstrated by the third example of legal developments in educational rights. This example involves who could be excluded and who must be included in state educational efforts. Fifty years after the recognition of parent's rights to control the education of their children, the Court, in *Wisconsin v. Yoder* (1972), upheld the challenge by Amish parents of a state law requiring all children under the age of 16 to attend public or private school. The Amish parents argued that their religion called for a way of life tied to local farming activities and shielded from the heterogeneous world of industrial and material distractions. The state argued that they represented the broader community interests and the interests of Amish children themselves in the manner it sought to insure that all children in the state received the same minimal amount of educational instruction. The Supreme Court concluded that the burdens placed on the Amish could not justify the state's espoused interests. The Court's reasoning was significant: the state's interests were being fulfilled by the Amish who were raising their children to become productive and law-abiding individuals. Although critics argue that the Court ignored the rights of children and the need to preserve their option to leave the Amish community, the case does reveal how tolerance and private freedom win as long as they comport with the goals approved by the majority of society.

Privatization

Although the above examples present significant developments in the Court's attempt to ensure individual rights and balance them with community interests, the 1980s and 90s reflected a significant move away from the notion of common schools. While we have seen that business groups gained the most from educational policies of the Reagan years and on, the move toward privatization of schooling emerged as even more revolutionary. Largely as a response to the religious right, both federal and state governments moved toward school choice and charter schools. The move has been critical; for the idea of choice runs counter to the common school ideal of having all children receive a common education that inculcates a common culture, and a common set of moral and political values. The choice movement thus represents a dramatic departure from previous school reforms: rather than aspiring to create one best system of public schooling run by experts for all children, charter, magnet, and voucher-based education proposals seek to multiply options, concentrate mechanisms for evaluation and accountability in the hands of individual parents.

Privatization plans vary considerably and the variations present significant developments in the manner the public will support schooling (Levesque, 1998c). Private options range from providing public support of a choice between public and private schools to limiting choice to schools within a school district or to schools throughout the state. Other variations include charter schools in which private companies operate public schools. A central idea of these schools is that they can be freed from local and state educational bureaucracies and thus operate more autonomously. Once freed from bureaucratic control, the schools would develop and maintain unique and innovative alternatives to traditional public schools. These variations converge around a confidence in market-style mechanisms to generate and sustain quality. Emphasis centers on consumer sovereignty, skepticism about experts, and a turn to plural solutions to disputes about substantive good.

In thinking of the new role of privatization, three points are significant. First, the Supreme Court has yet to review the massive privatization of public schools. The Supreme Court has allowed, however, public funds to be used in religious schools, but only for specific purposes which have yet to involve support for tuition (*Mitchell v. Helms*, 2000). Second, despite variation, the new reforms receive support from both liberal and conservative reformers. Both extremes of the ideological spectrum contend that competition will make both public and private schools stronger, that it will afford low income parents and students to choose better schools (Chubb & Moe, 1991). Lastly, despite considerable enthusiasm, voices of dissent do emerge. Choice programs may enhance pluralism but they do not erase the real potential that these programs could instead produce self-segregation that exacerbates intergroup misunderstanding along the familiar lines of race, class, gender, religion, disability and national origin (Smith & Meier, 1995). It remains debatable how massive privatization can respond better to the numerous disappointments regarding racial desegregation, bilingual education, gender equity struggles, school finance litigation, and special education reforms. Despite the continued reforms, public education's public mission still remains. Schools still seek to forge commonality, even though it could be the common need to respect and support the common rights of parents to direct their children's educational environments. Likewise, schools still must promote civic engagement and offer quality opportunities in a diverse and democratic nation. In thinking of the new privatization, then, much remains to be determined about how it will address the entire society's interests affected by individual's educational opportunities and their achievements' impact on the next generation.

CONCLUSION

Developments in public schooling reveal the manner society construes its collective obligations to adolescents and what it expects from adolescents themselves. Schools have become the primary institution through which the state attempts to monitor, regulate, protect, and control adolescents. As the needs of society change, so do the justifications for and limits placed on efforts to inculcate adolescents into society. This role ensures that schools become increasingly significant for the social development of adolescents and that broad social changes impacting family and adolescent life challenge schools' effectiveness. As we have seen, public schools emerged to inculcate values, morals, discipline and citizenship. Advances in technology, fluid social orders, economic depressions, recessions and recovery, wars, and conflict over the meaning of democracy led to demand for re-evaluating educational aims reforming society through education. When reforms were not quick or not effective enough, educational trends returned to more conservative approaches to education that focused on preparing students for careers and dismantling the traditional model of public schooling that aimed to provide a common education for all.

The magnification of the educational enterprise raised new issues concerning schools' relationships to other social institutions. Parallel to developments in formal schooling, for example, is the story of adolescents' place in their families and their communities. A look at the development of schooling reveals a challenge to the view that families are private and immune from community intervention. Although still prevailing, the ideology of families as private entities immune from community control has its limit in practice. As the state's powers grew, communities (both local and distant ones) increasingly became able to control adolescent life. As a result, although many values and ideals may seem so fundamental and unassailable to family life, communities explicitly assert considerable power to control the lives of adolescents. Also parallel to developments in public schooling is the new role state officials play as arbiters and protectors of community values or preferences, both in the sense of common values shared throughout society and in particular communities. The developments emphasize the inculcative or indoctrinative nature of schooling for a given purpose. Public schools not only may but should influence their students to adopt particular beliefs, attitudes, and values—all of which change with the times.

Mounting crises would lead to two of the most important trends in educational reform in the 1990s. The first trend would involve increased calls for a return to moral and religious education. Many of the public schools' most ardent defenders actually would conclude that schools had become so devoid of appropriate moral content that they would now champion the demise of public schools (McClellan, 1999). As defenders of public schools continue to abandon them, the public schools would face unprecedented challenges. Those challenges constitute the second trend: a move away from common, public schools. Both trends find full expression in efforts to privatize adolescents' educations and to do so without traditional legal restrictions originally seen as fundamental to ensuring educational experiences that would prepare adolescents for democratic, societal membership (Levesque, 1998c). How schools can maintain their public functions while abandoning much of its public nature remains to be seen. Public schools must implement public norms, including such democratic principles as racial desegregation, free speech protections, due process protections, and a general emphasis on socializing students into a society ruled by law. Although not directly challenged, these public dimensions may be jeopardized by the redistribution of public dollars through private organizations, management through private rather than public employees, and fundamental changes in democratic control.

Given developments in school reform, the most critical issue that remains is the extent to which current laws and social science evidence allow for rethinking the nature of educational rights so as to foster adolescent development that could help adolescents reach the goals set by broad, democratic legal principles. The investigation that follows explores how to foster such development. The next chapters cull social science research to help make sense of the legal and social themes relating to the current regulation of adolescents' development—laws and policies that impact schools' efforts to develop, control, and reform adolescents' potentials for aggressive and violent behavior and create opportunities for adolescents to develop into healthy and socially responsible adults.

II

Challenges Facing
Adolescents' Education

3

Dangerous Adolescents

Extreme tragic events involving adolescents' brutal actions shatter our sense of basic civility and call for immediate responses. Such was the response to recent incidents involving the killing of several students by classmates in apparently safe schools and sheltered neighborhoods (Jenson & Howard, 1999). Although these extremes represent the popular types of interpersonal dangers that may lurk in or around schools, the violence actually reflects only a fraction of adolescent aggression and violence and the environments that sustain offending and victimization. In fact, only 1–3% of extreme forms of violence among school-aged adolescents actually occurs on school grounds or in related school-sponsored activities (Anderson, 1998). *Serious* violent events pervasively occur in adolescents' neighborhoods or in their homes—only about 7% of serious assaults take place at school (Snyder & Sickmund, 1995). Regardless of the actual reality of adolescents' offending, extreme violence grips and creates social consciousness regarding the realities of adolescents' offending against others and of disorder in schools. As a result, juvenile offenses in schools and the failure of schools to respond to offenses committed outside of schools rank among the most important social issues facing adolescents, schooling, and society.

Although the offenses receiving attention may be extreme, such episodes actually reveal much about school violence and environments in which adolescents find themselves. It is difficult to dispute the precariousness of adolescents' environments. Adolescents do live in and contribute to serious violence; e.g., within any given year, from 12–20% of males aged 13-16 report committing serious acts of violence (including aggravated assault, robbery, rape, or gang fights) (Kelley, Huizinga,

Thornberry, & Loeber, 1997). These serious offenses reveal only the tip of offenses and victimization. Environments conducive to serious violence strongly associate with risk for injury, exposure to intimidation and threats, and perceptions of fear and vulnerability (Brenner, Simon, Krug, & Lowry, 1999). These dangerous environments also breed school official reactions that themselves contribute to other forms of victimizations that induce severe physical, psychological, and sociological consequences (Hyman & Snook, 1999). Likewise, the extreme environments foster changes in adolescents' rights, as made most obvious in the dismantling of the juvenile court by transferring violent minors to adult court (Levesque, 1996a) and the removal of aggressive and violent adolescents from their community schools (Levesque, 1998c). Perhaps more importantly for policy reform, focus on extremely serious violence hampers the development of alternative approaches to other forms of problem behavior that may better alleviate adolescents' rates of more serious violence and that would otherwise reduce schools' iatrogenic effects on delinquency. Thus, even though adolescents' deadly violence and many less severe forms of violence now exhibit downward trends (Brenner, Simon, Krug, & Lowry, 1999), the dangers found in schools and communities remain significant social concerns and create potent images of the place of schools in adolescents' offenses.

The dangers (and perceptions of dangers) associated with adolescents and their schooling leave an important legacy for policies dealing with adolescents' rights and education. This chapter evaluates the legacy to lay a foundation for Chapter 6's delineation of reform alternatives consistent with the evolving understanding of adolescents, their offenses against others, and schooling's place in society. To do so, this chapter first details the nature of adolescents' offending, which for the purpose of this review ranges from severe violent criminal behavior, delinquency, to less recognized forms of abuse. The analysis then highlights the place of schooling in the creation and responses to adolescents' offenses. Having understood the important role schools play in addressing the needs of adolescent offenders and their victims, the discussion charts current legal responses to adolescents' offenses and delineates these responses' limitations.

ADOLESCENT OFFENDERS AND THEIR OFFENSES

A necessary starting point for discussion involves the manner researchers, policy makers, and society actually define certain offenses as problems and define schools' roles in addressing those problems.

Defining the contours of offenses worthy of intervention and the nature of schooling determines policies, the allocation of resources, and the extent to which schools may measure their success in responses to adolescents' offenses. As expected, delimiting the policy relevant contours of adolescents' offending and envisioning schools' roles remain contentious matters. Vastly different views of schools' roles in the reduction and production of problem behavior exist and complicate responses to the extent that each may marshal important empirical evidence to support their claims. Since none of the perspectives can negate fully the validity of others, attempts to establish policies that move toward any one perspective and approach to schools' roles in offenses necessarily must address issues raised by other views. That is a critical point. Although research supports many positions, some positions might gain more support and suggest the need to move toward certain poles of a polarizing continuum. Thus, delineating possible directions for addressing schools' failures in addressing adolescents' offending first requires a review of guiding themes emerging from empirical assessments of adolescents' offenses.

NATURE OF OFFENSES DEEMED WORTH ADDRESSING

Research that responds to adolescents' offending typically must begin by addressing two related issues. The first issue involves defining the problem. Research on adolescent offending usually focuses on some forms of violence but generally continues to have difficulty determining what precisely constitutes violence or even problem behavior. As a result, analyses often conflate aggressive behavior, violence against property or individuals, delinquency, crime, misconduct, and vague concepts such as disruptive behavior or school disorder (cf., Loeber & Stouthamer-Loeber, 1998; Welsh, Greene, & Jenkins, 1999). The second issue involves the need to address policy focal concerns. Thus, once problems have been defined more clearly, research must pinpoint the types of problem behavior deserving attention in light of competing resources, goals, and existing knowledge about what to do about the offenses. These directly intertwined issues affect both negative and positive outcomes. Lack of differentiation helps call attention to actions and allows for more inclusive research into the nature of adolescent offending. On the other hand, failure to distinguish between types of problem behavior leads to expected problems: it obscures the nature of violence, hampers comparisons between research findings, and potentially renders intervention ineffective when efforts are not tailored to specific problems. These issues generally continue to be addressed in a haphazard fashion; and no commentator has yet to propose a definitive resolution.

Despite continued failures to focus concerns, a close look at existing commentaries and research reveals two dominant positions regarding the types of offenses needing urgent attention and careful response. By far the most popular school responses to adolescents' offending involves the need to prohibit or suppress any form of overt, physical violence or actions indicative of possible violence. This approach is exemplified well by several "zero tolerance" policies that have emerged to deal with criminal activity in schools (Bogos, 1997) and the general community (Tonry, 1999). These efforts seek to remove offending adolescents from schools and tend to take a very narrow view of violence as constituting, for example, assault, intimidation, use of weaponry and conduct that seriously disrupts the education process (Johnston, 1999). Another group of commentators urges the need to address low-level aggression, such as cursing, disruptiveness, bullying, and horseplay (Goldstein, Palumbo, Striepling, & Voutsinas, 1995; Wilson & Petersilia, 1995). In addition to these two dominant positions, several now highlight the need to reconsider the nature of violence so as to include more covert violence, such as harassing behaviors that go ignored (Stein, 1999; Rigby, 2000) or the manner school staff, in the name of discipline, physically and psychologically assault students and impose violence (Hyman & Snook, 1999).

Notwithstanding controversies regarding the forms of violence that should receive priority, no one suggests that schools should ignore overt physical violence and that school environments should not be free of guns and weapons that place the school community at risk. Efforts to address school violence through suppressing gang activity reflect well the need for aggressive responses. For example, although several criticize policy makers' excessive focus on gangs, it is important to realize that some surveys reveal that up to 30% of urban inner-city adolescents join gangs at some point (Howell & Hawkins, 1998). Even if the percentage were smaller, the numbers gain significance by what we know about the extent to which gangs influence criminal activity. While in gangs, adolescents commit serious and violent offenses at rates several times higher than do non-gang members; and while in gangs, adolescents commit offenses at higher rates than before joining or after leaving (Thornberry, Krohn, Lizotte, & Chard-Wierschem, 1993). Their violence clearly impacts school life. A multi-state study of youth gangs reveals that 70% admit their gangs assault students and more than 80% bring weapons to school (Parks, 1995). Alleviating violence in several school districts, then, necessarily involves suppressing gang membership and the violence such membership produces.

Despite the significance of overt violence, research findings do support commentators' claims regarding the significance of addressing more subtle forms of offending behavior. Commentators concerned with covert behavior receive support from three recent lines of research. First, episodes of subtle violence and the environments they create actually may be more harmful in terms of the number of students they impact, largely because less severe violence tends to be less addressed. For example, psychological maltreatment in the schools remains an area pervasively ignored by researchers and policy makers (cf., Hyman & Snook, 1999; Levesque, 1998b). Thus, addressing extreme forms of violence actually fails to respond to the major forms of aggression and violence adolescents receive and perpetrate in the form, for example, of bullying and harassment by peers (Pellegrini, Bartini, & Brooks, 1999). Second, addressing the more extreme forms of violence requires addressing the more subtle and ignored forms of violence (Goldstein & Conoley, 1997). Research convincingly reveals how subtle forms of violence contribute to adolescents' criminal activity. For example, low-level school disruption clearly increases the likelihood of serious school violence (Heaviside, Rowand, Williams, & Farris, 1998). Likewise, subtle violence relates to adolescents' needs to join gangs. Adolescents who are particularly drawn to gangs include those who are failing in school, not involved in school activities, have few perceived opportunities and come from socially depriving conditions (Spergel, 1995). Third, reductions in violent crime do not necessarily impact perceptions of the school's level of safety. For example, research clearly reveals decreases in adolescents' more violent crimes, especially fatal homicide and assaults at school (Brener, Simon, Krug, & Lowry, 1999). However, research also fails to document parallel decreases in the percentage of students who feel too unsafe to go to school, being threatened or injured with a weapon on school property, or having property stolen or deliberately damaged at school (Brener, Simon, Krug, & Lowry, 1999). One of every ten students fears being shot or hurt by other students; and more than 20% avoids going to unsupervised areas (such as restrooms) to dodge victimization (Elliott, Hamburg, & Williams, 1998). Although subject to different interpretations, the figures do highlight the extent to which fear does seem to infiltrate places which historically have been viewed as safe havens. Perceptions of school safety, the actual safety of adolescents in schools, and the contribution of low-level aggression to overt violent behavior suggest a need to respond to all forms of violence.

CHARACTERISTICS OF ADOLESCENT OFFENDERS

Perceptions of violence worth addressing color images of adolescent offenders. In general, those who take a narrow, more overt view of violence suggest that adolescent offending involves essential character flaws.

This position is revealed by the general and increasing tendency to view aggressive and violent adolescents as super-predators. Underlying the view of impulsive, remorseless, assaultive adolescent offenders is the proposal that violent adolescents suffer from "moral poverty" (Bennett, DiIulio, & Walters, 1996, p. 59). Countering the view of adolescent violence as a character trait is the recent proposal that much of adolescent violence, delinquency and other problem behavior may stem from the nature of the adolescent period itself. From this view, violence and aggressive behavior during adolescence pervasively tends not to involve ingrained pathological character traits but instead involves manifestations of adolescents' peculiar place in society, a position based on the claim that the overwhelming majority of adolescent violence actually remains limited to that stage in the life cycle (Moffitt, 1993).

Although perceptions of adolescent offenders seem so at odds with each other, research actually supports both perceptions of adolescents who offend. The most relevant area of research deals with adolescents' life-course trajectories. Several longitudinal studies have identified different trajectories; and the most influential and useful grouping of offenders tends to involve two groups: life-course-persistent offenders and adolescence-limited offenders (Moffitt, 1993). Systematic attempts to sort out offenders' background characteristics, criminogenic influences, amenability to intervention, and cessation of offending repeatedly produces those two broad categories. Regardless of some controversies in grouping offenders (Loeber & Stouthamer-Loeber, 1998), few doubt that the largest group of adolescent offenders, up to 90%, limit their transgressions to their own adolescence. These adolescents typically begin offending after the age of 11 to 13 and desist criminal activity by age 18 (Loeber, Keenan, & Zhang, 1997). Although this group of adolescence-limited offenders also includes those who commit serious violent acts, these offenders typically do not progress in offense seriousness (Id.). The smaller group, those deemed life-course-persistent offenders, are distinguishable by many characteristics: early onset of offending, family adversity and neuropsychological impairments, active offending during adolescence, persistence in crime in adulthood, and escalation of offense seriousness (Loeber & Hay, 1997; Laub & Lauritsen, 1993; Moffitt, 1993). The persisters group is substantially more likely to be violent, to display antisocial personalities, and to leave school early. Commentators' perceptions of adolescent offenders, then, do seem to reflect reality, with the notable exception that the prevalence of certain types of offenders may be disputable.

The existence of different types of offenders gains considerable significance to the extent that they present different patterns of violence that place them at risk for engaging in problem behavior. Risk factors for life-course persistent offending present a distinct group of factors. First, these offenders typically reveal difficult temperaments during the first four years of life. For example, early displays of aggression and frustration toward adults and peers predict later aggressive behavior (Loeber & Hay, 1997). Early oppositional and aggressive behavior appears related to several difficulties that exacerbate conditions relating to adolescence-limited offenders. For example, although the association between prenatal and perinatal difficulties and adolescent violence may be weak, the association becomes strong among children reared in unstable home environments (Howell & Hawkins, 1998). Second, life-course-persistent offenders exhibit early cognitive deficits in learning, reading, speech, writing, and memory (Loeber & Hay, 1997). For example, early offending relates to how social cognitive difficulties contribute to aggressive behaviors. Some aggressive children consistently misunderstand others' intentions and reinterpret prosocial overtures as aggressive (Dodge, 1991). Third, certain social environment characteristics increase the risk of early offending. Most notably, family violence, including spouse abuse and childhood maltreatment, contributes to life-course offending (Smith & Thornberry, 1995; Loeber & Hay, 1997). Likewise, neighborhoods contribute to the early initiation of violent behavior (Loeber & Hay, 1997) and poverty presents a risk for violent behavior during and after adolescence whether measured in childhood or in adolescence (Lipsey & Derzon, 1998). Importantly, some groups of early aggressive children do desist from aggressive behavior by adolescence, but those who continue aggressive behaviors that become violent more likely exhibited more deviancy and more serious forms of aggression in childhood (Loeber & Stouthamer-Loeber, 1998).

Adolescence-limited offending typically relates to four groups of variables that place them at risk for offending. First, lack of parental interaction and involvement in their children's lives contributes to the spread of violence during adolescence. For example, poor family management practices and low degree of bonding to the family consistently relate to higher crime rates (Hawkins, Herrenkohl, Farrington, Brewer, & Catalano, 1998). Second, poor school performance and attitudes contribute to adolescent delinquency. For example, a recent meta-analysis of academic performance and delinquency found that poor academic performance relates not only to the prevalence of adolescents' offenses but also to the escalation in the frequency and seriousness of offending in adolescence (Maguin & Loeber, 1996). Similar analyses indicate delinquency's link to dropping out of school, low interest in education, low school achievement, poor quality school, and truancy (Lipsey & Derzon, 1998). Third, adolescence-limited

offenders seemingly acquire aggressive behavior patterns through victimization by others which exacerbate the likelihood of offending. For example, combining victimization experiences with school failure and mental
health problems more than doubles the likelihood of violent offending
(Huizinga & Jacob-Chien, 1998). Lastly, adolescent offending also is embedded within the peer group. Peers are the strongest predictors of violent
behavior during adolescence, but neither life-course persistent offenders
(Lipsey & Derzon, 1998) nor those who begin to offend in adulthood
(Loeber & Stouthamer-Loeber, 1998) are so highly influenced by peers. The
large majority of school-related crimes stem from peer interactions occurring in the course of routine daily activities that escalate, so much so that
normative expectations support incidents of violence (Lockwood, 1997).

Research, then, suggests that the vast majority of adolescents who
commit delinquent or even violent acts do not exhibit ingrained character
flaws. This research gains support from numerous other research findings
that highlight the extent to which the adolescent period itself often functions to support disruptive and violent activity. Most notably, the adolescent "culture" rewards and accepts certain violent behaviors to the extent
that they link to adolescents' unique developmental needs. For example,
adolescence involves social comparisons, processes that impact identity
formation and naturally give rise to competition, disputes and misconduct (Kazdin, 1995). Likewise, the significance of peers to adolescents,
such as the manner they confer or withdraw status, increases the importance of bystanders in the escalation of violence. The point is significant
given the critical role bystanders play in escalating disputes into violence
(Tedeschi & Felson, 1994; Pellegrini, Bartini, & Brooks, 1999). In addition,
adolescents have limited avenues to obtain the types of social status and
roles that come from participation in community life. For example, the
demand for personal respect, coupled by limited avenues by which to
attain it, sets up conflicts that can be resolved through available pathways
to high status which, for males, leads to the use of manifestations of physical power or fighting to establish positions in social hierarchies (Guerra,
Nucci, & Huessmann, 1994). Adolescence also involves the establishment
of sex-roles and even an intensification of gender roles. Sex-role considerations gain significance since, for example, expressions of masculinity and
their utility in social positioning links to numerous forms of violence
based in the need to establish and prove "manhood" (Bowker, 1997). Yet
another area of supporting research derives from the manner the period
of adolescence involves learning ways to read social cues and developing
cognitive capacities to engage in abstract reasoning. As a result, adolescents may lack the cognitive capital to understand the range of potential
consequences or to fashion strategies that may exempt them from

violence (Steinberg & Cauffman, 1996). These different levels of competence help account for difficulties in deterring adolescents from committing crimes; research has long failed to find an impact of deterrent sanctions on delinquency, self-conceptions, or perceptions of risk (Thomas & Bishop, 1984). Another consideration involves how adolescents commonly defy authority structures. Although that defiance varies considerably depending on their individual and cultural location, adolescents oppose social controls from different sources, including police, peers, neighbors, or social institutions such as schools (Arnett, 1999). Lastly, adolescence involves risk taking and managing impulsivity. Compared to adults, for example, adolescents engage in much more risky or sensation-seeking activities and adolescents also may be unaware of the nature of their risks and calculate risks differently than adults (Scott, Reppucci, & Woolard, 1995). All of these robust empirical findings confirm the significance the adolescent period itself plays in fostering offenses.

THE PLACE OF SCHOOLS IN ADDRESSING ADOLESCENTS' OFFENDING

Having understood the offenses adolescents commit, this section examines schools' responses to those offenses. Schools actually play numerous roles in efforts to address adolescents' offending behavior. Schools variously serve as environments for victimization, as root causes of offending inside and outside school grounds, and as sites for intervening and preventing violence. Although much still may remain unknown about schools' roles, important themes emerge from existing research and help lay a foundation for reform and analysis of existing legal mandates.

CONTROL MEASURES

The most obvious role schools play in addressing violent, delinquent, and disruptive behavior involves the numerous ways schools seek to control adolescents. Not surprisingly, schools' responses to violence reflect the images of adolescents reported above. The most popular approach to controlling adolescents responds to the perspective that views adolescents as essentially primed for offending. This view tends to champion suppressing violence through "hard" special security measures, such as instating weapons detection equipment, police in schools, searches of school lockers, drug-sniffing dogs, closed-circuit television monitors, and photo identification (National School Boards Association, 1993). The view also is seen in broad, authoritarian school responses that use traditional disciplining (e.g., punitive and controlling strategies) in responses to disruptive behaviors (Bear, 1998). Without doubt, suggested reforms to address adolescent violence tend to adopt this approach which seeks to "get tough" on adolescents and foster environments with low tolerance for problem behavior.

The currently less popular approach to controlling adolescents responds to the perspective that views adolescents' offending less as symptoms of character traits and more as parts of transitions to adult responsibilities. This view suggests that efforts to alleviate violent and disruptive behavior reach effectiveness when they address school climate: the unwritten beliefs, values, and attitudes that become the style of interaction among students, teachers, and administrators. This alternative view proposes that less crime-inducing school environments allow for firm but fair governance of the school environment, an environment in which authoritarian and policing measures become a secondary means of allowing students to concentrate on education. This view emphasizes respecting adolescents' rights as fundamental to educational endeavors that gain their legitimacy only to the extent that they reflect democratic measures they expect adolescents to exhibit in and outside of school. This approach champions, for example, a focus on establishing democratic schools, participation of students in developing school policies, and a general focus on enhancing students' sense of community and connection to schools and to themselves (Devine, 1995). The approach also proposes that teachers are more effective when they adopt authoritative (rather than authoritarian) measures (Brophy, 1996) and when schools reject aggressive responses, such as corporal punishment (Elbedour, Center, Maruyama, & Assor, 1997). The different views of adolescents' offending, then, impact schools' approaches to dealing with adolescents' potential for disruptive and violent behavior.

Existing research reveals much about the effectiveness of the two general approaches to dealing with offending behavior. A close look at research and school policies reveals a negative relationship between what schools do and what research and commentators suggest would be most effective. Schools increasingly embark on repressive, authoritarian measures (National School Boards Association, 1993). Yet, researchers tend to champion a need to move toward authoritative measures that provide students with more voice in disciplinary matters and increase students' participation in creating safe school climates (e.g., Anderson, 1998; Hyman & Snook, 1998).

Despite receiving considerable criticisms, aggressive and authoritarian measures clearly do have their place in effective responses to adolescents' offending. For example, research does reveal that metal detectors do work to the extent that they do reduce weapon carrying in schools and weapon related harms (Cohen, Weiss, Mulvey, & Dearwater, 1994; Samples & Aber, 1998). Dress codes also may reduce the number of gang related apparel as well as the risk of theft and concealed weapons; all of which may lower the incidence of violence (Cohen et al., 1994). Invasive searches, such as strip searches and drug testing, also may work to the extent that they necessarily do identify perpetrators and send important messages regarding the school's lack of tolerance for delinquent behavior (Hyman et al., 1997). These important findings support the general view that incapacitation is an effective crime-control measure and, in fact, that incapacitation now serves as the principal justification for criminal justice efforts to restrain crime (Zimring & Hawkins, 1995).

Although reflecting criminal justice policy trends and responding to public demands, data documenting the effectiveness of tough security measures in *schools* remain extremely scarce (Skiba & Peterson, 2000). Even if data do indicate that policing measures function to reduce some types of crimes and delinquent behaviors, aggressive measures still raise important concerns. The major concern involves the manner policing measures impact school climates. Schools' aggressive and seemingly totalitarian responses may be creating climates of fear and increasing adolescents' actual victimizations. Commentators who urge caution before enacting repressive strategies argue that current aggressive enforcement measures schools adopt to stop violence actually corrupt students' respect of liberty, privacy, self-identity, autonomy, personal integrity and personal expression (Myhra, 1999). Commentators further note that traditional segregationist responses to adolescent problem behavior result in further alienation of more students and enhances the likelihood of violence (Stone & Boundy, 1994). The failure to improve schools' behavioral climates by balancing positive and negative responses to students' behaviors seemingly yields a coercive cycle that increases the likelihood of disruptive behavior (Skiba & Peterson, 2000).

Although many commentaries about the proper approach to dealing with adolescent offending remain theoretical, emerging empirical evidence tends to urge more caution about the aggressive authoritarian approaches than those based on more authoritative models. Schools that rely heavily on zero tolerance continue to be less safe than schools that implement fewer components of zero tolerance (Heaviside, Rowand, Williams, & Farris, 1998) and overreliance on physical security measures associates with an *increased* risk of school disorder (Mayer & Leone, 1999). Reviews of "get tough" approaches propose that such efforts fail to create safe environments simply because coercive strategies interrupt learning and produce environments of mistrust and resistance. For example, the use of metal detectors discourages the use of alternative strategies that would encourage a sense of community and collective responsibility necessary to reduce violence within and outside of schools (Noguera, 1995). Gang suppression efforts reveal similar results. An important conclusion of research results from a two-year project investigating gangs in three inner-city high schools concluded that the common repertoire of suppression strategies used by schools generate unintentional antieducational consequences (Brotherton, 1996). Perhaps more dramatically, research on responses to gangs reveals that schools must separate gang members from one another as they emphasize democratic learning processes that focus on respect and recognizing talents in gang-affiliated adolescents instead of doing what has become the most frequent response to gangs: segregating gangs from other students which strengthens bonds among gang members, preps gang youth to drop out of school, and ensures that they are differentiated and stigmatized (Vigil, 1999). These studies reveal that aggressive, controlling, and punitive measures undermine the legitimacy of both teachers and administrators, stifle the pursuance of democratic public pedagogy, and essentially become futile (Brotherton, 1996).

In addition to the above research, other important sources of research examine the effectiveness of disciplinary measures. Several analyses of programs for adolescents at risk of dropping out and of being thrown out of school find that these programs blame young people for their problems, ignore institutional barriers to success, and silence voices of dissent and resistance (Hamovitch, 1996; Ennis, 1996). Other provocative research reveals that "humanistic" approaches to discipline, rather than more traditional coercive approaches, more effectively increase school safety (Lab & Clark, 1996). Humanistic discipline includes consultation with and involvement of students in setting punishments, students' and teachers' assessments of punishments' fairness, and the existence of a student court. More coercive measures include teacher monitoring of student activities, rates of suspension or expulsion, and aggressive security measures like guards, alarms, and locks. The study concluded not only that low victimization rates related to student humanism but also that student humanism was the only variable related to each type of victimization (Lab & Clark, 1996). This area of research emphasizes that school officials must make safety an important educational issue without sending a panicked message about their lack of moral authority. In general, the findings urge social integration to foster an atmosphere of inclusiveness, open communication, and shared decision making on safety and other important issues with students, staff, and parents.

Despite controversies, then, some efforts to control adolescents do seem more effective than others. Research increasingly suggests that the power asymmetry between teachers and students in school, when coupled with the former's use of negative and assertive strategies, encourages and supports aggression and victimization among students (e.g., Pellegrini, Bartini, & Brooks, 1999). Although not necessarily intuitive, these findings parallel an established body of research in the parenting literatures. That literature supports authoritative rule-making environments, which focus on building relationships marked by warmth, acceptance, openness, high standards and expectations, consistency in enforced rules, and promotion of autonomy by encouraging active participation in decisions regarding their behavior (Steinberg, 1996). These parenting styles contribute to the alleviation of delinquency, as revealed by research finding that effective parenting in childhood (use of consistent, child-centered, and nonaversive strategies) associates with adolescents' internal attributes that allow them to resist delinquent behavior (Feldman & Weinberger, 1994). The significance of these findings cannot be underestimated; existing technology suggests that schools can respond effectively (or at least much better) to violent, delinquent and disruptive behaviors.

CURRICULAR RESPONSES

In addition to school climate and school discipline research, a series of studies has examined curricular responses to adolescents' offending. Recent comprehensive surveys reveal that many school districts have instituted many curricular programs that vary in popularity and intensity. These programs range from mentoring programs, multi-cultural sensitivity training and law-related education, classes in coping with adolescent problems, and classes in conflict resolution, mediation training, or peer mediation (National School Boards Association, 1993). Given the popularity of many of these programs, they actually have been one of the most evaluated responses to adolescents' offending.

Research on curricular reforms reveals important findings. The most persistent conclusion confirms the pervasive ineffectiveness of programs that simply disseminate information, arouse fear, or appeal to morals (for a review, see Gottfredson, 1997). As a result, even highly ubiquitous programs tend to be ineffective, as revealed by the consistent failure of the enormous D.A.R.E. (Drug Abuse Resistance Education) program involving over 25 million students in 70% of school districts in the U.S. (Anderson, 1998). Likewise, community service programs and recreational activities (such as midnight basketball) fail to impact delinquent behavior (Anderson, 1998). Importantly, preventive programs, especially those based on peer groups, generally fail to decrease delinquency rates and some even tend to reinforce bad behavior rather than motivate

students toward doing well (Dishion, McCord, & Poulin, 1999). Even programs that do reach levels of effectiveness, such as intensive gang resistance education programs, actually reveal modest effects (Esbensen &
Osgood, 1999). The modest findings from effective programs are especially significant. The more effective programs, like the gang resistance
programs, deal with destruction and violence associated with gangs and
cover issues that unlike D.A.R.E. do not enjoy widespread acceptance in
the adult population. This material difference suggests that the acts to be
resisted should be more easily distinguishable as improper for adolescents to engage in and thus attempts to dissuade adolescents' participation in the activities should be more easily accepted and followed by
adolescents.

Although the above curricular attempts do not lead to optimism, evaluation research does suggest that effective programs have at least four
common characteristics. First, effective programs generally provide long
term services. Second, effective programs focus on a wide range of social
competency skills, such as developing self-control, stress management,
responsible decision-making, social problem-solving, and communication
skills. Third, effective programs rely more on cognitive-behavioral training
methods (such as feedback, reinforcement, and behavioral rehearsal) than
on traditional lecture and discussions. Lastly, effective programs involve
adults who offer control, guidance and support rather than leave interactions to adolescents and their peers. In essence, the more effective
programs involve "social competence promotion" and actively involve
adolescents in activities that model and reinforce responsible behavior.
These findings suggest the fundamental point that schools can impact
adolescents' dispositions and that adolescents' offending behaviors need
not necessarily derive from deep-seated character flaws.

COMMUNITY INFLUENCES

A last important element of schools' responses to adolescents'
offenses involves the extent to which societal violence and disorder necessarily spill into schools and impact levels of offending in schools and
schools' responses to adolescent offending. This area of research also par-
allels that which addresses the extent to which adolescent offending
results from either deep character flaws or the adolescent period itself.
Thus, schools either mirror society's (and families') problems or may be
structured in ways that suppress offending and offer adolescents protective shields against future offending. By far, the most dominant view
insists that schools reflect violence in communities. Under this view,
alleviating school violence requires ridding communities and families of

violence (Lawrence, 1998; Lockwood, 1997). An emerging view reveals that schools actually can be safe havens, regardless of the levels of violence found in the community (Anderson, 1998; Welsh, Greene, & Jenkins, 1999). The latter view suggests that schools can insulate themselves from violence and that schools in rather peaceful communities can induce violence.

Few doubt that levels of school disorder and violence relate to levels of community factors and societal forces. For example, regardless of the context (homes, schools or neighborhoods), certain sociodemographic subgroups of adolescents, such as minority and urban adolescents, are at greater risk of being victims of violence (Sheley, McGee, & Wright, 1995). Several community characteristics also can impact adolescents' actual misconduct in schools. Communities can heighten exposure to risks as students go to and from school, can import norms and behaviors conducive to the use of violence in dispute resolution, and weaken community controls over the behavior of children who attend schools in specific neighborhoods (Lockwood, 1997; Pearson & Toby, 1991). These findings comport with ecological studies of crime and delinquency that highlight the need to consider how community characteristics influence crime rates (Sampson & Lauritsen, 1993).

Although often ignored in analyses of school violence, families remain an important aspect of communities' influences on adolescent offending both in and outside of schools. In fact, families are primary sources of violence and primary sources of factors that place adolescents at risk for violence (Hawkins, Herrenkohl, Farrington, Brewer, & Catalano, 1998). The significance of families is readily obvious in the manner mobilizing adult caregiving frequently emerges as a critical and viable intervention target for even the most severe adolescent delinquent (Chamberlain & Moore, 1998). Interventions with high-risk parents have shown results in improved parenting, concomitant reductions in adolescent behavior and improvement in academic skills (Dishion, McCord, & Poulin, 1999). In addition, clinical researchers who focus on adolescence argue that interventions targeting high-risk adolescents benefit from a family focus (Henggeler, Schoenwald, Borduin, Rowland, & Cunningham, 1998). These responses harness insights from developmental theory that highlight the need for comprehensive, ecologically-focused responses to violence.

Although recent reform efforts and commentaries increasingly focus on community involvement and reforms to address community violence, research indicates that it remains an imperfect panacea. In-school problems are not necessarily caused by local environments and not beyond schools' control. The surprising finding from national studies is that schools do not view themselves as possible sources of violence (Petersen, Pietrzak, & Speaker, 1998). Yet, several studies suggest that school disorder is more a function of internal school environments than communities themselves. Regardless of the nature and levels of crime in the community, schools have the capacity to become "safe havens" for students. A leading study of 44 schools found that school victimization figures failed to show relationships to levels of community violence, except for theft and neighborhood economic level (Lab & Clark, 1996). Yet another study concluded that the best overall predictors of school disorder and violence relate primarily to internal school factors and not community crime characteristics (Welsh, Jenkins, & Greene, 1996). These findings confirm results from the ground-breaking Safe School Study data (Gottfredson & Gottfredson, 1985). That study had revealed that schools with the worst discipline problems shared many common characteristics: schools used ambiguous or indirect responses to student behavior, teachers and administrators did not know the rules or disagreed on responses to student misconduct, teachers ignored misconduct, and students found the rules illegitimate. Within school environments undoubtedly play a profound role in effecting or exacerbating adolescents' offending.

Recent research, then, reveals that a school's location or student demographics do not dictate entirely levels of violence and disruption. Community levels of crime and disorder have less effect on student misconduct than individual student characteristics, such as beliefs in rules and positive peer associations that constitute the school climate (Welsh, Greene, & Jenkins, 1999). In fact, independent of both community *and* family factors, schools that are safe and help adolescents to differentiate right from wrong also buffer adolescents from engaging in problem behavior outside of schools (Kowaleski-Jones, 2000). These are important findings in light of the persistent and pervasive failure to increase parental involvement in children's schooling (Sarason, 1995) and the often fruitless efforts to mobilize communities and other public agencies (Anderson, 1998). Although it remains important to consider new strategies to reform communities' impact on schools, the central findings remain. The internal management of schools and their classrooms impact student aggression and violence; extremes of overly restrictive rules or lack of structure make violence more likely to occur, as do arbitrary applications of rules (Warner, Weist, & Krulak, 1999). Thus, school systems in which students have few rights or little say over the governance of the school or themselves are prone to violence, as are schools and classrooms characterized as authoritarian. These studies and commentaries emphasize the critical point that schools need not reflect the communities and families in which adolescents find themselves.

Existing research reports important results. Schools must adopt rules and regulations to control students, but they should take precautions to ensure that their rules and regulations result from meaningful and rational deliberation that seek adolescent involvement. Schools must provide rule-supporting environments. Efforts to change adolescents are likely to be unproductive or even counterproductive in the absence of attention to school climate policies that may be contributing to misconduct. Likewise, curricular programs reach their highest potential when they actively involve adolescents rather than simply provide students with descriptions of behaviors deemed appropriate. Communities and families also can play important roles; although important, the way they impact adolescents may not necessarily be entirely determinative. Regardless of students' familial and community backgrounds, schools still can engage adolescents in ways that can alleviate the otherwise negative effects of violence emanating from families and communities.

DANGEROUS ADOLESCENTS, EDUCATION AND THE LAW

Analyses of adolescents' rights always involve balancing their rights against the government's interest in supporting and protecting an ordered society. This is especially true of students' rights in the context of responses to adolescent offending. This area reflects the need to balance adolescents' individual freedoms and obligations with community interests (including the community interests of adolescents). In school contexts, community interests tend to limit adolescents' individual freedoms and impose obligations adolescents would not have in other contexts (e.g., in their families). The critical issue for analysis involves the nature of limitations, rationales for them, and the extent to which reform could be instituted that still addresses the rationales laws determine as legitimate reasons for balancing students' rights and community rights in particular directions. This section first examines rationales and boundaries found in federal mandates, the richest source of analyses of adolescents' educational rights. The analysis then examines state constitutions and state legislative mandates, which recently have emerged as well-recognized sources of civil liberties that may provide a source of *greater* protection for rights the federal government recognizes only narrowly.

CONSTITUTIONAL PARAMETERS

Through a series of decisions spanning over 25 years, the Supreme Court has developed a now consistent view of students' rights. Initially, the Court invited substantial judicial scrutiny to schools' efforts to limit adolescents' rights. That scrutiny, however, now has given way to substantial deference to decision-making by locally elected officials. Although providing substantial deference to school officials, the Court nevertheless has set important boundaries. These boundaries reveal critical themes and trends in efforts to deal with adolescents' disruptive or delinquent behavior and efforts to ensure appropriate school responses.

Regulation of student expression by school authorities involve the most common response to adolescents' everyday disruptive behaviors. The Supreme Court cases dealing with expression reveal a trend toward giving increasing weight to administrative decisions. The Court articulates the philosophy of climate-controlled education, one controlled by school personnel who have the responsibility to determine the degree of toleration in their school for lewd, indecent, or offensive speech. The Court announced the general rule in *Bethel School District No. 403 v. Fraser* (1986). In *Fraser*, a student challenged a three-day school suspension and removal of his name from a list of potential graduation speakers. The punishment derived from his sexually-laden speech nominating a fellow student. Although the Court recognized a student's "undoubted freedom to advocate unpopular and controversial views in schools and classrooms" (p. 680), it noted that the right must give way when it is disruptive and infringes on the rights of other students. By doing so, the Court recognized the school's need to inculcate "habits and manners of civility" (p. 681) and that schools must teach students the boundaries of socially appropriate behavior. As instruments of the state, schools were required to inculcate societal lessons of civil, mature conduct.

School district hegemony over the behavior and speech rights of students was enhanced further by *Hazelwood v. Kuhlmeier* (1988). In *Hazelwood*, students objected to a principal's censoring of the school's newspaper. The Court recognized the school's broad powers in censoring student speech and gave schools wide latitude to censor all school sponsored activities. The Court ruled that speech that appears to carry the school's imprimatur can be prohibited if a legitimate educational concern exists. Schools have the right and obligation to disassociate themselves not only from "speech that would 'substantially interfere with its work ... or impinge upon the rights of other students' but also from speech that is for example, ... biased or prejudiced, vulgar or profane, or unsuitable for immature audiences" (p. 271). Given legitimate pedagogical concerns, schools are thus free to set high standards for student speech disseminated under its auspices. These cases reveal how the Court accepts an education ideology that inculcates values and provides communities with freedom to control student expression in the name of protecting community values.

Despite broad discretion to inculcate community values and ensure that students abide by those values, the Court does set major limits on schools' control of students' expressive behavior. The Supreme Court invited judicial scrutiny of school district efforts to address student expression that may be characterized as misbehavior in *Tinker v. Des Moines Independent School District* (1969). In this leading case, students (ages 8, 11, 13, 15 and 16) were suspended from school for wearing black armbands in protest of the war in Vietnam. The Court held that the wearing of armbands constituted an exercise of pure speech entitled to First Amendment protection and that schools simply could not punish students for expression they simply disagreed with. The Court rejected the argument that the mere possibility of disruption was enough to justify regulations on student expression:

> Undifferentiated fear or apprehension of disturbance is not enough to overcome the right to freedom of expression. Any departure from absolute regimentation may cause trouble. Any variation from the majority's opinion may inspire fear. Any word spoken, in class, in the lunchroom, or on the campus, that deviate from the views of another person may start an argument or cause a disturbance. But our constitution says we must take this risk. (p. 508)

The Court, though, did not leave school personnel without control. The Court emphasized the need to affirm the comprehensive authority of the states and of school officials, consistent with fundamental constitutional safeguards, to prescribe and control conduct in schools:

> Conduct by the student, in class or out of it, which for any reason—whether it stems from time, place or type of behavior—materially disrupts class work or involves substantial disorder or invasion of the rights of others is, of course, not immunized by the constitutional guarantee of free speech. (p. 513)

The *Tinker* standard, although protecting students' rights, was indeed quite low. The Court simply had declared that schools could control students' expression so long as schools "show that its action was caused by something more than a mere desire to avoid the discomfort and unpleasantness that always accompany an unpopular viewpoint" (p. 509). Schools must show some proof of disruption or possible disruption rather than conjecture or supposition. Importantly, the expression must be deemed worthy of protection, which in *Tinker* involved political speech. Thus, in *Hazelwood v. Kuhlmeier* (1988), the Court would reject the application of the *Tinker* standard when the speech involved an allegedly disruptive sexual metaphor and would extend the power of school officials to any expressive activities that members of the public might reasonably perceive to bear the school's imprimatur. With respect to such activities, the Court held that school officials may regulate student speech in a manner they see fit so long as the actions remain reasonably related to legitimate pedagogical concerns.

Although some of the above cases may appear tangential to students' disruptive behaviors, they provide the rationales for controlling adolescents. For example, the cases are significant to the extent that schools now regulate students' expression in the form of speech codes, dress codes, and attempts to suppress gang activity. In these instances, at least two reasons support schools' efforts. First, school officials have a direct and legitimate interest in providing the uninterrupted, nondisruptive education of students. Second, the need to promote civil values in a democratic society furnishes schools with the authority to control speech. Thus, students' rights notwithstanding, the schools address violence and disruption through the "police power" of school officials and the authority of school boards to protect the health, safety, welfare, and civility of students and staff as the schools influence adolescents' current and future participation in society.

Schools also may regulate student conduct through more aggressive measures that involve another critical area of students' rights: Fourth Amendment claims. Broadly stated, this right protects everyone against unreasonable searches and seizures. The extent of the protection also is enumerated by the Constitution which explicitly states that "no Warrants shall issue, but upon probable cause, supported by Oath or affirmation, and particularly describing the place to be searched, and the persons or things seized" (U.S. Const. amend. IV). The Court has interpreted several exceptions to the general rule that allows for a much more lenient standard for conducting searches, such that some searches may be proper without a warrant and without probable cause (Luna, 1999). One of the most notable exceptions involves the extent to which the general rule applies to students.

Less than two decades ago, the Court announced that the Fourth Amendment protected the rights of public school students against searches (or seizures) by school officials. Although recognizing that the right applied to even a limited search, the Court took the opportunity to reduce the amount of protection students could receive. The case, *New Jersey v. T.L.O.* (1985), involved a search of a 14-year-old female student's purse for cigarettes. The problem arose when the search ultimately produced evidence of possession of marijuana and the issue of whether that evidence could be used in delinquency proceedings against the student. The student challenged that the search violated the Fourth Amendment's prohibition on unreasonable search and seizures which requires warrants and probable cause in criminal proceedings. The Court ruled that searches by school officials were governed by the Fourth Amendment but that the standard for authorizing searches in public school contexts was less rigorous than that in the criminal law enforcement setting. In school settings, the legality of the search depended on its reasonableness, both at its inception and with respect to its scope. The Supreme Court held that under ordinary circumstances, the search would be justified at its inception "when there are reasonable grounds for suspecting that the search will turn up evidence that the student has violated or is violating either the law or the rules of the school" (pp. 341–342). The search would be permissible in its scope when the measures adopted by school officials are reasonably related to the objectives of the search and not excessive in light of the student's age, sex, experience, and infraction. As with the First Amendment free speech cases, the rule developed by the Supreme Court grants considerable deference to local school officials. School personnel simply must act reasonably and their search must simply be justified at its inception.

Although the power of school officials to search students may have been broad under *T.L.O.*, the Court actually has broadened the power of school officials. The recent case of *Vernonia School District 47J v. Acton* (1995) offered considerable discretion to school officials in their effort to control student behavior. The case involved the validity of a school district's student athlete drug policy which authorized suspicionless random urinalysis drug testing of students who participate in the school's athletic programs. The case moved beyond *T.L.O.* to the extent that it involved searches without individualized suspicion. The Court ruled that individualized suspicion was not necessary before submitting students to random urinalysis drug testing. The Court emphasized that school officials exercised their duties as state actors, an authority that was "custodial and tutelary, permitting a degree of supervision and control that could not be exercised over free adults" (p. 655). The Court even took the decision beyond its immediate context to conclude that "when the government acts as guardian and tutor the relevant question is whether the search is one that a reasonable guardian and tutor might undertake" (p. 655).

The impact of these rules governing searches are far-reaching. Most notably, the rules allow for sniff searches, random drug tests, use of surveillance cameras, locker searches, automobile searches, metal detectors and strip searches. All of these searches are permissible under two related grounds. A search may be very invasive (e.g., strip searches) so long as school officials have individualized suspicion and the search is reasonable under the circumstances. A broader, less intrusive search (e.g., through metal detectors) may be conducted without suspecting particular individuals so long as the students' reasonable expectations of privacy are not "subject to the discretion of the official in the field" (*New Jersey v. T.L.O.*, 1969, p. 342, n. 8). Such broad, low-intrusiveness searches are permissible as long as schools can articulate a rational reason for their searches. Given the broad reach of these policies, the search and seizure rules promulgated by the Court undoubtedly play critical parts in the control of students and ways to address adolescents' offending in and out of schools.

Although schools may possess broad authority in controlling student speech and conduct, schools' broad authority finds important limits when they seek to deny disruptive and even violent students the benefits of education. This area of law deals with the Due Process Clause of the Fourteenth Amendment. The leading case in this area, *Goss v. Lopez* (1975), found that students had interests in their education that could support a due process challenge by aggrieved students. In *Goss*, several students had been suspended for disruptive conduct relating to a student demonstration. The student who appealed, Lopez, had been suspended in connection with a disturbance and damage to school property. Lopez denied the charges but was never granted an opportunity to influence the suspension decision even though the school had no evidence linking him to the incident and there was no evidence that he was lying. The Court held that students suspended from school for up to 10 school days have both liberty and property interests protected by the Due Process Clause of the Fourteenth Amendment. The Court found that compulsory laws created both a property right and a liberty interest in public education. When schools' actions jeopardize that interest, it cannot be taken without traditional constitutional safeguards. Although the Court ruled that suspensions for up to 10 days implicated student's rights, it also found that those rights could be protected by simply requiring school officials to give students oral or written notice for the charges against them, and if the students deny the charges, an explanation of the evidence the officials had and an opportunity for the students to tell their side of the story. The Court, then, provides students an opportunity to protect their right to education but does not ensure that students will be educated if officials ultimately decide to suspend or expel them. As in the right to privacy implicated in searches, students' right to education may be protected through rather minimal safeguards.

Although the Court requires schools to adhere to some basic safeguards before they can suspend, expel, or perform searches on students, few substantive limitations have been placed on school official's wide discretion to discipline students. Protections that could exist would be implicated in extreme situations that could fall under the Cruel and Unusual Punishment Clause of the Eighth Amendment to the Constitution. The Court, however, has held that the clause does not protect students from school official's punishment. The leading case on this issue, *Ingraham v. Wright* (1977), involved corporal punishment imposed as a discipline in public schools. The students in *Ingraham* had been subjected to such severe physical abuse and injury as to be grounds for an official state report for child abuse. One student had received more than 20 hits with a wooden paddle resulting in severe hematoma, while another had been struck in the arm so severely that he was unable to exercise full use of the arm for a week. The Court did find that the punishment involved important liberty interests. Again, however, the Court found that due process did not require notice and a hearing prior to the imposition of corporal punishment in the schools—students' rights could be respected with minimal protections. The Court refused to apply even the momentary verbal interchange required by *Goss*. The Court found that the students had enough protection without requiring any proceedings prior to punishment. Rather than being found in the basic principles of the Constitution, the protections were to be found in the openness of the school, the professionalism of those who impose punishment, and the civil and criminal remedies available to those who get too severely beaten. From this perspective, minors only have voice after their rights have been violated; they can be subject to unwarranted punishment without any voice whatsoever. Although commentators and the dissent note that the opinion leaves adolescents without rights and without realistic remedies (Levesque, 2000a), states are allowed and do continue to impose corporal punishment in the schools.

The above cases are significant. As we saw in Chapter 2, public schools always have defined their missions as promoting the sometimes contradictory themes of individual rights and community values. At this moment, legal decisions tip the balance in favor of community safety over individual rights, a response largely to perceptions of crime and violence committed in the larger society. Accordingly, school administrators and teachers have legal authority to emphasize community values and preservation over individual student liberty interests, and must inculcate "habits and manners of civility" and "the essential lessons of civil, mature conduct" (*Bethel School District No. 403 v. Fraser*, 1986, pp. 681, 683). The cases call for a return to discipline, respect for authority, and the singular values of the community's majority in the classroom. To do so, the Court grants authority to public schools to inculcate values and socialize students in accordance with the majority of the community's preferences. The Court allows schools to do so notwithstanding the possibility that those preferences may not be the ones that students may have chosen for themselves or, even worse, the possibility that the imposed restrictions actually may not be in adolescents' own best interests.

LEGISLATIVE MANDATES

Understanding the significance of legislative mandates requires understanding an established general principle about the U.S. legal system. The federal Constitution provides only the minimal protections all governments must respect; federal, state, and local governments are free to offer increased protections. The only limit to those protections involves the extent to which they may violate constitutional principles. These rules mean that a proper analysis of the federal government's response requires consideration of both statutory enactments and Supreme Court responses to those mandates. Although it is important to emphasize that laws consistently fluctuate and are subject to challenge, the relevant statutes already have been addressed by the Supreme Court to the extent that important, general themes emerge to serve as a basis to evaluate policy responses to adolescent offending and victimization in schools.

Federal Safe Schools Provisions

As we already have seen in Chapter 1, the federal legislature and the executive branches generally aim to leave school issues to state officials. In terms of school violence, however, these federal branches of government have passed significant initiatives. From the 1970s to 1990s, the most important provisions included the commission of the "Safe Schools Study" to investigate crime and violence in public schools; a "National School Safety Center" to provide legal and administrative assistance with school violence problems; and the "Safe and Drug-Free Schools and Communities Act" to help organize drug prevention programs and educate children about the consequences of violent behavior (Cloud, 1997). These provisions reflect the federal government's commitment to revamp education through its "Goals 2000: Educate America Act—Safe Schools" (1994). Title VII of the act states that its purpose is "to help local school systems to achieve Goals Six of the National Education Goals, which provides that by the year 2000, every school in America will be free of drugs and violence" (Title VII, § 701). Toward this end, the Act made several funds available for various projects. The funding contributed to the proliferation of conflict resolution and social skills development programs, student-led peer mediation, peer counseling and student courts, acquisition and installation of metal detectors, and hiring of security personnel. By 1994, the federal initiatives had expanded even more and resulted in the Safe Schools Act (1994). That act established a program to provide more funding for violence prevention programs, victim counseling services, and security personnel. In addition to focusing on prevention and responding to victim's needs, Congress also responded to the threat of extreme violence as it enacted the Gun-Free Schools Act (1994). That act moved away from simply giving schools broad discretion in responding to crime. Instead, the act contained provisions that dramatically intruded on local and state powers to control educational matters. Among its most intrusive provisions, the act provided for a zero-tolerance policy requiring one year expulsions for bringing guns to schools. Given that a school's penalty for not following such a policy would be drastic—schools would lose their federal funding provided under the Act—the legislature provided for some discretion by allowing for some case-by-case changes in this policy made on a case-by-case basis. By fostering research, funding violence-prevention programs, and guiding school policies, Congress undoubtedly has emerged as a significant partner in schools' responses to violence.

The above initiatives generally have not been viewed as legally problematic. These efforts generally aim to assist states in their efforts to address school violence. In fact, few dispute the need for a federal role and few challenge the focus on prevention, education, and harsher sanctions for dealing drugs or selling guns near public schools. When the federal government's attempts are more intrusive and preempt states' efforts, though, the statutes do become problematic. Those efforts infringe on the role of states to provide and control the provision of education, a role the Constitution generally defers to states.

The above point gains increasing significance and is illustrated by recent legislation and Supreme Court responses to mandates that usurp state's roles. The Gun Free School Zones Act (1990) (not to be confused with the Gun Free Schools Act described above) made the knowing possession of a firearm on or near school property a federal crime. That legislation preempted the state's traditional control over education and their police power to define and respond to crime. The major way that the federal government would be able to do so would be if the actions somehow impacted a federal concern. The traditional way the federal government has shown that concern has been through linking the actions to an impact on interstate commerce. The Commerce Clause of the federal Constitution provides the federal government with a very broad power to regulate activities in and affecting commerce. It was the extent to which that power has become so broad which makes significant the Supreme Court's response to the act in *United States v. Lopez* (1995).

United States v. Lopez (1995) started when Alfonso Lopez, a 12th-grader, brought a concealed .38 caliber handgun to his school in Texas. Acting on a tip, authorities confiscated the unloaded weapon and five bullets from Lopez, who told them he had been instructed to deliver it after school to "Jason" who planned to use it in a gang war. Lopez was charged under the Federal Gun Free School Zones Act, found guilty and sentenced to six months in jail followed by two years of supervised release. He appealed the constitutionality of the act on grounds that Congress had no power to legislate control over public schools. Congress had recognized the power of the state to control public schooling but had sought to circumvent that limitation by acting under the Commerce Clause. The argument had been that gun violence affected the "business" of schools which affected commerce. A slim majority of the Supreme Court, for the first time in 60 years, struck down a provision that relied on the federal government's power to regulate interstate commerce. The majority opinion found that gun possession on school property, criminalized by 922(q), had nothing to do with "commerce" and was not an essential part of a larger regulation of economic activity in which the regulatory scheme could be undercut unless the interstate activity were regulated. The majority rejected the dissent's central argument. The four dissenting justices had argued that the seriousness of gun-related violence adversely affect classroom learning and represents a substantial threat to trade and commerce. The majority countered that the Congressional power would become too broad under this principle since a school's curriculum had a significant effect on classroom learning because such learning had a substantial effect on interstate commerce. Under the impact theory, the majority reasoned, the federal government could dictate the local curriculum, a possibility clearly not envisioned by the framers of the Constitution. The majority also was unpersuaded by other arguments usually used to uphold Congress' broad commerce clause power. The majority did not find elements which would assure that firearm possession affected interstate commerce. The Court also was unpersuaded by evidence that the costs of crime on the national economy contributed to a less productive citizenry.

Lopez reaffirms what the history of educational policy making reveals. Although education clearly may have federal consequences, its regulation remains within the purview of the states. The federal government does not have the power to mandate a federal curriculum for local elementary and secondary schools. If the federal government seeks to impact schooling, it must do so through other means, primarily through providing states with financial incentives to follow federal mandates. By providing states with a choice, the federal government resists imposing itself in educational matters. The argument is that, if states feel so strongly about policies within their jurisdiction, they simply can forego federal monies. Although this may seem coercive, states actually frequently do opt against federal funding in numerous instances, as exemplified by federal limits placed on sex education mandates that states reject (Levesque, 2000a).

Civil Rights Actions under Federal Tort Claims

In addition to broad federal efforts to control violence, the federal government also provides broad statutory frameworks that may be used by students who claim deprivation of their rights. Students, and their parents, frequently have brought claims under 42 U.S.C. § 1983. That federal remedy allows for the imposition of liability on state actors (e.g., teachers and school officials) for the failure to observe a constitutional duty. According to 42 U.S.C. § 1983 (1998):

> Every person who, under color of any statute, ordinance, regulation, custom, or usage, of any State or Territory of the District of Columbia, subjects, or causes to be subjected, any citizen of the United States or other person within the jurisdiction thereof to the deprivation of any rights, privileges, or immunities secured by the Constitution and laws, shall be liable to the party injured in an action at law, suit in equity, or other proper proceedings for redress.

The constitutional duty potentially placed on parties that deprive citizens of their liberties stem from the Fourteenth Amendment's protection against state deprivation of liberties without due process of law. The critical point of these arguments derives from the suggestion that students are in state custody and that those who act on the states' behalf must protect students from deprivations of their liberties, e.g., from victimization by others.

Although the Supreme Court has dealt with § 1983 torts in a variety of contexts, three cases directly relate to the issue of a state actor's duty to protect a citizen. These cases serve as the appropriate starting point; for they distinguish between the rights of victims based upon whether they are in official state custody. The first two cases involved individuals in involuntary state custody, which allowed for the use of federal remedies under § 1983. The first case, *Estelle v. Gamble* (1976), dealt with a state's duty in relation to prisoners who, because of incarceration, could not care for themselves. Given that inability, the Court found the state had a duty to provide adequate medical care. The second case, *Youngberg v. Romeo* (1982), involved the state's duties to provide for involuntarily committed mental patients. As with *Estelle*, the Court found an affirmative duty to protect a citizen placed fully within the state's custody. The cases stand for the accepted principle that the act of state custody creates a "special relationship" that binds the state actor to protect those under the state's complete control.

The duty does not necessarily arise, however, when the citizen is not in full state custody. This general rule was the holding of the third case, *DeShaney v. Winnabago County Department of Social Services* (1989). In *DeShaney*, the Court refused to hold the state responsible for its failure to remove a child from a father's custody when the state had received complaints of abuse and actually had taken temporary custody of the child. While sympathetic to the child's plight, the Supreme Court found the obvious: "nothing in the language of the Due Process Clause itself requires the State to protect the life, liberty, and property of its citizens against invasion by *private actors* ... Its purpose was to protect the people from the State, *not to ensure that the State protected them from each other* [emphasis added]" (pp. 195–96). Thus, although it seemed obvious that the child had been in danger and that the state had taken steps to safeguard the child, the state still had no constitutional duty to protect the child from harm unless it had taken him into custody. Only the custodial event gives rise to liability because it triggers the Due Process Clause protections of a State's inability to deprive individuals of their liberties without due process of law because the state restrains the individual's freedom to act.

Some seek to derive a more liberal interpretation of the *DeShaney* rule that would attach liability when there would be other similar restraint of personal liberty than incarceration or institutionalization or when the state renders the citizen more vulnerable to the dangers, even though the state did not create them. However, the duty still only arises when there is a "special relationship" between the actors and the state formed when the latter takes the former into some form of custody. Despite the possibility of a more liberal interpretation of the *DeShaney* rule, the Court's open window to find control in other areas has proven difficult to lift. The lower courts follow a basic pattern in their logic: for example, in *D.R. v. Middle Bucks Area Vocational Technical School* (1992), the 3rd circuit court found, and the Supreme Court denied to grant review, that no custody existed since the state did not restrict the victim's liberty to access help after school hours.

The above line of reasoning dooms attempts to impose sanctions on institutions that fail to protect students from other students. Relying on *DeShaney*, several circuits have found that assaults from other students do not give rise to a 1983 claim. For example, in *Aurelia Davis v. Monroe County Board of Education* (1994), the Court dismissed a case dealing with adolescent sexual harassment on the grounds that the school did not have a special custodial relationship with its students and that the school thus had no special duty to protect them from other students. In dismissing the Section 1983 claim, the Court noted that, in spite of compulsory attendance laws and the common law doctrine of *in loco parentis* (in the place of parents), no special relationship existed between the school district and victim which required an affirmative duty on the part of school officials to protect her from harassment. The only exception thus far has been in the context of residential schools, in which one court has recognized the *possibility* that a "special relationship," and hence a duty to protect, could exist (*Walton v. Alexander*, 1994). Thus, without the special relationships, schools have no duty under this legal approach to imposing liability on a state and its actors.

The post-*DeShaney* decisional law has not discouraged plaintiffs from using alternative routes to seek imposing constitutional liability on schools. The most common alternative theory argues that schools can be held responsible if they affirmatively acted to create the danger that caused the harm, or to render the plaintiff more vulnerable to it. Support for this claim draws from a single comment in *DeShaney*: "While the State may have been aware of the dangers that [the palintiff] faced in the free world, it played no part in the creation, nor did it do anything to render him any more vulnerable to them" (*DeShaney v. Winnebago County Department of Social Services*, 1989, p. 201). In *Middle Bucks* (1992), the federal circuit court recognized the theory but held that the complaint was insufficient to support the claim since school personnel's failure to intervene, despite complaints of sexually assaultive behavior, to address the behavior. As a matter of law, the school did not "create the danger" that caused the harm (p. 1376). Mere inaction by school officials will not support a claim under this theory. As was found in *DeShaney*, the "most that can be said of the state functionaries in this case is that they stood by and did noting when suspicious circumstances dictated a more active role for them" (p. 1376). Thus, states must have created or enhanced the danger.

Attempts to impose sanctions on institutions that fail to protect students from the actions of school officials (rather than students) may lead to a different result. One of the few Supreme Court cases that did address Section 1983 cases in public schools actually dealt with the school officials direct actions toward students. In the leading case, *Wood v. Strickland* (1994), the Court heard the appeal of two high school students who had been expelled from school for spiking the punch at a extracurricular meeting attended by parents and students. The students challenged their expulsions and sought to hold school officials liable under Title 42 U.S.C. 1983 for violating their constitutional rights. The Court articulated a qualified immunity from liability for school and other public officials and to vest them with substantial discretion in interpreting their own policies. The majority imposed a rigorous standard that imposes liability if the school official new or reasonably should have known that the action he or she took within the official's sphere of responsibility would violate the constitutional rights of the students affected or if the school official took action with the malicious intention to cause deprivation of constitutional rights or other injury to the student.

In sum, school districts and their representatives generally owe students little protection under § 1983 mandates. Federal remedies arising from state actors' mandates to protect adolescents' constitutional rights are difficult to obtain. Although several may champion the need to recognize and expand the remedy (Levesque, 2000a), current jurisprudence severely limits its utility. Cases based on this legal theory have yet to garner adolescents with much protection from other students' actions (Hermann & Remley, 2000). When violation does involve victimization and rights deprivations from school personnel, the standards remain considerably high and limit access to the ultimate remedies such mandates would offer students.

Federal Education Amendments

Actions on behalf of students have alleged a violation of Title IX (1998). Title IX specifically only provides that "[n]o person in the United States shall, *on the basis of sex*, be excluded from participation in, be denied the benefits of, or be subjected to discrimination under any education program receiving Federal financial assistance" (20 U.S.C. § 1681(a), 1999) (emphasis added). Title IX defines an educational institution as "any public or private preschool, elementary, or secondary school, or any institution of vocational, professional, or higher education" (§ 1681(c)).

Legal actions based on Title IX contend that schools that allow victimization may be held liable if the actions constitute discriminatory behavior that denies students educational benefits. In terms of students' misbehavior toward other students, the most common allegations charge that schools that allow a hostile environment involving sexual harassment against students constitutes sex discrimination. The link between sexual harassment and discrimination is significant; absence of the link renders the statute inapplicable and none of its remedies may be had. The link that allows some forms of student-to-student sexual harassment to constitute sex discrimination has been firmly connected and even has received the Supreme Court's imprimatur in *Aurelia Davis v. Monroe County Board of Education* (1999). That case involved a fifth-grade student's repeated attempts to stop sexual harassment by another student. Her formal complaint alleged that school officials were slow to react and for a six-month period allowed harassing conduct by a boy who tried to touch her breasts, rubbed his body against hers, and used vulgar language. The harassing ended only after the mother filed criminal charges of sexual battery against the boy, to which he pled guilty. As a result of the behavior, the victim's grades had suffered and she had contemplated suicide. After a series of reversals, the Eleventh Circuit eventually affirmed the trial court's dismissal of the Title IX claim and held that Title IX does not allow a claim against a school board based on a school official's failure to remedy a known hostile environment created by student-to-student sexual harassment (*Davis v. Monroe County Board of Education*, 1997). Of 11 judges, 6 concurred only in part, and 4 dissented. The Supreme Court, in a highly heated exchange between the majority and four dissenting justices, reversed. The Court found that Title IX actually does place a burden on schools to respond to student-to-student sexual harassment (*Aurelia Davis v. Monroe County Board of Education*, 1999).

To find liability under Title IX, the Court needed to find that (a) the statute allowed for imposing a right of action by victims against the school and (b) harassing behavior by peers could actually constitute discrimination for the purposes of Title IX. In its reasoning, the Court invoked *Franklin v. Gwinette County Public Schools* (1992) to find an implied right of action under Title IX which allowed for private damages actions against schools that discriminated, which in this instance would be the failure to respond to the student's harassment which deprived her of the schools' educational opportunities (*Aurelia Davis v. Monroe County Board of Education*, 1999, pp. 1670–71). In finding for the student, however, the Court also transposed from precedents a very high standard of misconduct on the part of the school and on the part of the harasser. In terms of the school, those seeking claims against schools must prove that the school had acted with "deliberate indifference to known acts of harassment" (p. 1671). The deliberate indifference must "'cause [students] to undergo' harassment or 'make them liable or vulnerable' to it" (p. 1672). To reach that high standard, the school must have exercised substantial control over both the harasser and the context in which the known harassment occurs (p. 1672). In terms of the harassing behavior that was not responded to appropriately by the school, the behavior must have been "so severe, pervasive, and objectively offensive" that it had undermined and detracted from the victim's educational experience so that they were "effectively denied equal access to an institution's resources and opportunities" (p. 1675). To reach that level, the Court explicitly noted that the behavior must be serious enough to have a "systemic effect" of denying them educational opportunity Title IX is designed to protect (p. 1676).

The four dissenting justices in *Davis* objected on several grounds. Most notably, they objected on simple legal grounds that a case decided only the previous year had emphasized the illegitimacy of finding an implied private cause of action under a statute which has been silent on the subject (*Gebser et al. v. Lago Vista Independent School District*, No. 96-1866, 1998). That silence meant that the Court had to defer to Congress and thus not infringe on the branches of state and federal government that make laws and allocate funds (*Aurelia Davis v. Monroe County Board of Education*, 1999, p. 1677). The justices also asserted that, for the purposes of Title IX's prohibitions, schools could only be held liable for harmful discriminatory actions when they are actually done pursuant of in accordance with school policy or action (p. 1679), which would make the schools not liable in peer harassment since it is not, for example, school policy to harass students. The justices also noted practical problems regarding the limited control schools have on their students, the need for schools to educate all students, the limitations placed on disciplinary measures against disruptive students, lack of resources to monitor students, and the difficulty of actually applying the legal notion of sexual harassment to normative adolescent sexual behavior (pp. 1680–1691).

Although the dissent provided powerful rationales against holding schools liable for student-to-student harassment, their fears are not likely to materialize at least any time soon (for a review of limitations to adolescents' redress, see Levesque, 2000a). Evidence suggests that the legal standard used to find liability ensures that only extreme cases will be litigated. In fact, the standard on which schools will be found liable nearly reach as high as the "state created danger" discussed above which finds school officials liable when they created the danger or rendered victims more vulnerable to dangers. The limits of the high standard are supported by existing research about the nature of adolescent sexual harassment. For example, it remains to be determined that students will pursue actions. Many students properly perceive that complaints to school authorities will not be treated confidentially and fear retaliation from alleged perpetrators or his friends and/or family. Likewise, without school awareness and school programs, children and their parents may not even know of other avenues for redress. In addition, even if redress is available, parents may not find the behavior disturbing and may contribute to the harassment. Lastly, despite already existing mandates and the prevalence of sexual harassment in schools, relatively few complaints are filed, still fewer are heard, and even fewer are found actionable. When existing policies exist, they are not necessarily followed or enforced. Relatedly, time and financial investment renders problematic the pursuit of sexual harassment claims. These difficulties are reflected in a plethora of important precedent-setting cases. Currently, these cases indicate that attempts to obtain redress are fraught with obstacles even though the right to proceed legally *may* be recognized.

Federal Disability Laws

One of the major developments in dealing with disruptive and potentially violent students involves the protections some students may receive through federal disability laws. Although federal disability law affecting students originated in the 1960s (for a review, see Melvin, 1995), Congress revisited and expanded the rights of disabled students in 1990 when it passed the Individuals with Disabilities Education Act (IDEA) (1998) and its recent amendments. The IDEA provides federal money to assist state and local agencies in educating disabled children. Those provisions place important limits on schools' responses to disruptive students.

To receive these federal funds, states must comply with both substantive and procedural IDEA requirements. To conform with the substantive requirements, each state must submit a detailed plan for providing a "free appropriate education" to children with disabilities; a school district does so when it gives children with disabilities "special education and related services" at no cost to the children's parents (§ 602(8)). Each disabled child's education must meet state standards and conform with the child's individualized educational plan (Id.). The formal detailed plans must recognize students' enforceable substantive right to public education and ensure that disabled children are mainstreamed into regular classes to the maximum extent appropriate. Thus, the children receive special education and services at public expense, under public supervision and direction.

In terms of procedural requirements, the IDEA provides parents with numerous procedures to protect their children's rights when they disagree with schools' plans for the child's education. These requirements require schools to notify parents regarding changes in the individualized education plans and provides parents with the opportunity to participate in meetings regarding the child's evaluations and educational placement (§§ 615(b) to (e)). In addition to those rights, the IDEA confers on parents extensive rights to challenge the school's evaluations and decisions. The statute enumerates the following procedural safeguards to ensure that parents can properly protect the rights of their children: the right to counsel, the right to advice from special education professionals, the right to present evidence and cross-examine witnesses, the right to a written record of the hearing, and the right to written record of the hearing officer's findings of fact and ultimate decision (§ 615(h)). The parents also have the right to appeal the outcome of a due process hearing to a state or federal court and may recover reasonable attorney fees if they prevail in the hearing or court proceeding (§ 615(I)). Congress views these mechanisms as a way to correct a history of exclusion by guaranteeing disabled students the right to an appropriate education designed to meet their needs as well as to mandate that disabled students be integrated (or mainstreamed) with non-disabled students in regular classrooms.

Although seemingly providing expansive, fair, and necessary protections for disabled students through their parents, the provisions have become rather controversial because of students' potential disruptiveness. The due process hearings provided by the Act place important limits on school officials' responses to disruptive behavior, such as the prohibition against unilateral suspension for more than ten days, the need to provide alternative education, and need to quickly return the child to the classroom (Rachelson, 1997). Recent amendments go even further. IDEA amendments forbid the termination of educational services through expulsion or suspension in excess of ten days for disabled children, even if there is no connection between their misbehavior and handicapping condition (Individuals with Disabilities Education Act, 1998, § 615(k) (8)(A)). Except with some modification relating to students who bring firearms to school, the provisions prevent school officials from using the most extreme of the traditional means of disciplining disruptive and violent students who are disabled.

Although the above statutory mandates curtail school officials' responses and limit the power of parents to challenge those responses, controversies still surround the new policies. These disputes highlight the new protections' relative strengths and weaknesses. One group of commentators suggests that the policies create unnecessary risks to school safety and discriminate against non-disabled students. For example, school officials argue that they need the authority to punish disabled students for violent misbehavior in the classroom; they contend that the disabled's civil rights hamper their ability to maintain safe schools (Groeschel, 1998). Others argue that the protections simply are too broad; they emphasize important gaps in identifying disabilities in school and how repeated behavioral incidents resulting in expulsion may be sufficient to qualify a student as disabled under the Act (Bryant, 1998). In addition to issues of school safety, others challenge the effects of the protections on other students. As a result of the need for due process hearings, for example, several commentators highlight the double standards resulting in schools' responses to disabled students and those who are not disabled: non-disabled students are more likely to be expelled and not provided with alternative forms of education (Groeschel, 1998; Rachelson, 1997). Similarly, commentators argue that the focus on disabled students forces districts to reduce services to general students and improperly provides more services to disabled and often disruptive students (Corbett, 1999).

Another group of commentators suggests that the protections are necessary although they still remain insufficient to protect the rights of disabled students. Parents of disabled students are concerned that schools will deprive their children of essential services if they are suspended or expelled; they also fear that schools may use behavior problems as excuses to remove disabled students from their classrooms (Groeschel, 1998). Others argue that many of the problems children with emotional disabilities face in schools arise from improper school responses, which tend to view emotionally disabled children as willfully bad and deserving of punishment, including expulsion from school (Glennon, 1993). These latter commentators list many deficiencies, such as the failure to identify many of the seriously emotionally disturbed students, failure to provide effective programs to those students identified as in need of special education, and the use of overly restrictive settings for students, including residential schools isolated from the students' communities (Glennon, 1993).

Like other critical areas of school disciplinary approaches, the Supreme Court has addressed the issue; and its ruling suggests that it is unlikely to disturb the current statutory provisions. In fact, the Court's only case in this area ultimately served as the foundation for the 1997 amendments. That case, *Honig v. Doe* (1988), essentially closed the door to efforts to exempt dangerous students from disability law protections. *Honig* involved the expulsion of disruptive and aggressive special education students, one of whom, among other things, had choked another student with sufficient force to leave abrasions and, on his way to the principal's office, had kicked out a window. In evaluating the IDEA's original provisions, the Court specifically stated that provisions requiring the due process protections for disabled students applied to dangerous students. The Court stated that the rule explicitly meant to remove school officials' unilateral authority that they traditionally had used to exclude disabled students (p. 323). The only exception to the "stay-put" provision would arise if the school officials could show that the placement would likely result in injury to the student or others (p. 328). In this instance, the Court balanced the interests of the disabled student in receiving a free appropriate education against the interest of the state (and school officials) in maintaining a safe environment for all students, and found in favor of the student.

The Supreme Court's opinion is far from radical. The Court asserted that disabled students have a right to appropriate education, a right recognized through the federal statute. In addition, even though the Court had upheld the right of students with disabilities to attend school, it placed no other restrictions on school officials' alternative methods of discipline. Thus, the Court noted that school officials could use short-term suspension, study carrels, detention, and restriction of privileges. The Court also ignored the extent to which the school environment contributes to the misconduct; or whether the school properly tried to respond and teach the student ways to understand or control their conduct. Lastly, the

Court prohibited exclusion from school only in instances where the misbehavior related to the disability, and left the school with great discretion in determining that link. From this view, the Court has not offered disabled students as many protections as may have been hoped.

STATE MANDATES

Safe Schools Provisions

All states' educational statutes address adolescent violence and disruptiveness to the extent they recognize that schools must provide safe learning environments. Although states universally recognize the need to provide safe schools, the nature of the recognition varies, particularly in terms of the extent to which the state undertakes its obligation. Thus, for example, Texas simply lists as one of its primary educational objectives the mandate that schools maintain a safe and disciplined environment conducive to student learning (Texas Education Code, § 4.001, 2000). Similarly, Kentucky's General Assembly finds that "every student should have access to a safe, secure, and orderly school that is conducive to learning" (Kentucky Revised Statutes, § 158.440, 1999). Minnesota also finds that "The public schools of this state shall ... develop the students' intellectual capabilities and lifework skills in a safe and positive environment" (Minnesota Statutes, § 120A.03, 1999). North Carolina's legislature finds that "all schools should be safe, secure, and orderly" (North Carolina General Statutes, § 115C-105.45, 1999). Rhode Island explicitly states that "Each student, staff member, teacher, and administrator has a right to attend and/or work at a school which is safe and secure, and which is conducive to learning, and which is free from the threat, actual or implied, of physical harm by a disruptive student" (Rhode Island General Laws, § 16-2-17(a), 2000). States, then, recognize safety as a concern, one which they construe as a matter of fact, as an objective, as something that would be worthwhile, as an obligation, or simply as an actual right individuals possess.

Although some states seem to recognize the right to safe school environments more absolutely than others, the recognition does not necessarily translate into policies that foster safe schools and create effective violence prevention strategies. This section examines variations and common themes in states' statutory mandates responding to students' violence and victimization. The analysis reveals considerable diversity in the manner each state construes its obligations and examines that diversity's significance. To do so, the analysis examines states' regulation of schools' disciplinary measures and violence prevention initiatives.

Disciplinary Measures

The most common area of state regulation directly reflects early Supreme Court jurisprudence dealing with disciplinary responses to students' disruptive behavior. As we have seen, those cases established that, to the extent students had rights to receive an education, school personnel could not deny their rights without minimal due process protections. States generally have addressed this issue in two dominant ways: (1) by enumerating the types of conduct deemed appropriate on school premises and in school-sponsored activities and (2) by detailing measures that can be taken in response to inappropriate conduct.

All states specify numerous types of misconduct subject to disciplinary actions. A close look at statutes reveals that the prohibited conduct remarkably varies, and typically varies according to school officials' potential responses. The focus on schools' potential response is of significance: it actually determines what is permissible conduct and the extent to which schools take some conduct seriously. One of the most striking aspects of states' efforts to deal with violence is the removal of disruptive students from educational environments. The two most frequently regulated forms of discipline, suspensions and expulsions, both remove students from school classes and activities. State statutes bestow on school districts their power to suspend or expel students as long as they have developed appropriate policies. Districts then delegate the implementation of that authority to teachers and principals.

A few examples illustrate well the wide variety of regulated conduct and the possible repercussions that may ensue from such conduct. Many states permit suspension *or* expulsion of students who express immoral or disreputable conduct or use vulgar or profane language (Tennessee Code Annotated, § 49-6-3401, 1999; Wyoming Statutes, § 21-4-306, 2000). Other states distinguish between suspension and expulsion to limit, for example, expulsion to conduct that constitutes a substantial interference with school purposes, including sexual assault and weapon possession (e.g., Revised Statutes of Nebraska Annotated, § 79-267, 2000; Texas Education Code, § 37.007, 2000). A few states focus on expulsion by listing offenses that permanently bar students from attending any public school, such as first degree murder, forcible rape or sodomy, robbery in the first degree (Revised Statutes Missouri, § 167.171(4), 1999). Statutes, however, pervasively contain clauses that allow for flexibility in their statutes' application; they do so, for example, by giving school officials discretion in determining the outcome of disciplinary procedures (e.g., Id.). These statutes, then, bestow on school officials wide discretion in controlling student conduct and determining its consequences.

Although school officials enjoy considerable discretion in applying disciplinary policies, their discretion tends to be subject to three important legal restrictions. A first limit involves the extent to which officials must abide by laws addressing the discipline of students with disabilities. As we have seen, the federal government requires states to offer disabled students increased protections. All states have enacted special education statutes pursuant to the federal requirements of the IDEA, so much so that state laws essentially mimic federal mandates (e.g., Connecticut General Statutes, § 10-76b et seq., 1999; New Hampshire Revised Statutes Annotated, § 186-C et seq., 2000; Wyoming Statute Annotated, § 21-2-205, 2000). A second limit involves the types of offenses that the federal government has viewed as critical to responding more forcefully to public concerns about crime. Reacting to these federal mandates, schools now respond more aggressively to weapon and drug offenses, some of which may require student expulsion for not less than one year (Texas Education Code, § 37.001(e), 2000; Virginia Code Annotated, § 22.1-278, 2000; Utah Code Annotated § 53A-11-904, 2000). Affecting more students, however, is the third major type of limitation—the requirement that schools provide students with basic procedural safeguards prior to infringing on their rights. Although students' due process rights have now been recognized in numerous school contexts, such as in cases involving search and seizure of contraband evidence (e.g., Tennessee Code Annotated, § 49-6-4203, 1999), statutes pervasively do not reflect that development. The most extensive statutory developments in due process rights involve disciplinary actions against students. Statutes generally provide students with more procedural rights as disciplinary outcomes become more severe (as they move from in-school suspension, suspension, expulsion, to permanent expulsion). For example, in-school suspensions typically are not even regulated. Yet, on the other hand, students who are to be expelled generally receive the right to: (1) written notice of the charges, the intention to expel, and the place, time, and circumstances of the hearing, with sufficient time for a defense to be prepared; (2) a full and fair hearing before an impartial adjudicator; (3) obtain legal counsel; (4) present witnesses or evidence; (5) cross-examine opposing witnesses; and (6) a written record demonstrating that the decision was based on the evidence presented at the hearings (e.g., Ohio Revised Code Annotated, § 3313.66, 2000). Existing state statutes, then, do provide considerable guidance to schools and help shape their policy responses to disruptive adolescents.

Although regulations curtailing disciplinary responses do control discretion, limitations do not ensure appropriate responses to dealing with disruptive students and those who may be deemed dangerous. For example, school officials still retain great power to determine what sort of discipline should be imposed and who should receive it. As a result, for example, research documents well the differences in groups that are subject to the more extreme disciplinary measures: minority adolescents more frequently receive suspensions and expulsions (Reed, 1996; Townsend, 2000). Likewise, nearly half the states still permit the use of corporal punishment; and those that do allow this form of punishment generally do not list the types of infractions that would permit its use. For example, subject to local district policies, Ohio permits the use of corporal punishment "whenever such punishment is reasonably necessary in order to preserve discipline" (Ohio Revised Code Annotated, § 3319.41, 2000) and Florida permits its use as long as principals identify the types of punishable offenses and as long as the person who will administer the punishment informs another present adult (not the student) of the reason for the punishment and the disciplinarian, upon request, provides the pupil's parent or guardian with a written explanation of the reason for the punishment and the name of the other adult who was present (Florida Statutes, § 232.27(j), 1999). Again, discretion helps account for the disproportionate use of corporal punishment against minority adolescents (Townsend, 2000). Equally importantly, the statutes typically do not ensure that expelled or suspended students receive an education; e.g., Texas law only mandates that educational agencies "*may* provide educational services to an expelled student who is older than 10 years of age in an alternative education program" (Texas Education Code, § 37.001(d)(3), 2000) (emphasis added). Although it would seem that expelled students would still receive an alternative education, states do not necessarily mandate that requirement. And, again, minorities disproportionately receive sanctions leading to the denial of education (Gregory, 1997). Statutes, then, do leave important discretion to local schools and their staff who would address disruptive school environments *and* schools do not uniformly apply their discretion.

Violence Prevention Initiatives

Until recently, responses to violent and aggressive adolescents essentially focused on enacting disciplinary policies, ensuring that students and parents received due process rights, and ensuring that individuals in schools were aware of disciplinary policies and codes of proper conduct. Within the past decade, several states have adopted statutes to foster more comprehensive violence reduction and prevention initiatives. Given the recency of responses, states that have responded generally tend simply to create resource centers. For example, California has enacted a statute to help coordinate key personnel and conduct research, including collecting and distributing information about violence initiatives (e.g., California Education Code, § 32228.1, 2000). Likewise, Missouri recently adopted a statute that requires the department of elementary and secondary education to identify and, if necessary, adopt programs of educational instruction regarding violence prevention and include community members in violence prevention efforts (Revised Statutes Missouri, § 161.650, 1999). Georgia requires every public school to prepare a school safety plan to help curb the growing incidence of violence in schools, respond to such incidents, and provide a safe learning environment (Georgia Code Annotated, § 20-2-1885(a)–(d), 1999). These cautious and necessary first steps have now been supplemented by two approaches to violence prevention that move beyond simply disciplining students.

The first approach to violence prevention focuses on establishing links with law enforcement and creating more effective control strategies. For example, Mississippi provides a school violence prevention grant program that offers metal detectors, video surveillance equipment, crisis management teams and violence prevention and conflict resolution training (Mississippi Code Annotated, § 37-3-83, 2000). California also commits itself to creating safe schools and violence prevention programs that involve cooperative agreements with law enforcement and providing schools with personnel trained in conflict resolution (California Education Code, §§ 32228.1-32234, 2000). Rather than supplying funds for developing violence prevention curricula and train staff, Georgia focuses on supplying funds for safety equipment (Georgia Code Annotated, § 20-2-1885 (a)–(d), 1999). Compared to Georgia, Washington seems more ambitious as its violence prevention mandate focuses on providing training offered to school staff interested in conflict resolution and other violence prevention topics (Revised Code of Washington, § 28A.300.270, 2000). Tennessee requires that the commissioner of education, in consultation with the commissioner of safety, develop advisory guidelines for local education agencies to use in developing safe and secure learning environments in schools; and mandates that "such guidelines shall emphasize consultation at the local level with appropriate law enforcement authorities" (Tennessee Code Annotated, § 49-1-214, 1999). As we have seen, approaches that focus on better engaging law enforcement have become a popular approach to addressing violence in schools. A review of existing state statutes reveals, though, that few states have seen fit to mandate this response through legislative mandates.

The second approach simply incorporates violence prevention into health education and other existing programs. Although this would seem like a dominant approach given the new focus on approaching violence as

a public health and educational concern, few state statutes reveal systematic attempts to respond to violence by incorporating efforts into existing
programs. Those that seek to incorporate these efforts tend to focus on
violence that would occur outside of schools. Thus, Massachusetts established a comprehensive interdisciplinary health education program that
includes school counseling services, health service delivery, and efforts
to prevent substance abuse, tobacco use, family violence, child abuse
and neglect, and early intervention services for high risk students
(Massachusetts Annotated Laws, ch. 69, § 1L, 2000). Likewise, Minnesota's
violence prevention curriculum aims to be integrated into existing curriculum in order to help students learn how to resolve conflicts within
their families and communities in nonviolent, effective ways by focusing
on preventing physical and emotional violence, identifying and reducing
the incidence of sexual, racial, and cultural harassment, reducing child
abuse and neglect and targeting early adolescents for prevention efforts
(Minnesota Statutes, § 120B.22, 1998). Similarly, Alaska's general curriculum similarly focuses on violence, by encouraging health education programs (including instruction in the identification and prevention of child
abuse, child abduction, neglect, sexual abuse, and domestic violence, and
appropriate use of health services) and by requiring the state board to
establish guidelines for a health and personal safety education program
and supplying adequate funds for teacher training in health and personal
safety education (Alaska Statutes, § 14.30.360, 2000). Although researchers
and policy makers increasingly frame offending and victimization as
fundamental health issues, legislatures have yet to reflect the trend.

    Although schools that do adopt broad violence prevention initiatives
tend to simply integrate these efforts into the general curriculum and use
existing personnel, it is important to note that some do attempt to integrate violence prevention into the general curriculum in a manner that
addresses violence by adolescents. Illinois encourages schools to provide
violence prevention and conflict resolution education courses or units in
existing courses which focus on consequences of violent behavior, causes
of violent reactions to conflict; nonviolent conflict resolution techniques;
and relationships between drugs, alcohol, and violence (Illinois Compiled
Statutes Annotated, tit. 105, 5/27-23.4, 2000). Likewise, West Virginia
recently adopted a statute to address violence by requiring that "the
state board of education shall prescribe programs within the existing
health and physical education program which teach resistance and life
skills to counteract societal and peer pressure to use drugs, alcohol and
tobacco, and shall include counselors, teachers and staff in full implementation of the program. The board shall also prescribe programs to
coordinate violence reduction efforts in schools and between schools and

their communities and to train students, teachers, counselors and staff in conflict resolution skills" (West Virginia Code, § 18-2-7b, 2000). Other states actually have developed programs that directly addresses violence reduction. Statutes that do address the issue generally provide that schools may offer instruction in violence prevention, self-esteem, and peer mediation (e.g., Louisiana Revised Statutes, tit. 17 § 286, 2000). Likewise, North Carolina's basic education program now includes a list of recommended conflict resolution and mediation materials, models, and curricula that address responsible decision making, the causes and effects of school violence and harassment, cultural diversity, and nonviolent methods for resolving conflict, including peer mediation (North Carolina General Statutes, § 115C-81(a4), 1999). Again, however, existing statutes that actually focus on preventing adolescent violence are remarkably rarer than would have been expected.

Preliminary Conclusion

Federal legislation and related cases reveal well the extent to which the legal system poses many formal obstacles to those who would use federal education mandates to offer greater protections to students. Numerous limitations are important to highlight. First, adolescents can benefit most from the legal system if their actions fit into preconceived legal mechanisms, such as the manner sexual harassment must constitute discrimination to obtain federal protection. Second, even if adolescents' actions would fit into existing legal categories, the standards for redress actually are quite high. Efforts to hold schools responsible for failing to protect students from violence or from inappropriate school official action typically fail. Third, the federal government continues to balance federal and states' rights in a way that allows states to retain considerable free reign to control and discipline students even to the extent that school officials may even deny students educations so long as officials follow minimal due process protections. Despite impressive progress in developing laws that would address the needs of offenders and victims, much progress remains to be made.

Although federal legislation could benefit from reform efforts, the emergence of a new federalism especially impacts federal responses to violence in schools (U.S. v. Lopez, 1995). That new balance of federal and state power limits the role of federal initiatives and renders imperative a close analysis of the nature of individual state mandates. That analysis reveals, however, that depending on state legislative mandates to address violence would seem unwise. An analysis of state statutes makes mythic the notion that states have taken the lead in experimenting with responses to violence by enacting cutting-edge law reform. Rather, existing statutes unmask a reactive approach spurred by Supreme Court and federal legislative mandates, as revealed by the focus on ensuring minimal due process rights to students subject to disciplinary sanctions, mandating expulsion for conduct the federal government has deemed especially dangerous, protecting the rights of disabled students, and essentially ignoring prevention that would entail curricular reform. Where the Supreme Court and the federal government have bestowed states with considerable discretion, such as in the context of regulating students' freedom of expression, states' statutes remain surprisingly silent and offer little guidance. To amplify problems even further, local discretion runs the risk of exacerbating invidious discrimination against already disadvantaged adolescents. Existing state legislation, then, remains considerably undeveloped and variable.

Despite important gaps in legislating responses to violence, it is important to note that most state laws express a need to address violence in schools. Despite that important commitment, how states do address violence remains essentially unguided by state statutory initiatives. As a result, for example, most states do not provide official, legal recognition of the need to address victimization by instituting policies and ensuring victims with avenues for redress. In general, when protections exist, efforts are simply made to suggest that schools create policies. The nature of those policies generally remains to be determined, as does how they will address the needs of adolescents. Existing violence prevention policies focus on detailing the nature of offenders' rights and on listing prohibited activities rather than taking preventive approaches that would address schools' role in fostering violence and that would help prevent violence by developing student and staff's skills, attitudes, and environments in a manner conducive to healthy development and peaceful conflict resolution.

Although current statutes present a general failure to address violence in a systematic and comprehensive manner, it is important to note that existing initiatives do evince considerable promise. First, that some states have legislated mandates eliminates arguments that states cannot do so. Second, some states that have responded have done so cautiously, an approach that emphasizes well the need to consider the most effective methods and need to leave local decision makers some discretion to adapt methods to their local school environments. Third, the focus on inappropriate conduct and punishment, although not necessarily effective in and of itself, provides a necessary first step in addressing violence. Fourth, the current focus on violence and problem behavior outside of schools, such as the focus on family violence and drug abuse, provides an important component of anti-violence programs that address well-documented links to violent behavior. Thus, although far from comprehensive, existing efforts do provide important sources of progress and hope.

CONCLUSION

Schools play numerous roles in adolescents' offenses. Schools variously serve as environments conducive to victimization, as root causes of offending inside and outside school grounds, and as sites for intervening and preventing violence. Understanding schools' roles and their relative significance is critical to fostering more healthy adolescents who can resist engaging in violence and who can respond effectively to unsafe and violent situations. Although still very much in its infancy, research highlights key points relating to the nature of adolescence, offenses and schooling. Schools' responses must be weighed carefully for they may induce the types of problems meant to be addressed. Schools also must confront several levels of violence without losing legitimacy as policing agents. The extent to which schools reach effectiveness rests on the extent to which families and communities can be engaged in similar socializing initiatives that support adolescents' resistance to violence and provides them with psychological and social resources to overcome and prevent victimization.

Although schools' roles in stemming the tide of violence and disruptive behavior remains daunting, schools already do respond to such behavior. The most popular responses favor approaches reflecting incarceration, paramilitaristic control and abridged freedom. The popularity of punitive approaches helps explain why the most widely-used response to school violence still involves the traditional "individual sanctions" approach which includes sending students to disciplinary classes for in-school suspensions, sending them home for out-of-school suspension, or expelling them from school (e.g., Anderson, 1998). Rather than producing desired outcomes, repressive strategies affirm that schools are *not* the place to learn how to grow and learn: Students are denied permission to attend if they have not learned what schools are supposed to be instilling; they only are welcome into the school community if they already know how to behave. A similar focus on sanctions and prohibitions for those who remain in school reveals similar outcomes. Simple prohibitions, without conditions conducive to resisting prohibitions, remain ineffective. Students benefit most from supportive environments that lead to resisting disruptive behavior. Non-supportive environments ensure that students learn that rights are insignificant and infringement sends an impermissible message to adolescents who are in the process of learning about how society and individuals in power respect their freedom and assist them to become responsible adolescents.

The extent to which legal responses respond appropriately to the current understanding of schools' roles in adolescents' violence is best understandable by emphasizing three significant points that have emerged from legal analyses. First, education remains a state issue, yet the reality is that federal law provides the most comprehensive and far reaching regulations of education. Federal law has encouraged the development of state laws and continues to set the bottom floor on which to judge and foster appropriate responses to violence and disruptions. Second, state legislatures have responded to what several view as an epidemic of adolescent violence and victimization. Equally importantly, the legal system allows schools to respond even more aggressively to provide more protections. Third, despite retaining considerable power and recognizing the need to provide safe learning environments, states have yet to take more active roles in guiding efforts to address adolescent violence both in and outside of schools. The last point deserves the most emphasis at this juncture; it will serve to highlight the most critical point of our analysis.

Despite important progress generally spurred by federal mandates, state legislative responses actually remain minimal, and when states do respond, their responses become remarkable for their limitations. Statutes are limited in both breadth and depth. State legislation that moves beyond recognizing the need for safe environments focuses on creating policies regulating consequences for students' misbehavior. This focus remains limited to the extent it proceeds without providing staff with training and students with skills and competencies that would allow them to follow directives. Furthermore, existing policies all explicitly focus on removing problem students from schools rather than enabling them to respect rules of conduct both within and outside of schools. Despite that focus, some states do reveal concern for assisting students and preventing their removal from schools and even recognize the need to receive input from the community and parents. Even that important development, however, remains limited. Only three states (Alabama Code, § 16-1-24.1(a), 2000; Ohio Revised Code Annotated, § 3313.663(A), 2000; Virginia, § 22.1-279.3, 2000) explicitly ensure involvement of parents of disruptive students (e.g., by subjecting them to fines for failing to participate in reintegrative efforts or by making them financially responsible for students' actions). No statute similarly seeks to involve parents of adolescents at risk for victimization; and no statute seeks to foster community reform to address violence. As a result, schools may fail to address the bulk of adolescent violence and victimization, which actually occurs mostly in homes and communities and, in turn, impacts school climates and violence. Yet, limitations in existing mandates actually highlight the most critical point to emerge from our analysis. Limitations reveal that the legal system allows considerable room for reform. As a result, the legal system leaves room for social scientists to marshal evidence to guide reform toward more effective responses to violent, disruptive, and potentially dangerous adolescents.

4

Model Adolescents

Society tends to view adolescents as amoral and as lacking in concern or respect for other people (Youniss & Yates, 1997). Although statistics offer a complicated picture of the reality of adolescent life, much research supports the negative view of adolescents' basic orientation to society. Compared to the several decades prior to the 1980s, for example, adolescents clearly have reneged on their role as political idealists who challenge tradition and seek a better society through political and social reform (Boyte, 1991; Flacks, 1988). Likewise, adolescents increasingly place themselves at risk for behaviors that contribute to their own and others' difficult circumstances. Many adolescents experiment with socially inappropriate behaviors—especially those related to alcohol and drug use, violence, and sexual activity—that they will not practice in adulthood but that nevertheless place them and society at risk for negative outcomes (Arnett, 1999). Even adolescents who do not engage in problem behaviors disapprove of them much less than other age groups do (Cohen & Cohen, 1996). These generally disturbing findings, though, frequently emerge with important contrary evidence suggesting that the vast majority of adolescents essentially do not manifest excessive self-interest and do not exhibit moral decline beyond that observed in previous generations or in adults (e.g., Youniss & Yates, 1997; Yates & Youniss, 1996; Arnett, 1999). In some domains, such as violent crimes and risky sexual activity, rates of adolescents' problem behaviors seemingly have peaked and exhibit downward trends (Jenson & Howard, 1999; Levesque, 2000a). Although adolescents may not disapprove as much of certain problem behaviors, they are indistinguishable from other age groups to the extent that they actually do place high priority on achieving very positive goals (Cohen & Cohen, 1996). Despite more favorable evidence and persistent efforts to paint a more realistic picture of adolescents, society still seems unwilling to embrace a more favorable view of adolescents (e.g., Males, 1996).

Much debate surrounds explanations for emerging findings suggesting that society has countered some of the apparently negative shift in adolescents' morality and prosocial concerns (Jenson & Howard, 1999; Levesque, 2000a). Few, however, suggest that positive shifts result from systematic educational efforts to address them (Damon & Colby, 1996; Levesque, 2000a). Although some educational programs demonstrate promise and long-term benefits may accrue for some adolescents (e.g., Durlak, 1997), research pervasively documents the ineffectiveness rather than successes of currently implemented programs. Schools pervasively remain unable to respond to the adolescent period's apparent commitment to resistance, defiance, and lack of interest in prosocial activities; to adolescents' apparent amoral, anti-intellectual, and dangerous behaviors; and to perceptions that adolescents' apparent self-interest and hedonism renders them unable to adopt responsible adult social roles in an ever-changing society (Levesque, 1998c). To exacerbate matters, schools actually may be contributing to declines in adolescents' responsible behavior (Elliott, Hamburg, & Williams, 1998).

This chapter examines the pedagogical and legal tensions surrounding the extent to which schools must, can and should enhance the development of prosocial values and more exemplary orientations to society. To do so, the chapter presents the current social science understanding of adolescents' values and social development and schooling's place in fostering such development as a background to evaluate current legal mandates that both require yet limit schools' attempts to inculcate prosocial values in students. The analysis focuses on the manner adolescents reveal a commitment to others and contribute to community life. The review focuses on developmental topics such as identity, values, volunteerism, morality, and intergroup relations to frame them as issues of adolescents' positive social engagement. That analysis then serves, along with the previous chapter and the one that follows, as a springboard for Chapter 6's proposals for school law reforms to foster adolescents' healthy development and social responsibility.

MODEL ADOLESCENT SOCIAL DEVELOPMENT

Polls consistently reveal that the general public, educators, political and religious leaders, and students themselves support public schools' efforts to instill proper social values (DeRoche & Williams, 1998). Although schools' roles in instilling values in students still may remain highly controversial, commentaries increasingly concur on the broad contours of values deemed worth fostering in adolescents. Examining the nature of values deemed worth inculcating, coupled by the current understanding of the nature of adolescent social and moral development, serves as a foundation for examining schools' efforts to provide opportunities and foster environments for students to express, experience, and internalize values critical to fostering and sustaining a civil society.

NATURE OF SOCIAL VALUES DEEMED WORTH DEVELOPING

Public schools necessarily confront a central paradox: They must ensure freedom while restraining it. Schools must both impose and oppose the inculcation of values. Although schools must deal with numerous and often conflicting values, their efforts fundamentally involve the need to promote the highly regarded value of individual students' self-determination (as well as that of their families and communities) while simultaneously denying that determination. Schools do so as they shape and constrain present and future choices to ensure a smooth functioning society in which adolescents (as well as their families and communities) take their social responsibilities seriously. Thus, adolescents must submit themselves to the yoke of educational demands in order to develop their own capacity for autonomous actions. The submission is not at all unusual, social institutions typically ask individual citizens to yield some degree of short-term personal freedom for the sake of long-term communitarian values. Although ubiquitous and necessary, the balancing undoubtedly poses many challenges as educational systems seek to support both individualistic and communal concerns and as they consciously indoctrinate and create values so that individuals, groups and communities will be capable of doing the opposite.

Existing efforts to understand moral development that is both healthy for individuals and for society constitutes an appropriate starting point to discuss the model social values deemed worth developing. Despite numerous potential controversies that can emerge (as we will see in the following section), scholars of morality and moral development increasingly concur on what constitutes model moral development and moral identity worth fostering. Researchers and commentators generally view effective moral identity as constituting a sense of self marked by empathy, altruism, and cooperation committed to promoting and respecting others' welfare (Hay, Castle, Stimson, & Davies, 1995; Berkowitz & Grych, 1998). This view implies a concern for society's well-being and a sense that one can make a difference in society—moral maturity involves the willingness to grasp the moral aspect in everyday events and take action on its behalf. Thus, despite the tendency to distinguish socially focused morality and self-interest as separate and orthogonal orientations, individuals deemed moral exemplars and model citizens define others' welfare and their own self-interest as inseparable in that their socially-oriented moral goals constitute their very identities (Colby & Damon, 1995).

The values deemed worthy of developing generally involve those that allow individuals to develop and exhibit moral identities that fuse self- and socially-oriented interests (Hart, Atkins, & Ford, 1998). From this view, there actually may be numerous values worth fostering so long as individuals exhibit, and eventually end up exhibiting, concern for themselves and others. These values derive from different dimensions of personality, intellectual style, temperament, and other dimensions that influence individuals' general approach to their social world. These dimensions allow for the existence of many different types of individuals deemed "of good character." From this view, character involves ways by which individuals pursue a consistent yet flexible path around social and ethical dilemmas; character involves the manner individuals mesh their ability to make moral judgements and their tendency to engage in prosocial behavior.

The type of moral identity deemed mature and worth developing emerges during adolescence. The moral identity that unifies the self's basic orientation to society requires individuals to combine complex cognitive, emotional and behavioral elements. Given the need to combine these elements to achieve a coherent sense of one's social orientation, researchers aptly argue that developmental and social transformations that occur across the threshold into adolescence allow, for the first time, for the development of a moral identity integrated into adolescents' sense of self (Blasi, 1995; Davidson & Youniss, 1991). Moral judgments and behaviors are tied intimately with strong judgments of self-worth and values. A strongly articulated self-identity, concern for that concept and the individualism that gives rise to it, provides the basis for moral action (Hart, Yates, Fegley, & Wilson, 1995). Thus, although it is important to emphasize that even infants exhibit moral behavior (Trevarthen, 1993), researchers increasingly view the adolescent period as one of changes that lead to moral identity construction. Coupled together, research on adolescence and moral identity allows researchers to understand better the socialization that leads to the development of positive moral development and productive engagement with communities. The next section examines these changes and understandings.

CHARACTERISTICS OF ADOLESCENTS' SOCIAL DEVELOPMENT
AND MODEL SOCIAL ORIENTATIONS

The adolescent period constitutes a time of remarkable changes in thinking, development and action. The transition fundamentally impacts both adolescents' current and future orientation to society. As with any other fundamental transition in human development, the changes in basic orientation to society emerge as part of other critical social, biological, and psychological developments. Although profoundly interrelated, five domains of development critically impact socio-moral development during adolescence.

The first critical transformation involves rapid and sweeping developments in adolescents' cognitive abilities that profoundly impact adolescents' orientations to their social environments. The cognitive transition allows adolescents to think conditionally (by using "if" and "it depends") and in terms of uncertainty. The transition also allows adolescents to be less egocentric and to engage in sociocentric functioning: unlike children, adolescents are better able to understand others. Thus, the period generally involves a move away from a focus on concrete information and personalized attributions of responsibility for certain actions and a move toward a focus on abstract conceptions of systems, ideologies, institutions and values. These critical changes allow adolescents to consider alternative possibilities, to engage in thinking about thinking, and to explore different value systems, political ideologies, personal ethics and religious beliefs. As a result of these changes, adolescents experience a heightened interest in ideological and philosophical matters, such as conceptions of individual freedom, civil liberty and social justice, and more sophisticated ways of looking at those matters.

The above cognitive developments are actually important to consider. They challenge negative views of adolescents' concerns for society and confirm adolescents' concern with social, political, and moral ideologies. Rather than selfish concern for themselves, adolescents exhibit a need to link themselves to communities and evaluate society's moral foundations. Adolescents' cognitive developments in perspective taking—the ability or tendency to understand internal and external states of others, including their social context—clearly benefits moral development and behavior. Overall, research suggests a positive relationship between the ability to engage in perspective taking and prosocial behaviors, all of which are associated with levels of moral reasoning. That is, higher levels and states of moral reasoning and other-oriented modes of moral reasoning relate positively to prosocial behaviors (Fabes, Carlo, Kupanoff, & Laible, 1999) and higher levels of moral reasoning relate negatively to delinquent and antisocial behaviors (Eisenberg & Fabes, 1998). These findings receive considerable support from studies of criminal behavior that highlight the significant roles empathy and perspective taking play in crimes of violence. Especially aggressive adolescents, for example, tend to exhibit problems processing information in a non-hostile manner; they tend to adopt a hostile attributional bias which makes them more likely to interpret ambiguous situations as deliberately hostile (Lochman & Dodge, 1994). Adolescents' cognitive development, then, provides an opportune time for adolescents to identify themselves with social, political, and moral positions that give their developing identities direction and meaning.

The second major transformation adolescents experience involves the manner peers provide important developmental contexts. Compared to younger age groups, adolescents' peer groupings change both in significance and structure. Adolescents experience a precipitous drop in the amount of time spent with parents; much of the time is replaced with time spent alone or with peers (Larson & Richards, 1991). Adolescents' peer interactions also dramatically change in the way they function much more often without adult supervision than they did during childhood (Brown, 1990). Likewise, adolescence marks the emergence of interest and concern for interacting with larger groups of peers, a movement toward belonging in cliques and more vaguely defined crowds (Kinney, 1993). Finally, interactions with others increasingly differentiate themselves, such as in terms of the extent that they involve opposite-sex peers and the extent to which peers tend to associate with those from the same social class, race, age, and grade in school (Ennett & Bauman, 1996). These transformations gain significance to the extent that they provide adolescents with positions in social structures, channel adolescents into associations with some individuals rather than others, and provide contexts for rewarding or disparaging certain lifestyles and behaviors (Brown, 1996). Peer groups and peer interactions, then, provide adolescents with opportunities to evaluate and define themselves and their interactions with society.

Although researchers have long accepted the existence of a peer group that constitutes a "youth culture" that evinces values different from traditional adult values (Coleman, 1961), adolescents themselves distinguish among individuals within that broad culture and select their own peers. Adolescents differentiate among peers based on values that correspond to adults' wide array of reasons for social associations. Equally importantly, adolescents associate with peers who express similar values. Three major types of values seem to determine adolescents' associations with certain peers. Adolescents associate with peers who have similar attitudes toward school, school achievement, and educational plans (e.g., Berndt, 1999). Adolescent peer groups also generally have a similar orientation to popular culture, as evidenced by tastes in music, dress, and leisure activities (e.g., Kinney, 1993). Lastly, adolescents tend to associate with those who reveal similarity in aggressive, antisocial and delinquent behavior and attitudes (Fergusson & Horwood, 1996). Although peer associations need not require concordance on all salient values, adolescents' peers clearly play critical roles in expanding, affirming, and reinforcing certain values as they contribute to adolescents' social environment.

Given the significance of adolescents' associations with others with similar values-orientations, peers undoubtedly play a powerful role in promoting (or hindering) adolescents' social development. In fact, clear links exist between peer networks and adolescents' prosocial development. Commentators, however, continue to debate the significance and exact nature of those links as well as the magnitude of positive and negative peer influences on adolescent behavior. Despite controversies, several findings emerge from recent research. Adolescents' peer interactions are different from those of adults to the extent that peers respond to prosocial behavior in a prosocial manner and engage in cycles of prosocial exchanges, a response viewed as unique to the adolescent period (Schonert-Reichl, 1999). Likewise, adolescents who have friends not involved in deviant behaviors also are likely to avoid deviant behavior (Eisenberg & Fabes, 1998). In addition, the impact and function of peers change through the adolescent period: adolescents' peer relations move toward more intimacy, which in turn impacts moral development and behavior through increasing adolescents' capacity for sympathy and empathy (Eisenberg & Fabes, 1991). These findings counter popular perceptions that peers provide a source of deviancy from societal norms. Maintaining interactions with peers requires sustaining cooperation, dealing with conflict, and achieving mutual understanding (Youniss & Smollar, 1985). Peer interactions, then, provide rich contexts in which to learn the intricacies and dangers of helping others, develop principles by which to judge when moral obligations arise, gain support for involvement in assisting others, and encourage those with less motivation to commit themselves to others (Hart, Yates, Fegley, & Wilson, 1995). These examples highlight how changes in peer group functions and structures impact the extent to which adolescents can and do engage in prosocial behavior; the core of peer relationships are inherently conducive to other-oriented prosocial norms.

The third major transformation adolescents experience involves basic physical changes—generally subsumed under the broad rubric of "puberty"—that necessarily interact with the changes highlighted above and that affect adolescents' behaviors and functioning. The biological changes that mark the existence of puberty directly affect behavior. For example, increases in testosterone directly link to an increase in sex drive, sexual interest, and sexual activity (McClintock & Herdt, 1996). Research also has long established that pubertal changes impact self-image and appearance which in turn elicit different reactions from others. For example, early maturing boys tend to be more popular; they also more frequently report positive feelings, such as being in love (Richards & Larson, 1993). Girls who mature earlier tend to exhibit more emotional difficulties, including lowered self-image, and higher rates of eating disorders and depression (Alsaker, 1995). Although physical changes may be the most obvious, pubertal changes involve much more than biological forces impacting adolescent development. Indeed, the impact of biology on social behaviors is not necessarily unidirectional: environmental conditions and adolescents' behaviors may effect biological changes. For example, adolescents who mature in less cohesive, or more conflict ridden, family environments mature earlier; girls who grow up without their fathers mature earlier than girls whose fathers are present (Graber, Brooks-Gunn, & Warren, 1995). These findings serve to highlight well how adolescents' social conditions impact their development which, in turn, impacts their interactions with others. Regardless of the causes of pubertal changes, the effects of puberty and its related psychosocial changes tend to be dramatic.

The onset and experience of puberty clearly influences moral development. That influence, however, may not necessarily move development in a positive direction. Illustrative of the complexity is puberty's impact on increasing interest in sexual activity and romantic relationships. Interest in intimate relationships may foster prosocial and moral development by focusing adolescents' attention on behaviors that promote and foster intimacy, such as helping, caring for, and sharing. These relationship patterns provide adolescents with a context to explore other-oriented emotions and increase adolescents' capacity for sympathy and empathy, both of which highly correlate with prosocial and moral behavior (Eisenberg & Fabes, 1991). On the other hand, puberty related characteristics also may diminish prosocial tendencies. Physical maturation may increase self-consciousness, impulsivity, anxiety, embarrassment, irritability, mood swings, and aggressiveness (Alsaker, 1995; Connoly, Paikoff, & Buchanan, 1996). In addition to the general impact of puberty on adolescents' social interactions, the timing of puberty may influence the moral development of adolescents. Both early maturing girls and boys are more likely than late-maturing adolescents to become involved in deviant activities, including delinquency and use of drugs and alcohol, school problems, early sexual intercourse and other risky activity (Orr & Ingersoll, 1995).

No dramatic changes linked with pubertal development have been so firmly established as puberty's differential impact on the sexes' moral development. To a large extent, sex-specific effects should not be surprising given the extent to which adolescents generally experience a heightened need to act consistent with traditional gender-role expectations (Balk, 1995). Why and how such gender role intensification occurs is not clear, but reviews of the moral development literature continually reveal that, across late childhood and adolescence, girls are more prosocial than boys and the differences increase with age (Eisenberg & Fabes, 1998). For example, girls are more likely to engage in volunteer work and more likely to hear messages of social responsibility emphasized in their families (Flanagan, Bowes, Jonsson, Csapo, & Sheblanova, 1998). Likewise, girls exhibit more altruism and empathy and are more likely to feel guilty when they fail to act compassionately (Williams & Bybee, 1994). In addition, research relating to delinquency, relationship skills, and community concerns continually place girls in a much more positive light (Chapin, 1998). These differences in prosocial orientations are significant yet frequently ignored. Sex differences emphasize the need to take a broad view of social commitment, rather than a narrow view that would reveal the consistent finding that girls express less interest in politics than boys. Girls, then, consistently exhibit more prosocial behavior than boys.

The fourth transformation relates to adolescents' relationships with authority figures, particularly relationships with parents and family members. Evidence suggests that adolescents' development of value autonomy occurs later than does their emotional or behavioral autonomy from family members. Emotional and behavioral autonomy typically occurs in early and middle adolescence. As that autonomy increases, adolescents develop their own sets of values which may reflect but nevertheless emerge as distinct from their parents' values and beliefs. The period of adolescence also typically involves questioning the extent to which parents are omnipotent and infallible authorities, a process that allows adolescents to reevaluate their fundamental sets of ideas and values about their interactions with others. Although adolescents may be reevaluating their values, it is important to note that adolescents' core values tend to mirror those of their parents, such as parents' expressed commitment to educational and religious institutions and parents' views of civic involvement (Fletcher, Elder, & Mekos, 2000).

Although successful transitions out of the adolescent period vary and do not necessarily involve intense rethinking of values, some patterns of parent-child relationships generally relate to healthier outcomes.

Parenting styles and behaviors impact the extent to which adolescents exhibit moral behavior, self-discipline, and social responsibility. Relationships deemed more democratic, or "authoritative," seemingly produce the most effective parent-child relationships. The findings are increasingly robust as cross-cultural considerations reveal that the most effective forms of parenting still are those characterized as warm, responsible, responsive and demanding (Baumrind, 1991; 1996). Authoritative parenting is neither exclusively child-centered nor exclusively parent-centered but, instead, seeks to integrate adolescents' needs with those of other family members, as it treats the rights and responsibilities of adolescents and those of the family as complementary. The distinguishing features of authoritative parenting—its emphasis on discussion, explanation, clear communication and responsibility—all relate to healthy social adjustment.

Authoritative parenting styles clearly impact adolescents' levels of moral development and community engagement. Several studies link advanced levels of moral reasoning to authoritative families (Boyes & Allen, 1993; Speicher, 1994; Walker & Taylor, 1991). In addition to those studies, several have examined the relation of parenting styles to components of moral development; these areas of research generally note that authoritative parenting produces higher moral functioning (Berkowitz & Grych, 1998). These findings reinforce those from other studies that continue to link this form of parenting to higher academic achievement, lower rates of delinquency and sexual activity as well as other important psychosocial outcomes (Collins, Maccoby, Steinberg, Hetherington, & Bornstein, 2000). The extent to which familial relationships and internal familial dynamics are significant is further highlighted by cross-national research emphasizing how adolescents who view public interests as important life goals come from families that emphasize an ethic of compassion, empathy and social responsibility (Flanagan, Bowes, Jonsson, Csapo, & Sheblanova, 1998). In addition, parents' own involvement in community activities predicts their adolescents' civic participation; when parents are not involved, the extent to which they parent authoritatively predicts their adolescents' civic participation (Fletcher, Elder, & Mekos, 2000). Even civically uninvolved parents, then, can influence their children's civic engagement, a finding that reinforces the pervasive finding that warm parents inculcate a general sense of social competence in their children (Janssens & Gerris, 1992); and social competence fosters and reinforces adolescents' efforts to seek out social relationships with others through civic opportunities. Thus, adolescents are more likely to engage in prosocial behavior and positive community activities if their parents are emotionally available, supportive and teach the importance of helping others (Eisenberg, 1992).

The fifth critical change that occurs during the adolescent period relates to a general move from authoritarian values to more democratic tolerance and need for voice in institutions outside the family. Early adolescents tend to believe more in the goodness and correctness of authority and its ability to control evil and wickedness. Early adolescents also reflect rigidity in their thinking, especially as they respect the law and favor strong punishment for wrong-doings. They also tend to be uncritical and trusting of authority. Later adolescents experience a shift in attitudes toward increasing tolerance of alternatives, more openness to change, and more receptivity to democratic principles (for a review, see Flanagan & Galay, 1995; Helwig, 1995). The movement away from authoritarianism, obedience, and unquestioning acceptance of authority's rulings relates to adolescents' cognitive development—to their ability to think in a more flexible manner, perceive more conflicting principles and systemic causes, and increasingly use a coherent and consistent set of principles. These changes influence adolescents' involvement in political movements, civic organizations, community work and other opportunities that foster civic engagement. The extent to which adolescents exhibit this change is important to consider to the extent it reveals a broader view of prosocial behavior, one that moves beyond close relationships to relationships with communities.

Adolescents' views of how civic life functions and of their place in civic life clearly vary. As we have seen, the dominant view is that adolescents reject community interactions and communities fail to make room for adolescents. In reality, though, adolescents exhibit trajectories that mirror adults' own levels of engagement in communally-oriented activities that would improve civic life (Verba, Schlozman, & Brady, 1995). The diverse orientations in adolescents' community interactions necessarily includes adolescents who manifest deep commitment to communities, as evidenced by community volunteerism and social activist stances (Colby & Damon, 1995). These adolescents, viewed as moral exemplars, reveal a marked shift from an individualistic orientation to being able to consider community needs (Colby & Damon, 1995). Adolescents who engage in civically responsible behaviors further demonstrate a more well-defined set of value structures and an increased awareness of community life (Merelman, 1985). Most unlike their less socially-committed peers, these adolescents exhibit a highly idealized image of themselves that supports their prosocial activity. The idealized image performs the critical function of motivating and sustaining when the commitment makes difficult demands; that commitment, in turn, results in new attributions supportive of the ideal self consistent with the activity (Hart, Yates, Fegley, & Wilson, 1995). Those who maintain active community involvement further enhance their idealized selves by justifying their actions to others, as well as the self, all of which heighten the salience of moral perspectives and actions in evaluating the self and others (Hart, Atkins, & Ford, 1998). As a result, adolescents who sustain active community service articulate a close connection between their activism and their sense of self-understanding. Morally exemplar adolescents define themselves in terms of their own moral actions, so much so that they take their altruism and prosocial behavior for granted and view it as not deserving special mention because it becomes part of their self-definition (Colby & Damon, 1995; Hart & Fegley, 1995). Despite variations, then, some adolescents exhibit exemplary social commitment as an ingrained character trait.

The varied extent to which adolescents do experience the transition in a manner that broadens their concerns for society and participation in civic life reveals adolescents' commitments to society and society's commitments to adolescents. The social context in which adolescents find themselves influences deeply their political attitudes and prosocial behaviors. Thus, minority adolescents, particularly adolescents living with limited opportunities, tend to be more cynical about politics than their nonminority counterparts (Torney-Purta, 1990). As a result, national surveys suggest that a higher percentage of Black adolescents than White adolescents judge as extremely important goals such as correcting social and economic inequalities, being a leader in one's community, and making a contribution to society (Hart, Atkins, & Ford, 1998). Social conditions, however, frustrate the development of socially-oriented, model behavior. Poverty and the concentration of poverty in minority neighborhoods reduce the opportunities important to the development of voluntary service, community involvement and political connections (Hart, Atkins, & Ford, 1998). Communities lacking in social capital and community attachment cannot provide the wide range of institutions (such as teams, clubs, and youth programs) that allow adolescents to experiment with moral identities and that connect adolescents with responsible adults from outside the family. Although particular adolescents may be motivated to volunteer and be involved in community efforts, they do not necessarily do so in obvious ways because infrastructures must be developed to provide opportunities, resources, and guidance necessary for involving adolescents (Freedman, 1993). Social structures in which adolescents find themselves link to adolescents' community involvement.

In addition to these broad community impacts, social trends influence the extent to which adolescents will engage in activities that benefit the common good. Trends reveal a decline in commitment to the welfare of the broader community and an increase in materialist aspirations. During the late 1970s and 1980s, for example, research noted adolescents' retreat from civic or group concerns. For example, adolescents increasingly sought occupations for financial remuneration rather than public service or self-fulfillment (Easterlin & Crimmins, 1991). Increasing focus on capitalism and remuneration are obvious in even mundane activities as household chores and expectations of allowances. Adolescents who expect allowances for chores are given chores as a way to learn self-reliance; adolescents who do not expect (and even oppose) allowances for chores are those who view their chores as a responsibility to their group (Bowes, Chalmers, & Flanagan, 1997). Self-interest generally has eclipsed the public interest in the goals of young people (Flanagan, Bowes, Jonsson, Csapo, & Sheblanova, 1998). The impact of communities, even through historical time, should not be surprising. The properties of strong civic society, as exemplified by trust, reciprocity, a dense network of community institutions, and caring adults, keep adolescents out of trouble and foster integration into the broader community (Blyth & Leffert, 1995). Problematic relationships between adolescents and society are more a function of institutional structures than of inherent deficiencies in adolescents.

Preliminary Conclusion

Events occurring between the time adolescents enter and exit adolescence dramatically alter adolescents' approaches to and views of their social world. Changes in the adolescent period reveal an opportunity to nurture social development. Although adolescence is commonly portrayed as a period of internal struggle to find an authentic and satisfying sense of self, it also involves a struggle with defining one's place in society. Understanding adolescents' moral development and commitment to social life requires that it be addressed contextually and in relation to opportunities. Family values and dynamics inform adolescents' developing concepts of community and responsibility to the public interest. Experiences of membership in institutions outside the family, such as volunteering and active participation in schooling and other institutions, are necessary for adolescents' successful integration into society and their identification with the common good. Adolescents' peer relationships further prepare them to respond to others; indeed, these relationships help them respond to inequalities relating to gender, race and class. All of these changes reveal how adolescents seek to be part of society. Adolescents' disenchantment with the political system and broader community life need not be viewed as a necessary part of adolescent life nor as peculiar to the adolescent period. The adolescent period provides developmental opportunities to draw on adolescents' existing strengths and their desire to be meaningfully involved in society. The extent to which adolescents' moral identities relate to their social conditions provides an important opportunity to assist adolescents achieve more healthy and responsible orientations toward others.

THE PLACE OF SCHOOLS IN FOSTERING MODEL SOCIAL DEVELOPMENT

Schools aim to inculcate values, despite the popular view that the types of values inculcated throughout adolescents' socialization generally should be left to and guided by parents and other social institutions. Schools actually foster adolescents' sociomoral development in numerous explicit and implicit ways. This section examines both curricular efforts and the often ignored moral atmosphere schools exude in their efforts to inculcate certain values and behaviors in students. Although much research still needs to confirm emerging trends in research findings, important trends do exist and lay a foundation for discussing the type of education necessary for fostering moral and socially minded behavior.

CURRICULAR RESPONSES

Fads generally determine the values that influence educational approaches and their reform, and educational approaches to instilling moral and socially-favored values provide no exception. Despite changes in names and pedagogical approaches—from moral education, values clarification, civic education, character education to service education—school-based efforts to address adolescents' moral and prosocial development all address similar concerns and raise similar debates. Ensuring the development of socially responsible citizens generally leads to championing responses that fall under the general and necessarily interrelated categories of moral deliberation or moral action.

Moral Deliberation

Approaches that focus on moral deliberation generally adopt two stances: education as the development of rationality and education as a means of cultural assimilation. The first approach seeks to enhance adolescents' abilities to make sound decisions by encouraging students to think through moral dilemmas. The second approach focuses more directly on moral inculcation of specific values so that adolescents will develop good habits and espouse specific values. Although both approaches show promise to the extent that both may be necessary to foster the development of adolescents who exhibit high levels of moral development, both approaches also remain problematic as efforts to address the inculcation of values in students in public schools.

The most established approach to fostering adolescent moral development involves teaching the processes of reasoning about values while avoiding the transmission of definite moral content. The approach derives from early psychological research on moral development. That research suggests that reasoning about values raises moral consciousness and that moral consciousness tends to be related to moral behavior. Educational programs that adopt this model rest on the finding that moral development emerges with cognitive development, both of which are amenable to enhancement through deliberate discussion of moral dilemmas (Kohlberg, 1985). The approach suggests that adolescents will pass through predictable stages of moral development and that, by doing so, they will reason in ways ethically superior to the preceding stage. Student discussion and cooperation allows students to enhance their cognitive capabilities which, in turn, allows for more sophisticated moral reasoning. The underlying assumption is that all values may be entertained seriously as long as adolescents reason in accordance with the approved process of thinking about moral problems. Under this approach, then, teachers serve as discussion guides who help raise adolescents' levels of moral reasoning simply by providing an environment that exposes adolescents to higher levels of reasoning. Rather than teaching right from wrong, teachers guide the process for deciding right from wrong and resist intentional normative input. Thus, it is not enough to learn to focus on independent reasoning abilities; rather, students learn to think and discuss moral problems as a community. This approach seeks to promote a value-free or relativistic values education and places a focus on the procedures by which students adopt their own values as they interact within a community of students guided by teachers (Duncan, 1997).

Although the moral reasoning approach may appear relativistic, it does seek to foster important values. The approach exposes students to all relevant viewpoints and seeks to have students entertain the viewpoints equally seriously. Proponents of the approach suggest that doing so fosters reasoning and the values of justice, equality, tolerance and freedom (Kirschenbaum, 1977). As the approach encourages students to locate and embrace their own personal moral code, it inevitably promotes values of self-inquiry over, for example, unquestioned allegiance. In this regard, the approach may be relativistic in substance but not procedure—teachers must aim to provide structure for enhancing moral reasoning. Placing emphasis on procedures necessarily means that the moral deliberation approach fosters certain values. Although instilling values, the approach manages to avoid important controversies to the extent that the inculcated values comport with some fundamental democratic values that may serve to guide society's goals for adolescent development.

Several challenge the effort to provide a value-free approach and champion the need for an education that inculcates selected values. Some argue that too much reflection and reasoning stifles moral responses and erodes respect for authority and that focusing merely on debating ethical issues leaves students without core values and principles (see, most notably, Bennett, 1993). This view appropriately notes the impossibility of teaching without at least unconsciously transmitting the values of the teacher or school. These commentators generally conclude that teachers should express a preference for certain values and attempt to transmit those preferred to their students. The approach generally argues that students need to attain a certain degree of moral literacy in order to be capable moral thinkers and that classrooms must focus on role modeling, rules, and discipline.

Approaches that envision a more active role for a mediating teacher generally become as contentious as those that envision a narrower role for teachers. Although considerable agreement could be reached regarding the need to reject some values, the need to inculcate certain values opens itself to the possibility that schools can bow to external pressure to inculcate values not necessarily seen as appropriate by some community standards. For example, leading commentators suggest that some opinions, such as racist attitudes, simply cannot be tolerated and are anti-democratic (Gutmann, 1999). Others view the need to inculcate values as including the need to embrace minority experiences in teaching. If, for example, a class had no students to articulate a minority perspective, the teacher would present materials that provided the perspective and subject all views, including their own, to a close scrutiny (Ashton & Watson, 1998). This approach underscores the importance of cultural and class experience in the community and transforms school policy making into a more deliberative process that prepares adolescents for interaction in diverse, democratic communities. Although seemingly appropriate and just, the reality is that schools tend to do the opposite. The general trend in addressing adolescents' moral education in schools increasingly moves efforts toward more traditional, conservative, and indoctrinating approaches to moral education (Tappan, 1998). This tendency is reinforced by the manner teachers, school boards, and policy makers tend to pay attention to more conservative voices (DelFattore, 1992; Emihovich & Herrington, 1997) and the manner school administrators pay attention to families (generally those who are non-minority and from higher SES) that have a disproportionately high access to schools and ability to influence the way schools respond to students' needs (McGrath & Kuriloff, 1999). Although providing the appropriate criticism that schools necessarily transfer values, then, the approach nevertheless still leaves itself open to criticisms for the values it will select and actually impose in practice.

Although both approaches may garner much criticism that detracts from their virtues, both tend to be pedagogically appealing even though neither may be as effective as proposals hope. Both actually comport well with the traditional nature of schooling. Efforts that focus on moral deliberation or the simple teaching of specific values have considerable appeal to the extent that educational efforts predominately aim to enhance cognitive functioning. These efforts also have considerable appeal given the dominant view that "learning" involves the acquisition of factual information. These views of schooling ensure that schools' primary focus and overt approaches to teaching values involves dissemination of selected information and rules of conduct from teacher to students. However, the simple dissemination of information, even when coupled with active deliberation, seems insufficient to foster model moral development. Although some programs may report benefits, programs directly aiming to foster moral development by deliberation or simply relaying information increasingly disappear because of their inability to reveal effectiveness (Tappan, 1998). These programs are being replaced by programs providing experiences deemed morally commendable and directly socially beneficial. We now turn to those programs.

Moral Action

Although education still simply aims to disseminate information, schools now also provide other approaches to increase adolescents' moral development, civic behavior and concern for others. Rather than focusing solely on deliberation and transfer of information, schools increasingly aim to provide opportunities to take actions consistent with moral beliefs deemed worthy of inculcation. Currently, two approaches dominate curricular programs: community service and service learning.

By far, the most common opportunities schools provide for adolescents to develop socially-minded behavior involves community service. Typically, those programs require students to volunteer a number of hours of their own time outside of school hours in any type of community organization. The service generally involves a concrete task and is framed in terms of giving back to the community from which students receive benefits. The hope is that, by giving to the community, students will learn the importance of charity, giving, and civic duty (Kahne & Westheimer,

1996). The only significant variations in this type of community service involves the number of hours that different schools may require.

Service learning, the other dominant approach to fostering moral action, simply integrates community service with academic work. Unlike community service, service learning encourages students to reflect on their experiences and integrate those experiences with academic work. Service learning enhances classroom work not only by complementing academic skills and content but also by providing structured reflection on the service experience. Because of its focus on having students reflect on their place and the place of others in society, service learning involves more than responding compassionately to those in need. Service learning often involves a social action perspective. Students frequently aim to analyze and question the status quo and society. Program goals tend to include change, caring, social reconstruction, and a transformative experience (Wade & Saxe, 1996). To a large extent, service learning has a more liberal orientation that hopes to increase political efficacy and stimulate political processes.

Although often viewed as appropriate and significant parts of schooling, both community and service learning have been the subject of important criticisms. Students and parents frequently make the first general form of criticism. Some object that service requirements essentially involve indentured servitude since students must perform services without remuneration (Chapin, 1998). Others object that students should not be required to perform certain activities they deem inconsistent with their values or their parents' rights and duty to direct and provide moral education (Minden, 1995). Others still object to reformist efforts that seek to reform traditional social structures (Purpel, 1999). Teachers and schools themselves tend to make the second general form of criticism. Public school structures actually discourage collaboration with communities, as exemplified by the limited time teachers have to plan, coordinate and supervise regular curriculum and the lack of resources to supervise, transport, fund and make other logistical arrangements for service learning. Relatedly, schools place pervasive emphasis on learning as memorization of factual information. The notion that important information lies in students' experiences and the processing of those experiences, rather than only in external authorities or textbooks, still remains alien to most school settings (Wade, 1997). All constituencies directly involved in these programs seemingly have much to complain.

Despite complaints, several support the claim that the positive benefits of efforts to involve adolescents in community and service experiences far outweigh their criticisms. Although the extent to which efforts reach effectiveness remains highly debated (Chapin, 1998; Kraft, 1996), some consistent trends emerge. Service learning programs, for example, report a variety of benefits for students, especially self-esteem, clarification of values, social and personal development, moral development, civic responsibility, and enhanced academic performance (for reviews, see Johnson, Beebe, Mortimer, & Snyder, 1998; Kraft, 1996; Moore, 1999; Raskoff & Sundeen, 1999). In addition, a number of authors have found that service fosters more positive attitudes toward adults and provides a crucial link between life in school and life in the community (O'Keefe, 1997). The general hope, and frequent conclusion, is that students with effective service experiences exhibit more concern for their own citizenship and societal involvement.

Despite potential to enhance adolescents' personal growth and social responsibility, not all programs achieve positive changes in students' attitudes or performance. Research, however, does identify key features needed for successful programs. The most effective programs take volunteers seriously. Reviews reveal that immediate satisfaction from service experiences largely derives from taking on adult responsibilities, developing collegial relationships with site staff, feeling challenged, and making a visible contribution (Raskoff & Sundeen, 1999; Root, 1997). Volunteer work also yields the most beneficial outcomes when students self-select their activities, enjoy their interactions, feel challenged to think about future goals, and learn new skills (Allen, Kuperminc, Philliber, & Herre, 1994; Wilson & Musick, 1999). Satisfactory experiences, though, do not necessarily ensure an enduring impact. However, the same focus on taking adolescents seriously and ensuring their need to actively participate in programs finds clear reflection in programs identified as having more long-term impacts. Programs most likely to have enduring influence on adolescent development require students to reflect on the dynamics of volunteerism, the responsibilities of citizenship, and an understanding of multicultural societies and the larger meaning of community. Meta-analyses of research studies on community service and service learning report that reflection about one's role in society constitutes the single necessary element in program's leading to learning by students (Wade, 1997). Yet, the vast majority of programs fail to provide opportunities for growing in moral, social, and civic awareness. Most efforts generally emphasize the need for service in terms of the personal benefits adolescents will receive, such as opportunities to improve basic skills, critical thinking, self-worth, and reliability (Kahne & Westheimer, 1996). The majority of existing programs also neither foster reflection nor integrate experiences into the regular curriculum (Raskoff & Sundeen, 1999). Most programs also frame the experiences as simply involving charity work or doing time, as exemplified by the focus on fundraising and similar activities. Rather than focusing on charity and experiences to develop work-related skills, effective programs focus on citizenship and encouraging adolescents to realize that they are not helping different others with their problems but rather on serving a public good that is also their own (Barber, 1992). The majority of efforts remain also ineffective because they fail to build communal relationships characteristic of effective service learning. Communal relationship experiences focus on others more than the self; these experiences help individuals understand their lives in relation to others, help them connect to others, and foster a sense of being part of a broader society (Youniss & Yates, 1997; Youniss & Yates, 1999). These efforts provide opportunities for students to develop knowledge, skills, and attitudes that can be applied to real-life situations and opportunities to develop moral identities that consider others' interests as part of one's own self-interest—the type of identities deemed worth developing. Research distinguishing from many forms of reflection and community service (including no service), finds that community service with reflection that emphasizes the ethical nature of community service is more likely to achieve service-learning goals (Leming, 2001). Importantly, service-learning not only can positively affect students' social responsibility but it also impacts academic success. Compared with other students, students with substantial hours of service learning, a focus on reflection, and a high degree of motivation attributed to service-learning, significantly increase their belief in the efficacy of their helping behaviors, maintain their pursuit of better grades and their perception that school provides personal development opportunities, and decrease less in their commitment to classwork (Scales, Blyth, Berkas, & Kielsmeier, 2000). Given our previous discussion that attachment to schools reduces delinquency, these findings seem rather significant and open many possibilities for fostering adolescent development.

SCHOOLS' MORAL CLIMATES

Analyses of schools' efforts to inculcate socially appropriate and even exemplary values generally ignore schools' moral climates. Yet, a focus on the moral atmosphere of schools reflects the reality that schools already teach moral and civil values that shape students' characters. Schools transmit values in three ways that deserve emphasis. First, the public school curriculum involves more than technical knowledge. Public schools seek to include a broad range of subjects, ranging from the natural sciences, history, family life, and ethics. These subjects intersect with fundamental questions of the nature of humanity and morality that traditionally have been the province of religion. Second, the structure of schooling transmits values. Even if schools explicitly resist the inculcation of values through pedagogical means, schools still convey values. Corporal punishment, textbook selection, drug-testing, metal detectors, or student-body elections all convey lessons about discipline, objectivity, speech and the types of values communities seek to instill in their young. Likewise, schools' responses to social and cultural realities extend a moral point of view. Together, the overt and covert curriculum teaches students about how to be good people and how to be good citizens; it also, of course, can teach the opposite. Third, schooling itself ensures that students adopt a particular social orientation as they participate in society. Education seeks to enable students to gain the skills necessary to become knowledgeable and productive social participants. Education, then, necessarily provides an inculcative function.

The above points suggest that schools impact moral as well as intellectual life and that education serves as a media for communities to transmit their selected values, beliefs, and ideologies to their next generation. Because of education's social role, the task for all constituencies involved in efforts to inculcate model social values and behaviors means reconstituting schools as effective communities, not simply learning communities, that orient concern toward adolescents' actual needs and their proper place in society. Society requires individuals to adopt certain practices; the need for these practices makes specific demands on schools and their students as students incorporate transmitted values into their understandings of society and relationships. The need to engage with others and efforts to raise adolescent's levels of responsibility toward others takes reform efforts in important directions. These directions are particularly significant to consider as they highlight the extent to which programs cannot hope to achieve change through isolated experiences; curricular programs must address the moral atmosphere of schools.

Despite criticisms of curricular programs, it is important to note that those that are taken seriously and effectively implemented reveal much about the moral atmosphere of schools that foster more model social relationships. Adolescents' interactions with others who take their positions seriously help ensure adolescents' prosocial development. When adolescents participate in resolutions of important issues and are heard, they are more likely to accept guidance and more likely to reflect on other people's strongly held beliefs. Both guidance and reflection contribute to positive moral development (Damon & Colby, 1996). Curricular models that focus on deliberation ensure knowledge and proper deliberation, approaches that focus on action ensure that adolescents have the skills for community action and problem solving in order to foster direct and deliberate participation rather than develop spectators who preoccupy themselves with rights talk. Curricular responses already exist that emphasize the significance of the approach. Effective civics education, for example, requires hands-on participation in democratic activities such as debating real views regarding, for example, affirmative action and immigration, views that have multiple sides, are not easily reconciled, and merit serious discussion (Parker & Zumeta, 1999). More active participation in community activities result in identity-forming habits that become part of the individual's self-definition and shape the individual's relationship to the political structure of the community (Fendrich, 1993; McAdam, 1988). These findings are significant to the extent that programs reveal the nature of the school's moral atmosphere that challenges more narrow approaches to moral education. Schools with moral atmospheres that foster socially-oriented behavior ensure that students are taught about civic life in a meaningful sense instead of through slogans or principles; that schools do not bow to popular pressure not to deal with unpopular views; that texts stimulate interest, debate and questioning; and that democratic authority really means that teachers and administrators can be challenged and should respond to challenges. Effective programs, then, affect the entire school's orientation to education.

School climates that provide adolescents with developmental opportunities to develop and express their "voices" help them shape their own lives and their communities in three ways. First, acknowledging the significance of voice comports with the manner adolescents define themselves within the context of others. Through self-expression, they assert their own social classes, culture and racial identities and participate in a common society that empowers them. Fostering student voice allows students to define themselves as individuals and provides a way to incorporate their values into the schools. Second, voice allows adolescents to bridge the gap between their own world and broader society. For example, providing adolescents with greater voice in schools allows them to connect with the world of administrators and teachers. It furthers students' understandings of the educational system and allows teachers and administrators to understand students' values; both adolescents and school personnel can realize how classrooms constitute institutionalized relationships of class, gender, race and power. Third, voice provides the opportunity for incorporation of other people's values and self and social transformation. For example, an emphasis on voice helps link the classroom with the experiences of the outside community and allows education to start from the standpoint of the community members themselves. Emphasis on recognizing and developing adolescents' voices, then, helps ensure that schooling reflects adolescents' everyday lives, responds to adolescents' needs, and addresses social concerns.

The focus on adolescents as active participants in enacting social change and constructing their own identities should not detract from the pivotal influence of social conditions outside of schools. Engagement in communities and societies occurs in environments that support them. Research emphasizes how adolescents need opportunities to identify with individuals, groups, and institutions beyond their borders of their families and friends. Adolescents may seek to form social cliques as they search for a sense of self-identity and a social niche. However, these cliques may pose dangers to society if adolescents are not provided with opportunities to link to broader society. As a leading commentator on adolescents' identity development emphasized, adolescents need meaningful institutional affiliations and connections to their communities, without which they may experience an "identity vacua," a lack of direction, no sense of purpose, and disaffection for their society (Erikson, 1968). A sense of membership that cuts across cliques in schools and even in broader society can enhance adolescents' identification with a common good.

These points are emphasized well by a leading analysis of a public school's failure to consider the needs of minority urban adolescents. That study, conducted and reported by Fine (1991), suggests that public schooling must be more community- and advocacy-oriented if schools are to serve students and society. Fine envisions schools as public spheres dotted with scenes in which multiple voices are heard and in which students participate in social change. She ultimately suggests that schools must aim "to enable young people to experience social problems as mutable, to position themselves as protagonists and makers of social history, to strengthen the sense of community and citizenship that schools intend to nurture, and to create among adolescents their own expertise and knowledge base which would migrate from community to school and back again" (Fine, 1991, pp. 216–217). Note that similar sentiments are expressed as occurring in private schools that achieve success in fostering adolescents' social and intellectual development. Catholic schools, for example, are deemed more effective than others to the extent that they are explicitly connected with communities; the schools tend to be highly communitarian and, as leading researchers put it, infused with an "inspirational ideology … informed by a generous conception of democratic life in a post-modern society" (Bryk, Lee, & Holland, 1993, p. 40). Catholic education is often countercultural to the mores of rugged individualism, self-sufficiency, and social indifference in that it seeks to socialize students into a way of life that cares about and contributes to the common good through an ethos of social consciousness and concern for the marginalized and suffering society. Education aimed to enhance adolescents' social values, then, must move beyond charitable activity to articulation of an explicit set of values. Community service programs reach effectiveness when they become part of an ethos of public community that permeates all aspects of the institution.

Contexts that facilitate moral commitment can be identified, and they generally require a move away from thinking of schooling as limited to learning in classrooms. They are characterized by warm relationships with persons who themselves evidence moral character. Adults other than parents can fulfil the role of setting a standard of moral conduct to which adolescents may aspire; but the adult must have an emotional bond to, and a relationship with, the adolescents. Supportive environments also involve opportunities to form and test moral commitments. Rather than simply focusing on already prescribed "community service," environments conducive to moral development actually arise from several social institutions that can fulfill the role so long as they provide a range of experiences in helping and caring for others. These experiences must involve more than actions that help others; adolescents need to discuss and reflect on their actions to understand themselves and the meaning of moral commitment and action. These experiences help facilitate the sense of effectiveness and connection to adulthood and future development. It is through self-initiated action that adolescents can develop the sense of effectiveness that can deepen their commitments and enable them to view their commitment as a clear reflection of their own interests and talents. Effective school environments allow for the construction of one's moral niche, which allows the adolescent to envision a future in which this niche can be an important of their life structure and development.

PRELIMINARY CONCLUSION

Effective programs address students' needs. These programs address adolescents' needs for autonomy by providing them voice, either in the school itself or in the services they provide to communities. They also address students' need to make a difference in community settings which otherwise can be positively or negatively expressed. They also address the need to experience emotional commitment and control impulses during a state of rapid growth and mercurial emotions. They assist students in their search for social identity and provide the opportunity to take risks within a context of affirmation and protection. They also allow adolescents to develop a range of relationships with adults and peers, permit them to make decisions within appropriate and understood limits, provide the opportunity to speak and be heard, and discover that they can make a difference. Effective programs also foster emphases on cooperation rather than competition and enhance competence at problem solving in a variety of situations. Programs maximize effectiveness in environments where orientations to caring for others permeate schools. Such institutional press reveals the extent to which the activities are part of an articulated school mission and taken seriously to have an impact. The necessity to recognize and appreciate developmental needs cannot be overstated.

MODEL SOCIAL DEVELOPMENT AND THE LAW

The above review of adolescent development and how it can be enhanced suggests a need to consider both the substance (content) and the procedure (process) of education. In light of the previous section's examination of social science findings regarding model development, this section details what the law mandates and the extent to which it permits schools to benefit from existing findings. The investigation is significant. Although research about adolescents' intellectual capabilities and the social influences on adolescent social development may lead to the conclusion that values inculcation is essential, the legal system may render the findings moot. What may be essential from an educational standpoint may be intolerable from the perspective of the Constitution or other legal mandates. Legal constraints define the role and mission of public education. In light of the view that values transmission is a necessary part of moral education and that education is a necessary part of moral development, an important legal issue arises regarding the governmental power to inculcate and the extent to which governments actually must do so. Addressing these issues requires a look at constitutional and legislative mandates. The legal questions that arise involve the extent to which values inculcation can satisfy constitutional mandates and, if schools can inculcate values, the nature of values deemed worthy of inculcation. Supreme Court jurisprudence and federal legislative mandates provide broad contours within which the states may inculcate certain values in adolescents. As with other areas of regulation, the states may offer more explicit mandates and expand adolescents' educational rights. States have expanded educational rights in both explicit and implicit ways, place different weight on the rights they recognize, and offer different ways to implement those rights. As we will see, the need to foster the model, civically-oriented development actually serves as the rationale for public schools, but how states ensure that they actually support such development remains surprisingly limited.

FEDERAL CONSTITUTIONAL PARAMETERS

While expressed in different ways, the Supreme Court repeatedly has supported the state's authority to indoctrinate adolescents so as to instill moral and civic values. Although the Court has advanced the proposition that public schools may seek to inculcate adolescents in fundamental values, it also has placed important restrictions on the school's authority to do so. The nature of those restrictions are significant to the extent that they reveal the purpose of schooling and what the law fosters.

Governmental Power to Inculcate Values

The earliest cases involving challenges to the states' educational authority, *Meyer v. Nebraska* (1923) and *Pierce v. Society of Sisters* (1925), actually operated on the explicit assumption that governments have an interest in promoting basic morality and civic virtue in both public and private schools. The ruling in *Meyer* involved a challenge by a parochial school teacher to a statute that prohibited the teaching of foreign languages of students who had not yet passed the eighth grade. The rationale for the statute was strictly assimilationist: it was to promote civic development consistent with American ideals. In a broad decision, the Court found that the statute impermissibly intruded, among other rights, on the rights of parents to direct the upbringing of their offspring, the teacher's right to teach, and the student's freedom to acquire useful knowledge. While the Court struck down efforts to limit the language curriculum, the Court also stated that its ruling did not preclude states from making reasonable regulations for *all* schools. Thus, despite other competing interests, both public and private school curriculum could be subject to reasonable regulations and "the state may do much, go very far, indeed, in order to improve the quality of its citizens, physically, mentally, and morally" (p. 401). Under this approach, states could seek to improve the moral quality of its younger citizenry and may go so far as to stand in the way of students' acquisition of knowledge from private providers.

The potentially broad reading of such power was quickly limited in *Pierce v. Society of Sisters* (1925). In that case, the Court indicated that it might not accept a model that provides states with such control. *Pierce* involved a challenge by two private schools to an Oregon statute that compelled all students to attend only the public schools. In upholding the claim that the statute violated the rights of parents to control the upbringing of their children; the Court held that "The child is not the mere creature of the State; those who nurture him and direct his destiny have the right, coupled with the high duty, to recognize and prepare him for additional obligations" (p. 534). What is significant about the case is the Court's continued receptivity to values inculcation in the schools. The Court made clear that states could still regulate private schools to assure "that teachers shall be of good moral character and patriotic disposition, that certain studies plainly essential to good citizenship must be taught, and that nothing be taught which is manifestly inimical to the public welfare" (p. 534). The Court was both ambivalent yet still clear. The Court clearly struck down standardization, mainly because the state lacked a reasonable relation between the legitimate state ends and the law, while allowing for continued state authority to require education "essential to good citizenship" be provide in the private as well as public schools.

Both *Myer* and *Pierce* had made clear that states may seek to inculcate adolescents in fundamental values, but the cases left open two critical issues. The first issue involved the question of whether the state's authority to regulate private education was so extensive as to permit the state to require all schools to offer similar curriculum which could be wholly indoctrinating. The Court answered the question negatively in *Farrington v. Tokushige* (1927). In that case, the state had abrogated the control of the curriculum of a private school, attended mainly by Japanese children, in order to ensure that the schools did not foster disloyalty to the country. The second issue involved the extent to which the state can go to indoctrinate its own pupils in public schools. Illustrative of the Court's approach was a leading case involving students' rights: *West Virginia State Board of Education v. Barnette* (1943). *Barnette* involved a challenge to a school board's requirement that all students participate in a ceremony saluting the flag while repeating the pledge of allegiance. According to the regulation, the compelled salute served to create a proclivity toward national unity during children's "formative period in the development in citizenship" (p. 628). The Court found that school boards do retain important, delicate, and highly discretionary functions, but "[t]hat they are educating the young for citizenship is reason for scrupulous protection of constitutional freedoms of the individual, if we are not to strangle the free mind at its source and teach adolescents to discount important principles of our government as mere platitudes" (p. 637). The Court continued in a highly cited phrase: "If there is any fixed constitutional constellation, it is that no official, high or petty, can prescribe what shall be orthodox in politics, nationalism, religious, or other matters of opinion or force citizens by word or act their faith therein" (p. 642).

Although emphasizing the limits of the school board's powers, the Court nevertheless recognized how the boards do retain broad discretionary powers. If anything, *Barnette* indicates that students' freedom of expression is not absolute. The Court discusses the importance of classroom instruction in history and government, including instruction that promotes the constitutional guarantees of liberty. *Barnette* also implies that as long as school boards do not force students to declare a belief, as compelling student to recite the pledge of allegiance does, local boards have the authority to implement a particular curriculum. Thus, schools may encourage national unity by persuasion or example, but not through compulsion. The Court found that school boards must perform their functions within the limits of the Bill of Rights.

Governmental Obligations to Inculcate Values

Despite some complexities, the one message that emerges with clarity from the above cases is that the Court accepts state inculcation and that the inculcation must serve state's interest in fostering development faithful to what the Constitution demands of its citizens. The Court has since amplified the nature of inculcation in four important lines of cases that require school to perform inculcative functions.

The first line of cases involves students' rights, and that line of cases both extends and limits *Barnette's* recognition of students' freedoms of expression. Three critical cases provide the foundation for analyses of students' rights that place obligations on states to inculcate certain values. The first highly-touted case to develop this line of cases, *Board of Education v. Pico* (1980) involved the rejection of a school board's decision to remove certain books from the library that the board considered vulgar and inappropriate for students. In an oft-cited phrase, Justice Brennan, delivering the plurality opinion, prohibited the board's action by finding that "the Constitution protects the right to receive information and ideas" (p. 867). The Court recognized the library as the principal locus of a student's freedom "to inquire, to study and to evaluate, to gain new maturity and understanding" (p. 868). That freedom, though, was plainly limited by the school's "duty to inculcate community values" (p. 869). The Court distinguished the library from the compulsory environment of classrooms as it stressed, in very crucial language, that the Court was "in full agreement … that local school boards must be permitted 'to establish and apply their curriculum in such a way as to transmit community values,' and that 'there is a legitimate and substantial community interest in promoting respect for authority and traditional values be they social, moral, or political' " (p. 864). Despite recognizing adolescents' rights by limiting the power of school boards to curtail students' rights to receive information, the Court also acknowledged that the school boards have wide latitude in determining what books to order in the first instance and in exercising non-arbitrary control over curricular matters.

The Court faced another challenge dealing with the reach of schools' inculcating role in *Bethel Sch. Dist. No. 401 v. Fraser* (1986). In *Fraser*, a student delivered a lewd speech before a mandatory school assembly. As a result of the speech, the student was suspended. On review, the Court espoused the importance of public schools for inculcating students in fundamental values and, more specifically, inculcating students in citizenship skills (p. 685). Most importantly, the Court noted that

> The inculcation of values is truly the 'work of schools' ... The process of educating our youth for citizenship in public schools is not confined to the books, the curriculum, and the civic class; school must teach by example the shared values of a civilized social order. Consciously or otherwise, teachers—and indeed the older students—demonstrate the appropriate form of civil discourse and political expression by their conduct and deportment in and out of class. Inescapably, like parents, they are role models (pp. 683–685).

The power granted to school officials in their efforts to limit students' expression so as not to undermine the school's basic educational mission served to sustain other important challenges to school official's ability to instill moral and civic values. Schools have an obligation to teach citizenship values and to act in loco parentis.

The Court again emphasized the role of schools to inculcate fundamental values in *Hazelwood Sch. Dist. v. Kuhlmeier* (1988). *Kuhlmeier* made another critical step in defining the inculcation of values in schools as it extended the school board's authority by explicitly recognizing that public schools may regulate students' actions outside of the classroom. In *Kuhlmeier*, students challenged the refusal of school officials to print a student paper that discussed, among other things, the impact of drug use and sexual activity on students. In finding in favor of school officials' control over the content of the student paper, the Court found that to find otherwise would unduly constrain schools from fulfilling their role as "a principle instrument in awakening the child to cultural values, in preparing him for later professional training, and in helping him to adjust to his environment" (pp. 272–273). The Court held that school-sponsored activities could be controlled by school officials so long as limiting actions reasonably related to legitimate pedagogical concerns. Schools may control any schools sponsored expressive activity, not only within the traditional curriculum but in any circumstances that are or may be perceived as being school-sponsored.

Kuhlmeier's focus on school-sponsored situations is of significance in the manner it curtailed a previously broad ruling in favor of students' rights. That broad ruling had originated in *Tinker v. Des Moines Independent Community School District* (1969). That case arose out of three students' suspension for wearing armbands to school to demonstrate their dissatisfaction with the Vietnam War. The Court supported the students as it provided the expansive dicta that students do not "shed their constitutional rights ... at the schoolhouse gate" (p. 506). The Constitution does not permit a prohibition against expression of opinion unless that prohibition is necessary to avoid substantial interference with school discipline or the rights of others. The Court recognized that students had a right to communicate with each other, that students may not be treated as "closed-circuit recipients" of communication imposed by the state (p. 511). Students may express personal opinions that do not comport with sentiments that are officially approved. From this perspective, students' rights serve to check the state-imposed communication that would otherwise effectively silence alternative viewpoints. Importantly, *Tinker* stresses that the individual classroom, and not only the public school in general, should provide a "marketplace of ideas" (p. 512). If the student expression simply happens to occur on school premises, the educators have a reduced interest. Under this approach, announced in *Tinker*, educators must justify their actions to the extent that restriction was necessary to address a reasonable fear of "material interference" with the school's mission (Tinker, 1969, p. 514). Thus, the voice of the student engaged in actual or symbolic expression receives protection, unless such expression is manifestly disruptive. *Kuhlmeier*, then, follows *Fraser's* success in reinforcing the public school's role to inculcating students in fundamental values as an integral part of the entire school program.

The second line of cases involving the government's regulation of what schools must inculcate involves teachers' rights. The leading case in this area explicitly impresses support for a focus on values in public schools. The Court, in *Ambach v. Norwick* (1979), reviewed New York's effort to exclude aliens from teaching in the public school system. The Court noted that public school teachers perform a task that goes to the heart of representative government. It stated that, "through both the presentation of course materials and the example he sets, a teacher has an opportunity to influence the attitudes of students towards government, the political process, and a citizen's social responsibilities ... a State properly may regard all teachers as having an obligation to promote civic virtues and understanding in their classes ... [and] take account of a teacher's function as an example for students, which exists independently of particular classroom subjects" (pp. 76–80). By finding that the inculcation of civic values and beliefs is a primary function of public schooling, the Court emphasized that schools should prepare students to be citizens interested in the "preservation of values on which our society rests" (p. 76). In the preservation of society, the Court had a specific view in mind as it explicitly approved of the schools' role in "inculcating fundamental values necessary to the maintenance of a democratic political system" (p. 76). Rather than focusing on the rights of teachers, then, the analysis focused solely on the importance of indoctrination as an educational tool in the public schools and used the case as authority to restrict the speech of students. The incantation of *Ambach's* resonate phrases regarding the inculcation of fundamental democratic values—endorsement of the teaching of "civic virtues"—would become ritual in cases dealing with public education.

The third line of cases that deal with the types of values schools can inculcate involves religion. Two fundamental religious liberty principles guide an analysis of the educational system's approach to religion. The principle of neutrality requires that the government, and hence the public schools, may neither prefer nor disparage any particular religion (*School District of Abington Township, Pa. v. Schempp*, 1963). Importantly, neutrality not only means that the government must remain neutral between religions; schools must also be neutral between religion and nonreligion. The leading case in this area, *Epperson v. Arkansas* (1963), acknowledged a state's right to prescribe curriculum for its public schools. Despite that apparently expansive right, the Court proceeded to invalidate a statute prohibiting the teaching of Darwinian evolution. The Court required schools to offer a balanced perspective of subjects they choose to teach. Under this view, then, states could avoid teaching objectionable materials by deleting courses or by deleting sections of courses from their curriculum. The state could not, though, mandate or delete only one view of the subject. Thus, states can be sensitive to moral and religious issues when it chooses topics, but it must be neutral in the presentation of topics that are chosen. By allowing states to present both sides or neither side of issues, however, the Court does not demand pure neutrality. The Court, then finds the study of religion constitutional but that schools must reach religion objectively or neutrally, such as by teaching a variety of religious traditions rather than indoctrinating any particular religion.

The Court also requires states to respect liberty of conscience. Broadly stated, this liberty affords religious citizens freedom from government coercion that would not allow them to worship, believe, practice, preach, proselytize and teach in accordance to the dictates of their conscience. In the educational context, the freedom allows parents and students to "choose [their] own course with reference" to "religious training, teaching, and observance, free of any compulsion from the State" (*School District of Abington Township, Pa. v. Schempp*, 1963, p. 222). The principle also reflects the right of students, as exemplified by the leading case, *Lee v. Wiesman* (1992). In *Lee*, the Court examined the legitimacy of a school official's efforts to direct public prayers. The official, a high school principal, decided that a clergyman would lead a graduation prayer, selected a rabbi, and advised him as to the prayer's content. The Court concluded that the principal, acting as a state official, had directed the performance of a formal religious exercise and that attendance at this state-sponsored religious activity was "in a fair and real sense obligatory" for students (p. 2655). The Court found that the principal's actions violated the constitutional principle that the government may not "coerce anyone to support or participate in religion or its exercise, or otherwise act in a way which establishes a state religion or religious faith, or tends to do so" (p. 2655). The Constitution forbids the state not only from coercing participation in religious exercises, but also from coercing the mere appearance of participation: "What matters is that, given our social conventions, a reasonable dissenter in this milieu could believe that the group exercise signified her own participation or approval of it" (p. 2658). The Court recently reaffirmed Lee's broad principle in *Santa Fe Independent School District v. Doe* (2000). In *Doe*, students and parents filed suit against the school district over school policies that governed speech at graduation ceremonies and sporting events. Under the first policy, the school selected students to deliver a brief speech at the beginning of each football game. The school district justified pre-game speech because it solemnized the event, promoted good sportsmanship and student safety, and established the appropriate environment for the competition. Although the school district argued that it would strike any proselytizing speech and emphasized that the speech may not even be a prayer, the Supreme Court found the arguments disingenuous. The Court found that every student knew the policy was about prayer and the school's establishment of an electoral mechanism impermissibly encouraged prayer by undermining the essential protection of minority viewpoints.

The last line of cases tends to be ignored in analyses of schools' inculcative functions but it nevertheless provides a critical example of what schools must be required to do. These cases deal with the states' treatment of minority children in landmark civil rights cases. A leading case, *Brown v. Board of Education* (1954), proves rather illustrative. It was in that case that the Court mandated an end to racially segregated public schooling. The Court was not concerned with the negative aspects of inculcation; yet the case provides a value-laden mandate to the public schools. The case compels students and schools to a nonneutral message about race relations. The lesson of their decision was that "education is the very foundation of good citizenship. Today it is a principal instrument in awakening the child to cultural values" (p. 493). Likewise, in *Plyler v. Doe* (1982) the Court examined state's duty to provide public education for children of illegal aliens. The Court struck down a Texas policy of excluding illegal alien children from public schooling. In determining that a state had to accord certain rights to the children of illegal aliens, the Court took occasion to comment on the significance of education to American society and that the state had an obligation and right to provide a morally based education. The Court reiterated precedent as it highlighted how schools were the most vital civic institution for the preservation of democracy an as primary vehicle for transmitting "the values upon which our society rests" (p. 221). The Court expressly reasoned that this policy denied children not only a general education, but also the opportunity to be inculcated in traditional values (p. 221). Although it is important to emphasize that the implementation of these principles continues to be the subject of immense controversy and difficulty, the principles remain good law.

Constitutional doctrine emphasizes that an adolescent's right to be educated is more substantial than the right to be let alone. Schools can foster the underlying values of the Constitution, such as free inquiry, personal expression, and participatory democracy, by directing educational processes rather than by staying out of student's way. The Court increasingly provides schools with institutional autonomy to develop students' educated capacities, so long as schools provide certain circumstances to promote rather than retard civic mandates.

FEDERAL LEGISLATIVE MANDATES

The federal legislative role seeks to not intrude on either the parent or state's power to direct the education of children. Despite the hesitancy to intervene, the federal government does impact the extent to which schools can foster model social development. First, it is difficult to argue against the notion that the government regulation against discrimination in the schools conveys values and images of appropriate social interactions. For example, education could not contravene equal protection mandates, such as the anti-discrimination statutes prohibiting discrimination on the basis of race (Civil Rights Act of 1964, 1994), gender (Education Amendments of 1972, 1994), and disabilities (Rehabilitation Act of 1973, 1994; Individuals With Disabilities Act, 1998). Through these statutes, the federal government implicitly views one role of educational systems as involving the inculcation of certain values. Second, concern over the mismatch between student needs and social interests has contributed to important efforts to impact the curriculum and programs offered by public schools. The passage of the National and Community Service Act of 1990 followed by the National Service Trust Act of 1993 has generated new enthusiasm for service learning at all levels of education. The funds inspire a proliferation of programs throughout the states and encourages educators and community-based organizations to seek new ways of collaborating. Thus, the federal government is free to offer financial incentives to help develop and support educational programs aimed at model social development.

STATE CONSTITUTIONAL MANDATES

All states' constitutions contain clauses that provide for and serve as guides to education. By providing and requiring education, which itself is value-inculcating, states provide important points of departure for ensuring the education of adolescents into common beliefs. The effort to inculcate common beliefs emerges explicitly from states' constitutional provisions. Constitutional clauses providing for free public education virtually mimic each other as they focus on the need to establish a "uniform," "general," "common," or simply "public" education. Thus, Washington State's Constitution provides that "[t]he legislature shall provide for a general and uniform system of public" (Washington Constitution, Art. IX, 2). The New Jersey Constitution states: "The legislature shall provide for the maintenance and support of a thorough and efficient system of free public schools ..." (New Jersey Constitution, Art. VIII, 4). The Kentucky Constitution provides: "The General Assembly shall, by appropriate legislation, provide for an efficient system of common schools..." (Kentucky Constitution, 183). The Pennsylvania Constitution provides: "The General Assembly shall provide for the maintenance of a thorough and efficient system of public education to serve the needs of the Commonwealth" (Pa. Const. art. 3, 14). The Connecticut Constitution provides: "There shall always be free public elementary and secondary schools in the state" (Connecticut Constitution, Art. 8, 1). The California Constitution provides: "The Legislature shall provide for a system of common schools" (California Constitution, Art. 9, 5). The North Dakota Constitution provides: "The legislative assembly shall provide for a uniform system of free public schools throughout the state" (North Dakota Constitution, Art. VIII, 2). The Virginia Constitution provides: "The General Assembly shall provide for a system of free public elementary and secondary schools for all children throughout the Commonwealth" (Virginia Constitution, Art. VIII, 1). The Wisconsin Constitution provides: "The legislature shall provide by law for the establishment of district schools, which shall be as nearly uniform as practicable; and such schools shall be free and without charge" (Wisconsin Constitution, Art. 10, 3). North Carolina obligates itself to providing for "a general and uniform system of free public schools, ... and wherein equal opportunities shall be provided for all students" (North Carolina Constitution, Art. IX, 2(1)). The

Maryland Constitution provides that "the General Assembly .... shall by Law establish throughout the State a thorough and efficient System of Free Public Schools" (Maryland Constitution, Art. VIII, 8).

By providing and requiring education, which itself is value-inculcating, states provide important points of departure for ensuring the education of adolescents into common beliefs. This is made most explicit by the extent to which these statements are much more than precatory. These clauses have led to important litigation to foster common experiences for all students. This is most obvious in recent efforts to include all students in public education efforts that have used constitutional clauses to effect school finance reform (Swenson, 2000) and to redress race, economic and gender inequalities (Ryan, 1999). Although these challenges to states' provision of educational opportunities have not been consistently successful, the litigation reveals how it has become either a supplement to or a substitute for important civil rights litigation bottomed on federal mandates.

In addition to simply providing for education, state constitutions serve as sources of information regarding the reasons for education, and those reasons remain important to developing the type of education mandated by law. State statutes do so by noting how citizenship, especially moral citizenship, serves as the primary rationale for education. Thus, Arkansas finds that "Intelligence and virtue being the safeguards of liberty and the bulwark of a free and good government, the State shall ever maintain a general, suitable and efficient system of free public schools and shall adopt all suitable means to secure to the people the advantages and opportunities of education" (Arkansas Constitution, Art. 14, § 1, 2000). North Dakota's Constitution provides that "A high degree of intelligence, patriotism, integrity and morality on the part of every voter in a government by the people being necessary in order to insure the continuance of that government and the prosperity and happiness of the people, the legislative assembly shall make provision for the establishment and maintenance of a system of public schools (North Dakota Constitution, Art. VIII, 1, 2000). The Minnesota Constitution provides: "The stability of a republican form of government depending mainly upon the intelligence of the people, it is the duty of the legislature to establish a general uniform system of public schools" (Minnesota Constitution, Art. XIII, 1, 2000). California finds as follows: "A general diffusion of knowledge and intelligence being essential to the preservation of the rights and liberties of the people, the Legislature shall encourage by all suitable means the promotion of intellectual, scientific, moral, and agricultural improvement" (California Constitution, Art. 9, 1, 2000). North Carolina's Constitution emphasizes that "Religion, morality and knowledge being necessary to good government and the happiness of mankind, schools, libraries and the means of education shall forever be encouraged" (North Carolina Constitution, Art. IX, 1, 2000). The Massachusetts Constitution provides: "Wisdom, and knowledge, as well as virtue, diffused generally among the body of the people, being necessary for the preservation of their rights and liberties; and as these depend on spreading the opportunities and advantages of education in the various parts of the country, and among the different orders of the people, it shall be the duty of legislatures and magistrates..." (Massachusetts Constitution, Part 2, Ch. 5, 2, 2000). Virginia notes "That no free government, nor the blessings of liberty, can be preserved to any people, but by a firm adherence to justice, moderation, temperance, frugality, and virtue; by frequent recurrence to fundamental principles; and by the recognition by all citizens that they have duties as well as rights, and that such rights cannot be enjoyed save in a society where law is respected and due process is observed ... . That free government rests, as does all progress, upon the broadest possible diffusion of knowledge, and that the Commonwealth should avail itself of those talents which nature has sown so liberally among its people by assuring the opportunity for their fullest development by an effective system of education throughout the Commonwealth" (Virginia Constitution, Art. I, § 15, 2000). These clauses provide further evidence that states do take education seriously and that education serves as a foundation of an orderly, civil society.

STATE LEGISLATIVE MANDATES

Legislative requirements that students be taught certain values and virtues in public schools come in three forms. One of the most explicit forms involves the manner states frequently require school districts to teach in a manner that promotes civic and moral virtues or require specific curricula directed to the development of those virtues. For example, Utah law requires that "Honesty, Temperance, morality ... and other skills, habits, and qualities of character which will promote an upright and desirable citizenry and better prepare students for a richer, happier life ... [must be] taught in connection with regular school work" (Utah Code Annotated, 53A-13-101(4), 2000). Tennessee law also focuses on moral development as it requires that classroom instruction include "character education" in order to teach students proper citizenship skills (Tennessee Code Annotated, § 49-6-1007, 1999). The Texas Educational Code provides that the public school curriculum shall "prepare thoughtful, active citizens who understand the importance of patriotism and can function productively in a free enterprise society with appreciation for the basic democratic values of our state and national heritage" (Texas Education Code, § 21.101(d), 2000). In Indiana, the legislature found that

"Good citizenship instruction integrated into the current curriculum instruction that stresses the nature and importance of being honest and truthful, respecting authority, respecting the property of others, always doing one's personal best, not stealing, possessing the skills necessary to live peaceably in society and not resorting to violence to settle disputes, taking personal responsibility for obligations to family and community, taking personal responsibility for earning a livelihood. It also includes respecting the national flag, Constitution, one's parents and home, one's self, and the rights of others to have their own views and religious beliefs" (Indiana Code Annotated, § 20-10.1-4-4.5, 2000). Others simply make general entreaties, such as Rhode Island's view that "Every teacher shall aim to implant and cultivate in the minds of all children committed to his care the principles of morality and virtue" (Rhode Island General Laws, § 16-12-3, 2000). Iowa's statute is even more expansive: "Schools should make every effort, formally and informally, to stress character qualities that will maintain a safe and orderly learning environment, and that will ultimately equip students to be model citizens. These qualities include but are not limited to honesty; responsibility; respect and care for the person and property of others; self-discipline; understanding of, respect for, and obedience to law and citizenship; courage, initiative, commitment, and perseverance; kindness, compassion, service, and loyalty; fairness, moderation, and patience; and the dignity and necessity of hard work" (Iowa Code, § 256.18, 1999). Some states, then, do address model social development. Even those states, however, do not necessarily provide education geared to help students develop model social orientations; a close look at statutory language reveals that the mandates remain largely precatory.

Although statutes dealing with moral, civil and other forms of character development generally do not involve directly enforceable mandates, other laws do regulate model development in largely ignored ways. For example, the second major way state statutes regulate the instruction of moral virtues involves the manner all states grant protection to parental autonomy and family privacy. These statutes come in different forms. Most frequently, statutes simply view parents as partners in educating children; e.g., Texas states as one of its first educational objective that "[p]arents will be full partners with educators in the education of their children" (Texas Education Code, § 4.001, 2000). Some states, however, explicitly recognize that "[i]t is the natural, fundamental right of parents and legal guardians to determine and direct the care, teaching, and education of their children" (Michigan Statutes Annotated, § 15.4005, 1999). Yet another way statutes evince concern for protecting parental autonomy comes in the form of excusing children from curricular requirements. For example, Utah law provides that when a parent or legal guardian may suggest a reasonable alternative to or request a waiver of required curriculum or activities that would infringe on the student or parents' superior duty to their religion or conscience (Utah Code Annotated, 53A-13-101.2, 1993). Under Utah law, however, in the event of a conflict between an assertion of conscience by a parent and a minor secondary student who wanted to participate in an activity or part of the curricula, the parent's assertion and request for waiver would prevail over student desire to participate (Utah Administrative Regulations, 277-105-5C, 1995). North Carolina provides school boards with the freedom to establish a comprehensive sex education program but allows for parents to withhold consent for their child to attend classes (North Carolina General Statutes, § 115C-81(e1)(7), 1999) or receive information deemed within parental discretion (e.g., regarding contraceptives) (§ (8)). Likewise, South Dakota prohibits schools form referring students to psychiatric treatment without parental consent (South Dakota Codified Laws, § 13-32-3, 2000). Although states do seek to respect parental rights, it is important to note that states all leave determinations of curricular matters to schools officials who, at most, may be required to gain input from parents and community members. The way states protect parental rights, then, reflects two critical points. Although parents may limit the inculcation of certain values, states do take it upon themselves to foster values. In addition, parental rights themselves may be limited when the values they would inculcate would violate community values.

Yet another way states legislate model behavior comes in the form that teachers and other school officials must role model civic virtues. Virtually all states require, through explicit statutes, that personnel must model moral character. For example, among the maximum requirements a board may require for teacher certification is that the "applicant is of sound mental and physical health and of good moral character" (Revised Statutes of Nebraska Annotated, § 79-809, 2000). Alabama requires, for example, that the members of the county board of education "shall be persons of good moral character, with at least a fair elementary education, of good standing in their respective communities and known for their honesty, business ability, public spirit and interest in the good of public education" (Code of Alabama, § 16-8-1, 2000). Alaska lists, among the three causes for revocation and suspension, immorality (defined as a crime involving moral turpitude) after incompetency and before noncompliance with school laws (Alaska Statutes, § 14.20.030, 2000). Florida limits eligibility "for appointment in any position in any district school system, a person shall be of good moral character" (Florida Statutes, § 231.02(1), 1999). In New Mexico, the "state board may suspend or revoke a certificate held by a certified school instructor or administrator for incompetency, immorality or any other good and just cause (New

Mexico Statutes Annotated, § 22-10-22, 2000). In Nevada, conviction of a "crime involving moral turpitude" provides a basis for suspension or dismissal (Nevada Revised Statutes Annotated, § 391.312, 2000). These broad statutes provide a clear example of how far-reaching the power of school officials may be; officials have broad discretion to use concerns of moral character as they see fit.

PRELIMINARY CONCLUSION

Federal law sets the parameters guiding schools' efforts to inculcate values deemed necessary for fostering model citizenship. Although courts generally hesitate to intervene in curricular conflicts and in school environments, they do intervene when constitutional principles expressly prohibit values states attempt to inculcate, such as when states inappropriately infringe on the free exercise of religion or restrict expression. Federal legislative mandates pervasively do not seek to regulate the inculcation of values. Legislative mandates, though, still impact the inculcation of values to the extent, for example, that they foster basic democratic principles by prohibiting discrimination which, in turn, impacts the moral and social atmosphere of schools. Otherwise, the states typically have free reign to control the curricular and extra-curricular educational environment that would mold social development.

Although states set curricular agendas and retain plenary power to control the moral atmosphere of schooling, state legislative mandates rarely guide efforts to foster exemplary moral character. The only consistency to emerge in state mandates involves the manner all states recognize the significance of education and the role it plays in the development of a civil society. Statutes typically neither guide nor support the development of programs that would help foster model citizenship. States that do respond pervasively do not focus on students and the atmosphere (or even determining the type of atmosphere) needed to foster student moral development. Rather than focusing on students, states focus on regulating the moral character of those who would educate them: teachers, parents, and community members involved in schools. States pervasively fail to take the lead despite retaining the most discretion and power to take action to promote model citizenship.

CONCLUSION

Existing research presents adolescents as reflective agents who grow up within specific social and historical contexts and who idiosyncratically interpret their options, opportunities, and restraints. These contexts provide the foundation for the type of character development civil society and its laws would deem model, moral, and worthy of reproduction. This interpretive and contextual view of adolescent development finds considerable support from moral and civil development research. The central message of that research emphasizes that students' voices must be heard not only by other students but also by teachers, administrators, and community members. Engaging with others supplies the critical catalyst for effective social development that necessarily does much more than simply reproduce existing social structures. Engaging with others allows adolescents to become model democratic citizens—individuals actively concerned about others' welfare and the betterment of society. By fostering concern for social transformation within their schools and in their external communities, effective school environments engage individuals in the betterment and reconstitution of society based on communally accepted and negotiated ideals.

This view of model development may seem at odds with popular perceptions of schooling. Schools continue to be sieged by the dominant myth that public educational enterprises must remain unbiased marketplaces of ideas, especially of ideas with explicit moral content. Yet, schools do much more than transmit information. Schools necessarily inculcate values simply by providing a social context for development. Schools do so by placing emphasis on certain ideas and attitudes and by providing social and emotional experiences that impact social development. Schools, then, help students form certain dispositions by providing ways to organize thoughts, actions, and emotions. School environments necessarily play important roles in the preparation and understanding of values and ideally transmit values appropriate for the survival of civil society. Yet, schools pervasively fail to convey the value and importance of model social disposition and community engagement (Raskoff & Sundeen, 1999).

Although research may seem non-extensive and inconclusive, certain school environments do tend to foster more model social behavior—more participation in society, more concern for others, and greater desire to foster fundamental democratic values. Schools identified as most effective in fostering model development involve adolescents in their own education and preparation for responsible citizenship. Schools directly address moral behavior and civic responsibility when they help students confront individual, social and cultural heterogeneity in addition to the more traditional focus on civil and political relations that constitute the foundation for democratic societies. These experiences most likely arise under conditions that require adolescents to engage in meaningful activities and to evaluate their experiences. More meaningful activities address real social needs and consider the unique qualities of participants. By considering adolescents' unique social position, these experiences provide developmental opportunities, as evidenced most by efforts that encourage adolescents to take personal responsibility for their actions and engage in activities with different people, especially individuals outside of schools who have been stereotyped and marginalized by society.

The many ways schools may foster or inhibit the development of more model citizenship reveals how laws regulating moral development's place in education address only part of social development deemed critical to civil society. The most explicit regulations involve laws that provide for common educational experiences by focusing on the roles adults play in transmitting values and controlling the transmittal of values. As a result, legal mandates currently grant greater power to parents' choices or the authority of school officials. Although discretion may allow for responding effectively to local conditions, bestowing enormous discretion on parents and school officials also means that it remains unclear what schools must do to actively promote model development. The most comprehensive source of guidance remains Supreme Court cases that place some limits on school officials' responsibilities to limit adolescents' freedoms in the name of protecting communal interests. Legislative mandates essentially ignore those obligations, a point that serves to reinforce the reality that school officials wield considerable discretion. Laws have yet to determine what it would mean to recognize adolescents' own educational rights more affirmatively and to delineate the substance of those rights. Only a few states guide the development of programs directly aiming to develop students' social development in ways that would be deemed exemplary; none require schools to develop comprehensive programs. The only dominant, but still limited, legislation involves the regulation of students' misconduct, as reviewed in the previous chapter. Regulations do not address students' positive conduct. Effective legal responses to education's role in fostering model development would seek to include adolescents in their education and seek to develop programs that allow them to learn how to relate cooperatively, tolerantly and respectfully with people from diverse backgrounds and to actively affirm the equal worth of others.

Although enormous, the challenges facing legal reform simply reflect the complex realities adolescents face in and outside of school. Effective reform in the regulation of education would bind citizens together in a broad political community; such reform also necessarily would involve reforms outside of educational environments so that they too could support the development of more exemplary citizenship. From an adolescents' perspective, educational rights would involve much more than an entitlement to have their freedoms respected. The law would recognize their membership in a community that actively recognizes the need to foster basic democratic principles. Schools would do much more than devote themselves to student learning through inclusion of diverse experiences and beliefs; schools would help shape experiences that contribute to bettering society and fostering more positive everyday relationships. Although existing mandates may not fully embrace this needed reform, existing legal mandates both permit their development and also require their development to the extent that they recognize the centrality of education to the survival of civil, democratic society.

5

Thriving Adolescents

Efforts to alleviate rates of violence inflicted by adolescents and efforts to encourage model social development necessarily must include adolescents' emotional (mental health) development. Adolescents' risk-taking, aggressive, delinquent and violent behavior, for example, consistently link to adolescents' lack of emotional health, particularly the most prevalent psychological dysfunction reported during adolescence—depression (Kowaleski-Jones, 2000; Rutter, Giller, & Hagell, 1998). Adolescents' mental health also relates to the extent they will engage in risk behaviors, which in turn influences their responses to challenges placing them at risk for negative emotional health outcomes (Cocozza & Skowyra, 2000; Larson, 2000). Many of the adolescents affected by violence have, or are at risk of developing, a mental health disorder (Porter, Epp, & Bryan, 2000). Likewise, adolescents' positive psychological health, such as their level of happiness, directly links to numerous forms of prosocial behavior, such as community service, altruism, creativity and leadership (Colby & Damon, 1995). Adolescents' healthy emotional development—the extent to which adolescents thrive—simply cannot be extracted from their effective social development.

   Given the important role schools can and do play in fostering social development, schools also necessarily play a critical role in students' emotional development. Educational experiences and outcomes reciprocally influence emotional health and thus determine the extent to which adolescents emotionally thrive. The most robust research supporting links actually focuses on adolescents' failure to thrive. School environments that undermine basic psychological needs generate negative emotional responses, negative motivational beliefs and negative behaviors

(Eccles & Midgley, 1989). Schools also can create emotional distress to the extent that schools socialize adolescents in particular ways of making sense of their worlds. Implicit and explicit ways schools emphasize different ways of appraising one's sense of self and signify the purpose of schooling also impact how adolescents view themselves, their abilities, and thus their emotional development. Likewise, early academic problems (such as grade retention, poor motivation, and declining academic performance) predict a wide variety of subsequent emotional or behavioral difficulties that emerge in later adolescence, including drug use and abuse, delinquency, teenage pregnancy, and the failure to complete high school (Eccles et al., 1997). Of course, adolescents also obviously bring emotional difficulties to schools, and that emotional development impacts both adolescents' abilities to learn effectively and to engage competently with their social environment.

Regardless of the initial cause of failing to thrive in and out of educational settings, it does seem that the reciprocal interactions between emotional and educational problems eventuate in widespread comorbidity of academic and emotional difficulties as adolescents move through educational systems (Weist, 1997). Left ignored or addressed ineffectively, emotional difficulties compromise adolescents' ability to learn and become responsible and productive citizens. The effects on educational difficulties should not be underestimated. Approximately 25% of all 10- to 17-year-olds in the U.S. function behind their grade level in school (Roeser, Eccles, & Strobel, 1998) and up to 20% of students are retained at least once in their academic careers (Durlak, 1995). Emotional challenges also influence adolescents' decline in academic motivation and school engagement as they progress through school (Roeser et al., 1998). In addition to the broad impact of emotional development on motivation, adolescents also suffer debilitating emotional disorders that truncate their educational attainments, which affects about 7.2 million Americans (Kessler, Foster, Saunders, & Stang, 1995). Low academic motivation, and lack of support that fosters motivation, also accounts for the failure of students to even finish high school (Rosenthal, 1998).

Fostering adolescents' healthy emotional development undoubtedly constitutes a necessary, but frequently ill-addressed, component of effective socializing institutions. Current systems of care pervasively fail to serve adequately adolescents' mental health needs and do not even consider providing services that would allow adolescents to thrive. The ground-breaking Congressional Office of Technology Assessment's (1991) report on the state of adolescent health found that up to 20% of adolescents present emotional and behavioral disorders severe enough to warrant intervention, but less than one-third of that percentage actually receive any form of mental health services. Other reports confirm that between 15 to 20% of adolescents are identified as needing, but not receiving, mental health services (Weist, 1997). Thus, despite high prevalence rates of mental health needs by public school students, society currently fails to respond. Reports examining adolescents' mental health do not even mention the nature of positive, thriving mental health, let alone try to index its existence.

The current failure to address adolescents' mental health needs and the necessity to address those needs in order to foster less violent and more model behavior leads to the need to link mental health concerns with broader school reforms aimed at educational outcomes. This chapter addresses the nature, extent, and opportunities to reform that link. The analysis first examines the nature of adolescents' mental health dysfunction and their positive mental health. The discussion then focuses on the peculiarities of adolescent development that challenge efforts to foster positive mental health, a discussion that serves as a springboard to discuss the role of schools in shaping mental health outcomes across adolescent development. As with previous chapters, the social science analyses provide the necessary background for a legal analysis of current and emerging efforts to address adolescents' mental health issues in school settings and the roles schools can play in fostering positive mental health.

ADOLESCENT MENTAL HEALTH: ITS DYSFUNCTIONS AND PROMOTION

Popular perceptions of and academic attention to adolescent development tend to focus on adolescents' negative responses to the significant changes and challenges associated with the adolescent period. The focus on disruptive transitions and negative outcomes, though, centers attention to only part of the adolescent experience. Transitions of this magnitude also bring the opportunity for positive growth. Commentators and researchers recently have begun to attach great significance to sites and opportunities that foster positive growth, a focus which promises to provide an understanding of mechanisms and processes by which adolescents reared in adverse and dysfunctional circumstances develop into competent and productive adults. Understanding adolescent mental health, then, requires an examination of both dysfunctional and optimal responses to developmental challenges. Much significance attaches to this examination. The analysis lays the groundwork to consider the extent to which and manner by which prevention programs and restructured socializing institutions can provide opportunities to foster adolescents' resilience and optimal development.

The vast majority of adults view the adolescent period as more difficult in some ways than other periods of life and a period difficult for both adolescents and for the people around them (Arnett, 1999). Adolescents actually do exhibit conflicts, even to the point of serious dysfunctions, as they respond to normative challenges. Available evidence also indicates that conditions that led to the negative view of the adolescent experience actually increase as adolescents face new challenges and present a greater diversity of needs. This section examines trends in the nature of dysfunction adolescents experience and in our understanding of the roots of conditions leading to dysfunction.

Nature of Dysfunction

The most frequently reported symbol of adolescent development is their apparent experience of emotional turmoil. Research confirms the existence of emotional difficulty associated with the adolescent period. Adolescents report more extreme and negative moods than either preadolescents or adults (Larson & Richards, 1994). Adolescents also report higher rates of depressed mood than either children or adults, and their depressed mood peaks in midadolescence (Petersen et al., 1993). The extent of negative emotional experiences is highlighted by the persistent finding that depression constitutes adolescents' most common clinical diagnosis. Studies of prevalence rates of disorders that occur during the adolescent period reveal that the most common diagnosis is for unipolar depression, with a 20% prevalence rate over the adolescent period (Lewinsohn et al., 1993). Other studies reveal even higher rates; a highly cited evaluation of 24 studies of nonclinical samples of adolescents concluded that depressed mood above scores thought to be predictive of clinical depression apply to over one-third of adolescents at any given time (Petersen et al., 1993). Although adolescents may experience swings in moods, their experiences do tend to be marked by negative experiences that reach clinical levels.

Adolescents' familial relationships also provide a common domain of adolescent functioning often perceived as an area wrought with dysfunction. The popular image of adolescence suggests that adolescents' familial relationships are marked by excessive and continued conflict. Conflict with parents does seem to increase during early adolescence and typically remains high until its decline during late adolescence (Laursen, Coy, & Collins, 1998). Although conflict may be more frequent in early adolescence, intensity peaks in midadolescence. Despite high rates of conflict, however, parents and adolescents do tend to report that their relationships are overall positive, that they share a wide range of core values, and that they retain mutual affection and attachment (Arnett, 1999). The majority of families do not report continued and excessive conflict. The adolescent period does not predict serious conflict with parents; however serious conflict with parents does predict an increase in adolescents' engagement in numerous risk activities that lead to physical and mental health hazards.

By far, the greatest hazards adolescents face emerge from the risks they take. Adolescents engage in risk behavior at greater rates than either children or adults. As a result, adolescents, especially those in their late adolescence, reveal the highest prevalence rates of a variety of behaviors that carries the potential for harm to themselves or others. Rates of crime, substance use, automobile accidents, sexually transmitted diseases all appear higher during adolescence (Moffitt, 1993; Arnett, 1992). These risks and associated hazards account for the primary causes of adolescents' ill health and early death. For example, according to the Centers for Disease Control, only five behavior-based causes account for over three-quarters of all mortality and a great deal of morbidity in American youth: motor vehicle crashes, homicide, suicide, preventable injuries, and sexual activity (Centers for Disease Control, 1998). Research consistently reveals that the main threats to adolescents' health are the risk behaviors they choose (Resnick et al., 1997).

Despite findings emphasizing that adolescents' unhealthy development emerges from the behaviors they engage in, it is important to recognize enormous individual differences and the relatively low percentages of disorders the behaviors actually indicate. For example, problems regularly attributed to adolescents typically include drug use, acting out, and eating disorders. Yet, prevalence rates for several diagnostic disorders among adolescents reveal that only 8% ever meet the criteria for any type of substance use disorder, 7% meet criteria for any form of disruptive behavior disorder, and less than 1% meet criteria for any type of eating disorder (Lewinsohn et al., 1993). Far from a period of excessive rates of chronic and serious dysfunction, the adolescent period does not appear more dysfunctional than other periods.

Although it is important not to diminish or trivialize problems regularly associated with adolescents, such as the seriousness of delinquency, eating disorders, and other problems, the current understanding of adolescent mental health and the image of adolescence suggest important points to consider as we evaluate the nature of adolescent mental health. Findings suggest a need for a more balanced conceptualization of adolescence. Experts typically direct their attention to the minority of adolescents who respond negatively to the significant changes and challenges associated with the teenage years. Although marked by some episodes of parent–child conflict, for example, rates of conflict are not that high and when conflict does exist it tends to indicate important areas of concern. Likewise, the excessive focus on disruptive behaviors results in a relative lack of concern for serious problems associated with the adolescent period, such as depression. The focus on adolescents' own risk behaviors also runs the risk of assuming that certain social conditions do not predispose them to engage in certain activities; it is important to focus on processes that contribute to dysfunction and alleviate their development among adolescents. Lastly, low rates of actual severe disorders do not necessarily vitiate the need for mental health services. Although adolescents' problems may become exaggerated, approximately one of five students in public schools exhibits significant mental health needs (Pfeiffer & Reddy, 1998).

Roots of Dysfunction

An appropriate starting point in considering the nature of troubled adolescence is to examine the factors that contribute to problematic developmental outcomes. No single developmental factor predicts dysfunction. Although unfavorable outcomes clearly remain multi-determined, research does reveal several constellations of interrelated social hazards that associate with problematic outcomes. Rather than detailing the massive amounts of specific findings, this section examines these social hazards' contributions to highlight the roots of dysfunction and challenges to positive mental health.

Although admittedly complex, research does identify several conditions that contribute to dysfunction. Child poverty and other factors associated with lack of resources remain the most consistent predictors of adolescents' problematic transition to adulthood (Doll & Lyon, 1998). Community factors also impact adolescents' outcomes; e.g., institutional resources and community norms serve as powerful pathways through which neighborhoods influence adolescent development (Leventhal & Brooks-Gunn, 2000). Ineffective parenting is the second powerful predictor of dysfunction, a finding suggesting that the attachment system is central to the general well-being and development of adolescents (Masten & Coatsworth, 1998). In addition, adolescents reared under conditions of physical and or emotional abuse are more likely to experience negative developmental outcomes as adults (Doll & Lyon, 1998). Lastly, chronic family conflict predicts adolescents' current and future maladjustment. Although research tends to focus on familial conditions, it is generally understood that social influences impact family dynamics and that the adolescents themselves impact the nature of their families and how well families create environments supportive of positive mental health (Rutter, Giller, & Hagell, 1998).

In addition to understanding specific factors that contribute to negative outcomes, researchers also tend to agree that the rate and intensity of undesirable outcomes appears to increase with exposure to each successive risk factor. Constellations linked to undesirable outcomes are understood as creating hazardous niches. The hazards identified by research suggest important points. First, the factors most predictive of dysfunction tend to be chronic life conditions rather than acute hazards. Second, the hazards involve conditions over which adolescents do not necessarily have direct control, such as poverty and ineffective parenting. Third, constellations of risk tend to be interconnected so that adolescents grow up within a "systemic niche" of multiple and interconnected life hazards (Pianta & Walsh, 1996). Fourth, factors that would contribute to resilience from hazards have a cumulative impact with greater levels of risk requiring greater accumulated protective factors to address them (Masten & Coatsworth, 1998). Fifth, risks are not absolute, risks fluctuate and change relative to new circumstances and developmental periods of life; and the experience of risk depends greatly on subjective meanings individuals attach to what may appear to be adverse life circumstances (Pianta & Walsh, 1998). Lastly, the phenomenon of accumulated risk argues against prevention/intervention programs that target students with a single risk factor. Thus, dysfunctions tend to be multi-faceted and require responses that address various needs depending on the nature of risks adolescents face.

MENTAL HEALTH PROMOTION

Few ever examine the nature of positive mental health or optimal functioning. Just as dysfunction tends to be framed in terms of the failure to move successfully into adulthood, researchers and commentators who study optimal functioning generally frame adolescents' mental health in terms of what would constitute the acquisition of necessary skills and experiences for a positive transition to adulthood (Lerner, 1995). The stance is significant: it is future-oriented and implicitly uses another age group to measure success. Under this approach, what may foster adolescents' happiness may not contribute to adult happiness, just as what may make adults happy may not contribute to their overall future happiness.

Although basing notions of well-being on what they will be like as adults, the approach is far from peculiar; well-being necessarily involves delayed gratification, unwelcomed experiences, and honing of skills to increase the chances of long-term well-being (Seligman & Csikszentmihalyi, 2000). Thus, the manner one deals with and controls current experiences and the attributions placed on those experiences largely determines mental health. From this view, then and as similarly proposed by leading experts, optimal mental health involves possessing appropriate coping skills, retaining a positive self-image, and maintaining a self-understanding that allows for engaged and proactive involvement in determining one's development and interactions with others (cf., Larson, 2000). This section examines this view of positive mental health and factors that seemingly contribute to its promotion.

Nature of Positive Mental Health

Standards for determining the nature of positive mental health easily lend themselves to accusations of bias (e.g., Fassinger, 1996). That some behaviors, thoughts, and emotions constitute optimal development necessarily implies that others are less than optimal. Questions of explicit and implicit bias arise, for example, when considering adolescents in relation to their potential racial/ethnic, gender, sexual orientation, and religious cultural diversity. These concerns, discussed in greater detail in the following section, do remain important to consider. The diversity, however, does not mean that underlying factors may not be identified. Diversity simply means that underlying factors may express themselves differently; cultural and developmental influences produce variations in the salience of certain goals and experiences which, in turn, yield different satisfaction of basic needs and different levels of well-being. Diversity also means that any understanding (and promotion) of optimal health must consider contextual forces. Although healthy psychological development involves numerous key components and supportive environments, three interrelated factors repeatedly surface as critical.

Positive mental health, regardless of age, involves a sense of agency. Agency entails experiencing one's thoughts and actions as originating voluntarily within the self (Ryan, 1993). This sense of agency is critical to intrinsic motivation, the experience of wanting to do an activity and being invested in it. Research on motivation illustrates the significance of agency for positive mental health. Adolescents can be motivated because they value certain activities or because of powerful external coercion; that is, they can have internal motivation or externally pressured motivation. Self-authored motivation leads to more interest, confidence, and excitement which in turn results in enhanced performance, persistence, creativity and general well-being (Ryan & Deci, 2000). Acting on intrinsic motivation describes the inclination toward assimilation, mastery, spontaneous interest, and exploration deemed essential to cognitive and social development and the principal source of enjoyment and vitality throughout life, including adolescence (Csikszentmihalyi & Rathunde, 1993).

A second factor, fundamentally related to the first, involves a concerted engagement in the environment. This engagement must involve paying close attention to the constraints, rules, challenges, and complexities found in the environment. Researchers term this pattern of effective adaptation in the environment "competency." Given great cultural and social diversity in conditions adolescents find themselves, standards on which to find competence may take at least two directions. Competence may be broadly defined in terms of reasonable success with major developmental tasks expected of a person in the context of his or her culture, society, and time. Or, it may be more narrowly defined in terms of specific domains of achievement, such as academics, peer acceptance or athletics. In general, however, competency refers to good adaptation, rather than superb achievement and engagement with the social environment. Competency carries a dual meaning that the person has a track record of achievement and that the influential factors impacting the capacity to perform will persist in the future.

The third factor central to optimal functioning involves efforts directed toward a goal, which might include dealing with setbacks, re-evaluations, and adjustment of strategies. To a large extent, this factor involves a sense of resilience. While there exists no universal definition of resilience, the term generally refers to manifested competence in the context of significant challenges to adaptation or development. Resilient individuals are those who successfully cope with or overcome risk and adversity or who have developed a sense of competence in the face of severe stress and hardship (Garmezy, Matsen, & Tellegen, 1984; Rutter, 1987). Thus framed, the identification of resilience requires two judgments. First, there must have been a threat to the individual, such as the extent to which they live in a high risk environment. Second, the individual must have adapted or developed in a competent manner despite the adversity. This line of research examines how predictable and alterable characteristics, mechanisms, and interactive processes enable students to attain educational and personal success despite seemingly poor odds.

Taken together, the three factors reveal much about conceptions of positive mental health. Definitions of positive health tend to take an adult-centered standard. For example, risks are seen as creating problems not necessarily for the adolescent period but arguably more so for when adolescents reach adulthood. As such, conceptions of mental health are future-oriented. Definitions also focus on individuals in context. Mental health tends to be viewed in terms of responses to social environments. Evaluations of optimal functioning, although seemingly viewed in terms of self-determination and individual initiative, still must consider social interactions. In addition, views of positive mental health essentially involve individuals' active engagement with their surroundings. Healthy adolescents are those deemed involved in creating their own social world. Lastly, despite impressive progress in understanding the nature of positive mental health, research remains in its infancy and has yet to attract the amount of research that its centrality to human development would warrant.

Promotion of Positive Mental Health

Given the continued lack of focus on the nature of positive mental health, it is not surprising to find that the promotion of positive adolescent development also garners little interest and research. Existing studies of adolescent and child development, however, do offer important starting points. Particularly important to consider is research relating to conditions that foster resilience (Luthar & Zigler, 1991) and research focusing on conditions that foster intrinsic motivation and positive emotions some view as "flow" (Csikszentmihalyi & Rathunde, 1993).

Research concerned with resilience focuses on the psychological and social forces that allow adolescents to overcome adversity and successfully adjust to conditions that seemingly would otherwise contribute to dysfunction. Although this research does not focus directly on optimal functioning, it does suggest important factors that lead adolescents to adapt positively to their circumstances. The central finding of resiliency research reveals that resilience to adversity depends as much upon the characteristics of the important contexts in which adolescents develop (family, school, and community) as upon the characteristics of the adolescents themselves (Garmezy, 1991; Radke-Yarrow & Brown, 1993). The most important factor associated with resilient behavior highlights the necessary interaction between individuals and social forces. Good cognitive development or intellectual functioning frequently serves as the most broad and salient predictor of competence, the ability to respond to challenges. For example, generally good cognitive skills predict more than academic achievement; they also predict other aspects of competence as well, such as the ability to follow rules, direct attention, and control impulses. This more social aspect of competence reveals that adolescents' social interactions matter in fostering competence. It also reveals that the caretaking roles adults assume can foster competence and hold important potential for adolescents to overcome some of the hardships that life may press upon them, a point highlighted by efforts to enact policies and programs to protect and foster good cognitive development as ways of building human capital (i.e., early intervention efforts receive enormous popularity and relative success, see Ramey & Ramey, 1998). In short, resilient outcomes depend upon specific mechanisms and processes that help link resilient behaviors with prosocial adult responses in a variety of contexts.

In addition to research on resilience, important insights emerge from examinations of ways adolescents become motivated, directed, socially competent and psychologically rigorous adults. Rather than focusing solely on the individual, this area of research focuses on how individual's approach situations and how specific supportive conditions must be present to maintain and enhance positive, engaged, competent, and intrinsically motivated approaches to one's environment. The general finding suggests that social-contextual events, such as feedback, rewards, and communications, conduce toward feelings of competence during actions and can enhance intrinsic motivation; but behavior will be experienced as intrinsically motivated if it is experienced as self-determined. Thus, optimal challenges and effective feedback that fosters autonomous behaviors and beliefs facilitate intrinsic motivation and positive mental health (Ryan & Deci, 2000).

Numerous areas of research support the above claims. Choice, acknowledgment of feelings, and opportunities for self-direction enhance intrinsic motivation and positive adaptation because they foster feelings of autonomy. For example, teachers who are autonomy supportive (in contrast to controlling) catalyze in their students greater intrinsic motivation, curiosity, and desire for challenge; all of which allows students to learn more effectively (Utman, 1997). Likewise, autonomy supportive parents, relative to controlling parents, provide types of environments in which children exhibit more intrinsic motivation (Grolnick, Deci, & Ryan, 1997). These findings generalize to other domains, such as music and sports, in which supports for autonomy and competence by parents and mentors incite more intrinsic motivation and greater success (Grolnick, Deci, & Ryan, 1997).

Not surprisingly, then, the combination of warm, structured child-rearing practices in parents with reasonably high expectations for competence strongly ties to success in multiple domains and to resilience among children at risk. In general, the more involvement, structure and autonomy granting opportunities adolescents receive from their parents, the more positively teens evaluate their own conduct, psychosocial development, and mental health (Gray & Steinberg, 1999; Kerr & Stattin, 2000); and the lack of such opportunities between sibling relationships also contributes to adolescents' adjustment problems (Conger, Conger, & Scaramella, 1997). The same has been found for student success in schools, with such opportunities deemed as contributing, for example, to more engagement, better performance, lower dropout rates, and higher quality learning (Ryan & Deci, 2000). Whether in school or in families, adolescents who receive support, feel challenged, and experience a sense of autonomy rate much higher on measures of optimal development (Hektner, 1997). Similar findings even have been reported with adolescents' engagement in their communities; meta-analyses reveal that structured youth activities reach effectiveness in fostering positive growth when they foster independence, self-efficacy, assertiveness, decision making, and internal locus of control (Hattie, Marsh, Neill, & Richards, 1997). The abilities of communities to foster adolescents' sense of engagement with their social world, and even do so perhaps more effectively than schools and some parents, has led leading researchers to focus on community programs to enhance adolescents' positive mental health (e.g., Larson, 2000; Lerner, 1995).

The above findings help support the general conclusion emerging from research indicating that resilient adolescents and those who seemingly thrive actually do not possess unique qualities. Resilient adolescents simply have retained or secured important resources indicating the presence of basic protective systems in human development. Foundational systems that generally foster competence in development must operate to protect adolescents or counteract the threats to development (Masten & Coatsworth, 1998). Adolescents reporting the most intrinsic and optimal motivation do so in contexts surrounded by structures which support self-determination. Greater understanding of resiliency and optimal functioning teaches us better ways to reduce risk, promote competence, and shift the course of development toward more positive directions. Given the multifaceted nature of positive human development, no single person nor single institution can be charged with the responsibility of promoting positive adolescent development.

COMPLEXITIES AND PECULIARITIES OF THE
ADOLESCENT PERIOD

Given the changes and challenges adolescents confront, investigations of adolescent development must include greater attention to contextual and cultural issues. We already have seen how viewing some actions as optimal necessarily implies that others are not. We also have seen that this necessity translates into the need to consider the role context must play in determining the nature of mental health and how it also plays an important role in helping adolescents develop behaviors that result in psychological health. Critical to understand, then, is the extent to which certain behaviors and choices for adolescents and large segments of the adolescent population are possible when constrained by social forces that limit options and prevent optimization. These dangers, caveats, and considerations, as we will see in the section that follows, present important implications for schools, not the least of which is support for a renewed focus on schools as places to foster positive mental health and influence the educational climates in which adolescents find themselves.

DISTINCTIVENESS OF THE ADOLESCENT PERIOD

Evaluations of adolescents' emotional health face the fundamental problem of evaluating adolescents' functioning by a normative social standard. In terms of adolescent development, adulthood continues to be the norm and source of comparison. Despite that tendency (or the opposite tendency to see adolescents as child-like), the adolescent period remains distinctive. Key peculiarities of the adolescent experience impact the extent to which adolescents can be judged on adult standards and the extent to which adolescent development may require its own standard. The distinctiveness of adolescence raises important considerations when designing policies that the adolescent period may require in order to ensure that adolescents actually develop to meet adult standards. Without doubt, a view of the adolescent experience does reveal the need to take adolescents' perspectives.

As noted above, the adolescent period tends to be viewed as a transition wrought with conflict between adolescents and their parents. Despite the pains associated with such conflict, conflict remains normal. In fact, some view the conflict as beneficial to adolescents' development. Within the context of warm relationships, for example, parent-child conflict serves to promote the development of individuation and autonomy (Steinberg, 1990). Investigations of the effects of parental control on adolescent development reveal that the optimal control strategy, fostering a wide range of positive child outcomes, is participative and not conflict free. Effective parents share decision making with adolescents and negotiate through conflicts with their children. The use of reasoning, the information provided by parents, and the child's active participation in the decision making foster a sense of efficacy. Conflict involving everyday behaviors or transient attitudes, not enduring natures of relationships, appear not only normal but also necessary for healthy adolescent development.

The adolescent period also is viewed as problematic because of adolescents' assumption of the numerous risks. Yet, risk taking and experimentation seemingly typical of adolescence actually may be healthy. For example, to create and forge their own individual identity, adolescents must explore available options and potential ways of being. What may be viewed as problematic and pathological may actually be normal and quite healthy. The use of drugs by adolescents illustrates the problem with viewing adolescents' experiences from an adult model. Research identifies a curvilinear relationship between drug use and adolescents who are "anxious, emotionally constricted, and lacking in social skills" (Shedler & Block, 1990, p. 612). Adolescents who use drugs frequently present the most psychological and interpersonal problems. However, adolescents who engage in some drug experimentation are the most well adjusted both personally and socially. Although adolescents' antisocial behavior does increase their life stresses and internalizing symptoms (Aguilar, Sroufe, Egeland, & Carlson, 2000), moderate deviant behavior seems part of establishing effective personal identity. Risk taking and experimentation are typical features of adolescence.

The adolescent period also is viewed as problematic to the extent that peers influence adolescent development. The concept of peer pressure seemingly misconstrues the adolescent experience. The influence of peers on adolescents' risk behavior actually does not typically involve overt peer coercion or pressure. Rather, it is peer influence or peer preference that plays a dominant role in adolescent development. For example, adolescents play an active role in decisions of first drug use, already having the intentions or "readiness" to experiment, and tend to select users as peers (Paglia & Room, 1999). Thus, rather than coercion, it is the normal focus adolescents place on peer group involvement that leads to risk behavior. In fact, risk-behavior involving drugs, alcohol, and tobacco occurs predominantly in group settings; and the behavior is incidental to other social activities. Equating peer influence with peer similarities overstates the considerable extent of peer influence, because the equation fails to take into account selection effects: individuals tend to select like-minded friends (Berndt, Hawkins, & Jiao, 1999) and associate with peers to construct and maintain health-promoting identities (Ungar, 2000). Indeed, mutual friends' levels of aggression predict the continuance of aggressive behavior (Warman & Cohen, 2000). Likewise, even though peers may be deviant, it is important to not lose sight of the finding that even deviant peers play potentially positive roles in adolescent development. For example, friendships with deviant peers may buffer against emotional problems adolescents may otherwise experience, having friends seems to protect youth from emotional problems. Compared to adolescents who do not have friends, adolescents with deviant friendships report better emotional adjustments on key factors, such as loneliness, low self-worth, and depression; like relationships with non-deviant peers, relationships with deviant peers buffer adolescents from social isolation and feelings of loneliness (Brendge, Vitaro, & Bukowski, 2000). Although research does not translate into the need to welcome deviancy and encourage deviant friendships, it does suggest the need to proceed with caution when considering the powerful role peers play during adolescence and the need to consider adolescents' perspectives in determining the relative normalcy or health of adolescents.

Influences on adolescent development also reveal the distinctive place adolescents occupy in society. Recall that the behavioral component of morbidities linked to adolescents provides considerable hope to the extent that morbidities can be preventable under the assumption that behavior can be modified. The reality of adolescence, however, reveals that adolescents are not necessarily in control. The lack of control reveals three critical points. Adolescents do not necessarily gain freedom of personal choice. As adolescents begin to gain personal control over many areas of their lives, they are expected to use the control to choose for a presumed better lifestyle. Sets of moral imperatives restrict adolescents' choices to a particular set of choices which society not only advises but also expects adolescents to internalize, such as not engaging in sexual activity and not using alcohol. Those imperatives actually may backfire, especially for adolescents who already engage in risk behavior (e.g., as revealed by abstinence programs, see Levesque, 2000a).

The second reason that it is important to emphasize how adolescents do not control key aspects of their social environment deals with the manner it may absolve social institutions from blame. Efforts to alleviate dysfunction increasingly focus on personal control and responsibility and the approaches receive resounding empirical support that documents the victories of health education and public health strategies to modify behavior and empower individuals to take personal responsibility for their health (Glanz, Lewis, & Rimer, 1997; Tones & Tilford, 1994). Although a focus on personal responsibility may lead to positive development, focusing on personal control may underestimate the social and environmental determinants of positive mental health and runs the risk of playing down institutional responsibilities. As we have seen, alleviating health risks includes addressing familial and societal circumstances, such as poverty and lack of access to educational opportunities. Focus on personal responsibility may absolve the government from responsibility to support social programs and research into the social causes of ill health (McLoyd, 1998). In addition, despite the belief that people can exert control over their development, much remains outside their control, such as their body type, which may lead adolescents to inappropriate conclusions about their development. Although some risk taking is expected during adolescence, serving as an integral part of learning to be an adult, risk taking that surrounds survival issues, such as efforts to secure shelter and food, or even to satisfy drug addictions, reflects society's disregard for the needs of a vulnerable portion of the population.

The third reason it is important to realize the limits of adolescents' control over their social environment is that a focus on personal responsibility may lead to placing undue emphasis on personal blame and personal weaknesses. For example, viewing dysfunction as resulting from irresponsible behaviors and choices raises the concern that individuals will be viewed as solely responsible for their adversity. This, in turn, raises the concern that they will receive less sympathy and assistance (Weiner, 1995). Allocating responsibility to the victim divests others of responsibility for people in need. For example, many view personal irresponsibility in health-related behaviors as anti-social because it raises costs for the entire community and has a negative influence on the just distribution of relatively scarce resources. This results in a narrow (but dominant) view of health, rather than viewing health as part of one's social environment and as part of sharing responsibility for the social structure and the community.

The need to move beyond personal control as the key determinant of mental health raises the critical point that health information must be taught within a moral framework. Education must contain normative and moralistic messages. Preparing adolescents for personal responsibility requires preparing adolescents to examine issues relating to social justice and adolescents' responsibilities to others. The responsibilities are reciprocal: individuals bear responsibilities toward the community and the community bears the responsibility to ensure that individuals are in the position to exercise autonomy and make educationally informed decisions about their development. In a real sense, adolescents must be placed in positions not only to maintain their healthy development but able to engage in dialogues that shape policies relating to everyone's healthy development.

DISTINCTIVENESS WITHIN THE ADOLESCENT PERIOD

Although the adolescent period may be distinct relative to other age groups, adolescents by no means constitute a monolithic group.

Adolescents exhibit variations and inhabit different environments that deserve emphasis to the extent that they determine the variety of challenges to adolescents' mental health. A most significant consideration involves the impact of living in a cultural or community context that differs from larger society. The primary example involves adolescents living in highly dangerous inner-city neighborhoods where survival depends on views that may be deemed inappropriate in mainstream society (Coll et al., 1996). Some argue, for example that adolescents raised in ghettos are barred from opportunities in mainstream society and that they may seek achievement in alternative economic and social structures represented by illegal activities (e.g., Ogbu, 1981; Bourgois, 1995). Likewise, adolescents and parents from these environments may use different criteria for successful developmental outcomes, such as the "Revised American Dream" that results from severe restrictions in opportunities (Burton, Obeidallah, & Allison, 1996).

Research consistently reveals that responding to different environmental considerations necessarily impacts adolescents' mental health: the health of minority adolescents is generally poorer than the health of their dominant-culture peers (McCloyd & Steinberg, 1998; Wilson, Rodrigue, & Taylor, 1997). To complicate matters even more, adolescents experiencing extreme levels of stress (e.g., minorities in violence urban settings) seemingly do not conform to existing theories of resiliency. Adolescents suffering from chronic exposure to stressors and identified as resilient to those stressors (through academic performance and relative lack of externalizing behaviors) do not report higher levels of hypothesized protective resources such as perceived self worth, competence, and social support; nor do they report lower levels of depression or anxiety (D'Imperio, Dubow, & Ippolito, 2000). Although potentially protective resources are themselves compromised by chronically disadvantaged neighborhoods, these environments do help shape protective factors. Minority adolescents expressing greater religiosity and concern for correcting social inequalities, for example, tend to score high on measures of well-being (Moore & Glei, 1995). Despite these more positive findings, research continues to document links between adolescents' perception of their neighborhoods as more threatening and increases in adolescents' numerous negative outcomes, especially their symptoms of depression, opposition defiant disorder, and conduct disorder (Aneshensel & Sucoff, 1996).

The adolescent experience also varies tremendously according to gender. Gender differences are manifested in behavior, beliefs about health and health-related behavior, health-related knowledge, and behavioral determinants. Moreover, gender differences interact with culture, ethnicity, minority/immigrant status, and SES to create unique mental health risks for different groups of adolescents. These differences are important in that they reveal more variation within groups than between groups (Eccles, Barber, Jozefowicz, Malenchuk, & Vida, 1999). These differences suggest that declines in factors relating to mental health are not inevitable consequences of adolescence or gender development; the differences also show that some factors that place some groups at risk for some things buffer them from other problems. For example, girls have many strengths that serve them well as they move through adolescence. Girls are more confident than males in stereotyped female gender role domains, such as general social skills and general academic abilities; and these strengths allow them to adjust to schooling better than boys who are more likely to drop out or get into trouble (Eccles, Barber, Jozefowicz, Malenchuk, & Vida, 1999). However, narrow standards for girls' appropriate gender roles place a majority of girls at risk to suffer from subclinical eating concerns, body dissatisfaction, and what researchers view as normal discontent which places them at greater risk for depression (Striegel-Moore & Cachelin, 1999). The role gender plays in adolescent development emphasizes well the need to consider adolescents' place vis-à-vis other adolescents.

Subpopulations of adolescents also reveal different issues regarding their mental health. Although many adolescents express different mental health needs, particularly adolescents who are homeless (Bearsley & Cummins, 1999), immigrant (Harris, 1999; McLatchie, 1997), and non-heterosexual (Anhalt & Morris, 1998), adolescents in foster care and those in detention continue to receive the most attention. Although even literature relating to these two latter groups remains limited, it nevertheless provides important examples of the unique risks for morbidity they express, often to a greater degree. Although the majority of studies examining the health of adolescents in foster care tend not to separate adolescents from young children, the surveys that do exist provide important information regarding adolescents' need for mental health services. A leading study of adolescents entering foster care found that three-quarters required urgent mental health referrals (Chernoff, Combs-Orme, Risley-Curtiss, & Heisler, 1994). Adolescents in custody for delinquent behavior also reveal mental health needs. Reports from detention facilities indicate that more than half of adolescents experience depression, one-fifth are actually suicidal or self-violent, one-third exhibit disruptive behaviors, and one-fifth have thought disorders (Snyder & Sickmund, 1995). In addition, incarcerated adolescents reveal high-risk sexual and substance use behaviors, with one-third entering detention testing positive for a least one illicit drug (Snyder & Sickmund, 1995) and with nearly one-quarter reporting a history of sexually transmitted disease (Canterbury et al.,

1995). The status of some adolescents, then, exacerbates differences other adolescents' experience as normative.

SCHOOLS' ROLES IN PROMOTING MENTAL HEALTH

Despite growing consensus that adolescents experience an array of extraordinarily challenging familial, community, and societal stresses that put them at particular risk for behavioral and emotional problems and academic difficulties, controversy still surrounds efforts to engage public schools and determine their proper place in the provision of mental health programs and services to students. For example, various stakeholders voice fiscal, religious, sociopolitical, and value/belief system concerns. They note, for example, that schools cannot appropriately address the vast diversities found in society and therefore cannot legitimately address critical issues such as human sexuality, birth control, and dispense psychostimulant medication and therapeutic support (Pfeiffer & Reddy, 1998). Despite controversies, contemporary national health and mental health initiatives place schools at the center of efforts to address adolescents' mental health concerns (Kronenfeld, 2000). Commentators increasingly offer public schools as optimal settings to provide full range health and mental health services (e.g., Dryfoos, 1994).

As with any controversies, the role of schools in fostering adolescents' mental health presents numerous complexities and masks potential areas of agreement. As caretaking environments in which adolescents can find themselves, schools actually can and do foster mental health in numerous ways. Although schools' implicit and explicit efforts can be presented in numerous ways, schools essentially impact students' mental health in three major ways. These three ways reveal how schools actually are in ideal positions to promote and help consolidate efforts to ensure the development of competence. How schools may be replete with opportunities to foster academic, personal and social competence lays the foundation for our discussion of legal mandates, both how mandates fail and how they may be reformed to reflect the realities of adolescents' educational experiences.

MENTAL HEALTH SERVICES

The most obvious way schools can promote positive mental health takes the form of mental health services provided to students, either in schools or linked to the schools but provided in the community. Despite concern about the reach of mental health services in school, most school-based mental health services actually are limited to providing services to students in special education (Duchnowski, 1994). School psychologists, for example, spend the majority of their time conducting special education screening, assessment, and treatment planning rather than on prevention and consultation activities for the whole school population (Weist, 1997; Natasi, Varies, Bernstein, & Pluymert, 1998). The task which they do the least tends to be what would seem most frequent: direct involvement in therapeutic activities with students or their families (Conoley & Conoley, 1991). Mental health service provision, then, typically remains focused on discrete problems and involves a consultation model, one in which mental health experts assess needs and seek to work with others to develop targeted services for referred students. The focus on special education students and evaluating their needs is so central to the provision of mental health services that reviews of innovative models of service delivery purposefully do not address services for students with mental health needs that are part of the regular education program (Duchnowski, 1994). Thus, students with psychiatric disorders are more likely to receive the attention of school psychologists than students with health problems resulting form behavioral, social, and environmental factors related to their life-styles—the so-called "social morbidities" related to their risk-taking.

Although focused on the needs of special education students, school mental health services also provide some services for regular education students. Schools that do offer mental health services typically do so through their health centers. Although initially established to meet the needs of pregnant and parenting adolescents in low-income (primarily urban) areas, these centers have broadened their reach. Reproductive health issues constitute less than a third of all services provided (Jepson, Juszczak, & Fisher, 1998). As much as 50% of student visits to school-based or school-linked health centers involve psychosocial concerns (Adelman & Taylor, 1998). More specifically, for example, depression and suicidal ideation constitute over 20% of all mental health visits; conflict and violence represent up to 20% of mental health visits (Jepson, Juszczak, & Fisher 1998). Importantly, substance abuse represents only 3% of the reason for mental health visits (Id.). However, 34% of students using clinics for mental health reasons report problematic substance use among family members, a finding that suggests links between high risk behaviors among both adolescents and their families (Jepson et al., 1998). Other analyses of programs reveal that mental health concerns account for nearly one-quarter of the visits to health centers; they only rank second to illness or accidents, which account for one-quarter of visits (Lear, Gleicher, St. Germaine, & Porter, 1991). Other reports reveal that health care clinic workers view mental health counseling as their greatest unmet need (Dryfoos, 1994).

Although the vast majority of school-based and school-linked programs vary, the majority of programs involve simple, one-component partnerships between a school and an outside agency or organization. As such, these programs often focus on specific target populations and provide largely uncoordinated and unintegrated services to adolescents and their families (Motes, Melton, Simmons, & Pumariega, 1999). In addition, the availability of special services to address emotional and behavioral difficulties decreases as students advance through grades, particularly when students reach secondary levels. Services are especially limited for adolescents in regular education (Weist, 1997). Schools generally rely on interventions that are short-term, narrowly focused, and responsive to disruptive students with acute or otherwise serious problems (Adelman & Taylor, 1998). Moreover, the emphasis on school-linked services plays down the need for restructuring the various services. The movement toward school-linked services seeks to coordinate community services and putting some on school sites, which leads to the impression that the linked service suffices to address barriers to learning and mental health problems (Adelman & Taylor, 1998).

Although still primarily aimed at special education students, mental health programs reveal important changes in service delivery. A national movement seeks to place a full range of mental health services in schools, services that range from primary to tertiary preventive for adolescents. The expansion has resulted from the growth of school-based health centers that emerged in relation to general concerns regarding the psychological and educational risks associated with adolescent pregnancy and parenting (Dryfoos, 1994). Although health centers are primarily located in urban, medically underserved areas, they increasingly are being developed in rural and suburban areas (Jusczak, Fisher, Lear, & Freidman, 1995). Although school-based clinics and school-linked health centers may offer mental health services to address numerous problems, only about one-third of the programs providing those services use trained mental health professionals (Weist, 1997). In fact, schools typically have no, or very minimal, staff trained in mental health: The most recent representative sampling of school districts across the United States revealed that the ratio of school psychologists or social workers averages 1 to 2,500 students (Carlson, Paavola, & Talley, 1995). Thus, despite visions that schools could offer comprehensive mental health through "full-service schools" (Dryfoos, 1994), few schools offer services that approximate the vision of bringing mental health services to schools in conjunction with other services ranging from parent education, child care, cultural events to community policing.

The advantages of providing mental health services through schools have been well noted. First, treatments reach greater effectiveness if offered in more natural settings. Several now recognize the unrealistic hope of addressing emotional and behavioral problems in artificial settings far removed from adolescents' natural environments (Henggeler, 1994). The dominant model of treating adolescents' emotional and behavioral disorders, weekly outpatient therapy visits, receives only limited support for effectiveness from meta-analyses of adolescent psychotherapy outcome studies (Weisz, Weiss, & Donenberg, 1992). Importantly, analyses reveal that the location of the services seems to indicate best the service's effectiveness: positive effects of therapy are found systematically only when the services are offered in university based research programs, not in the general field (Duchnowski, 1994). Second, by offering services in schools, adolescents have a single point of access to services in a familiar, nonthreatening atmosphere in a more accessible setting. Providing such access is critical given that the dominant system for addressing adolescents' mental health problems—community mental health clinics—present many barriers and prevent adolescents from accessing clinic services designed for adolescents. As a result of barriers, only 3% of adolescents receive mental health services from community providers (Knitzer, 1993). Third, relying on parents to ensure adolescents' access to mental health services places adolescents at risk for not receiving services. Adolescents' poor mental health actually is connected to the mental health of their parents and the conditions contributing to their parents' mental health serves as obstacles to adolescents' obtaining services (Stern, Smith, & Jan, 1999). Likewise, stress in families can preclude adequate attention to adolescents' emotional difficulties, families may have poor knowledge of mental health services, and cultural barriers may reduce access to services. Even if they did get services, they may not remain long enough to receive the necessary assistance: dropout rates for therapies offered to children and their families reach higher than 50% (Durlak, 1997). Treatment effectiveness, access, and increased chances of using services certainly reinforce the need to provide mental health services in schools.

Although many advantages may arise from offering mental health services through schools, evaluations tend to lag in demonstrating actual effectiveness and their actual implementation suggests that they remain unlikely to reach their full potential. Evaluations of mental health services are limited and narrowly focused. Only scant research seeks to determine these services' cost-effectiveness as well as their possible iatrogenic effects (Adelman & Taylor, 1993a, b). Relatedly, research indicates that even though school-based mental health services may be offered, they are not necessarily used (Barker & Adelman, 1994). Likewise, research reveals the continued need to involve parents; yet studies consistently report a failure to reach parents (Atkins et al., 1998). These failures are especially serious given that individual psychotherapy seems ineffective and that parents play a critical role in the development and alleviation of problems adolescents face. These obstacles are compounded by the type of service needed: mental health needs create emotional barriers to obtaining assistance (Roberts, 1996). As a result, services actually may be offered too late since adolescents must show salient symptoms of emotional distress, such as acting out, in order to receive access to services (Flaherty, Weist, & Warner, 1996). Many adolescents with social, emotional, or behavioral difficulties never receive the services necessary to address these difficulties either within or outside of schools. Despite high prevalence rates of students with significant mental health needs, less than 1% are identified as behaviorally or emotionally disturbed (Werthamer-Larsson, 1994).

Despite challenges, existing research relating to the provision of mental health services still provides considerable promise. Studies on risk and resilience proscribe actions that schools might take to counteract the discouraging futures students may face. Schools and educators can establish programs to promote resilience to counterbalance the risk and adversity facing many contemporary students and their families. This important development benefits from research shifts from a static consideration of risk variables or factors toward a more dynamic consideration of negotiating risk situations (Rutter, 1987). That research already contributes to programs that can help address adolescents' mental health needs (Motes, Melton, Simmons, & Pumariega, 1999). The hope is that offering services in schools could alleviate many of the problems facing the current delivery of mental health services to adolescents: fragmentation of services, poor coordination within and between agencies, staff limitations, inadequate treatment facilities, and escalating difficulties in paying for services with managed care that eventually combines to make mental health services essentially a "nonsystem" for adolescents (Kelleher et al., 1992).

CURRICULAR PROGRAMS

Curricular programs continue to evolve to match the theoretical and empirical understanding of adolescent development. Initially, programs that addressed issues relating to health behavior emphasized informational approaches. Interventions were based on the premise that providing adolescents with accurate knowledge about certain issues, such as drugs or sexual activity, would lead adolescents to change their behaviors accordingly. These efforts relied on the assumption that adolescents behave in a rational manner and are able to alter their behaviors accordingly. Informational strategies, however, have failed to gain support from research. Summaries of informational approaches indicate that these strategies used in schools have not contributed to any area of prevention in which they have been used (Durlak, 1995). Providing information may increase knowledge and awareness of the adverse effects of certain practices, and at times increase negative attitudes toward practices, but they do not necessarily impact behavior (e.g., Botvin, 1995).

The next generation of efforts focuses on social learning principles to enhance the competency of adolescents. Programs based on these models emphasize building singular or core sets of skills. Empirical work identifies skills deemed worthy of focus by linking their absence to behavior problems or their presence to positive adaptation. Once targeted skills are identified, they are then modeled by adults or by peers. Children then are allowed to practice their new skills and receive feedback and reinforcement for effectiveness. This approach contributes to many curricular programs, such as those that focus on communication skills, assertiveness, goal-setting, self-control and self-monitoring strategies, and general problem solving to promote competence. The most popular programs teach interpersonal problem-solving skills (Spivack & Shure, 1974), assertiveness training (Rotheram-Borus, 1988), and resistance skills and life skills (Botvin & Tortu, 1988). The basic premise of these more popular programs asserts that adolescents engage in certain behaviors because of social pressures from peers, the family, and the media, as well as internal pressures (e.g., the desire to be cool and popular). Programs seek to counter those pressures and attempt to motivate students to resist them.

The most recent generation of programs operate from the assumption that most forms of adjustment and maladjustment are multiply-determined, that efforts must use multi-level interventions and modify multiple risk and protective factors. These programs adopt a more developmental, ecological, and multi-causal view of competence and its enhancement. These models train a wider variety of more elaborate skills over longer periods of time, link the teaching of skills to developmental trends, and attend to various developmental contexts for competence. The most common program seeks to prevent antisocial behavior and delinquency by targeting children's cognitive and social competence as well as parenting behaviors, family interactions, and social support. Results from these studies indicate that enhancing cognitive and social competence in adolescents and enhancing patterns of interactions in families can have long-term cumulative protective effects (e.g., Yoshikawa, 1994).

Despite focus on the multi-systemic nature of problems facing adolescents, current programs clearly remain narrowly focused. Current

WSU Lake Campus Library
7600 State Route 703
Celina, Ohio 45822
419-586-0360

Tue Jan 21 2003

#7

A hold has been placed on the following item by the patron
listed below. Please pull this item and forward it to the
library location given below.

AUTHOR: Levesque, Roger J. R
Dangerous adolescents, model adolescents : shaping the role and promise of
CALL NO: LC191.4 .L46 2002
BARCODE: 01406060667910
STATUS: AVAILABLE
LOCATION: Dunbar 3rd Floor
PICKUP AT: D. Lake Campus Circ Desk

KATHLEEN F HART
1449 JAMES DR
CELINA OH 45822

programs generally focus on enhancing adolescents' skills. For example, the leading program, Life Skills Training, uses social learning principles to systematically teach students a set of skills that may be useful in preventing drug use (Botvin, Baker, Dusenbery, Botvin, & Diaz, 1995). Students are taught coping skills, how to resist peer pressure, how to communicate effectively, and how to set and maintain personal goals. These programs have been consistently effective in reducing student drug use, including students from several school settings and for students from ethnically diverse populations. Some programs reduce the odds of smoking, drinking immoderately, or using marijuana up to 40% and report success rates of up to six years (e.g., Botvin, Baker, Dusenbery, Botvin, & Diaz, 1995; Durlak, 1997). Research generally confirms that programs like Life Skills Training that use interactive delivery modes, such as small-group discussions, role playing, and demonstrations, prove generally more effective than didactic presentations characteristic of earlier generations (Tobler & Stratton, 1997). Given the often pessimistic prognostications of prevention research, these findings seem nothing short of phenomenal.

Secondary prevention research presents even more striking findings. This research focuses on mental health intervention for adolescents with subclinical problems discovered through a population-wide screening approach. The vast majority of these programs is school-based and involves early adolescents who exhibit internalizing symptoms, poor peer relations, poor academic achievement or a mixed symptomatology. Likewise, the vast majority of interventions tends to be offered in a few sessions conducted in group formats. Meta-analyses of these studies reveal that the average participant in behavioral or cognitive-behavioral interventions surpasses the performance of approximately 70% of those in the control group (Durlak & Wells, 1998). These levels of effectiveness are much higher than treatment outcome studies and primary interventions aimed to prevent delinquency, smoking or alcohol use (Durlak & Wells, 1998). These impressive findings provide strong empirical support for taking secondary prevention seriously. Interventions can identify early signs of maladjustment and intervene with problems least amenable to change via traditional psychotherapeutic efforts when they reach clinical levels.

Despite considerable progress in designing programs, though, it is important to emphasize that the high levels of effectiveness do not necessarily reach similar levels when implemented in non-experimental settings (e.g., Gagor & Elias, 1997). The difficulties faced by non-multisystemic programs are exacerbated when programs seek to expand beyond school grounds and include other social systems in which adolescents find themselves. Most notably difficult, for example, are efforts to include families in service delivery. Efforts remain limited by the difficulty of obtaining and sustaining parental participation in programs. Parents who participate in prevention programs already have better parenting skills an relationships with their children, compared to parents who do not participate (Paglia & Room, 1999). Attracting and retaining family participation with high-risk families is even more challenging. Yet, researchers continue to view family skills training, geared towards improving communication and interactions, targeted to high-risk families as the most promising family-based selective prevention approach (Paglia & Room, 1999).

Current prevention projects support the view that effective programs focus both on competence enhancement as well as problem reduction. These projects provide global evidence that it is possible to change the course of development. The programs highlight the utility of health promotion and show how some adolescents need systematic skills training that considers the needs of adolescents' peculiar environments. Prevention has great potential to alter the odds of favorable development and simultaneously to test our beliefs about what makes a difference. Schools undoubtedly constitute a primary arena of adolescents' social environments that could make a difference. Numerous programs may reach high levels of effectiveness. In implementing programs, however, evaluation research persistently reveals that program success relates less to selecting effective programs and importing them into school systems than it does to implementing programs in a manner that adapts programs to particular schools, especially to the schools' culture, practices, and community.

SCHOOL CLIMATES

Positive aspects of mental health and optimal development associate with schooling. Schools may potentiate optimal emotional functioning by addressing basic psychological needs that generate positive emotional reactions, positive motivational beliefs, and positive behaviors (Eccles & Midgley, 1989). For example, adolescents' beliefs that school is interesting, important, and instrumental for attaining future goals relate to a strong connection between adolescents' personal identities and the socially sanctioned pathways to future opportunity in the United States. The integration provides a sense of hope, purpose, and direction that manifests itself in positive behavioral choices, a sense of well-being, and a positive outlook on the future (Roeser, Eccles, & Strobel, 1998). How schools address adolescents' needs for competence, autonomy, and quality social relationships have been seen as especially determinative. For example, leading approaches attach significance to the manner the fit or mismatch between adolescents' psychological needs and affordances (i.e., the demands and opportunities) in school context determines the quality of academic motivation, achievement, and mental health (Eccles et al., 1993). School settings that provide developmentally appropriate affordances for students to actualize their competencies, exercise autonomy, and participate in caring and respectful relationships create environments more likely to have children who feel more academically competent, value school, feel good about themselves, achieve, and act in prosocial ways. On the other hand, schools that undermine the fulfillment of these needs produce environments in which students feel academically incompetent, devalue school, feel poorly about themselves, act out, and underachieve.

Theories linking school climates with adolescents' optimal development take advantage of what we know about adolescents. Adolescents generally exhibit heightened self-consciousness. That tendency suggests that students would need safe, nonjudgmental settings to develop their competencies rather than competitive and socially comparative motivational practices. Likewise, most adolescents desire more decision-making power as they move into adolescence. That development reveals why schools that fail would increase effectiveness if they provided students with more decision-making power.

Support for the above person-environment fit theory derives from research examining the transition from elementary to middle-level schools. Prior research had revealed that many students experienced a deterioration in perceptions of self, affect, motivation, and performance during early adolescence, and in particular when they moved to middle-level schools (Eccles & Midgley, 1989). Rather than viewing the deterioration as an inevitable result of changes associated with puberty, research indicated that the deterioration was more due to the nature of the transition and its timing. The deterioration associated with less facilitative school environments. Contemporary research examining normative school transitions underscores how adolescents' developmental needs appear incompatible with the social and organizational structures of the middle, junior high, and high schools that they experience (Seidman & French, 1997). Although the timing of the transition to middle-level schools may render early adolescents particularly vulnerable and eventually place them on paths toward either educational engagement or disengagement, the studies indicate that they were vulnerable to both positive and negative influences. Those findings provide evidence that young adolescents do not inevitably suffer declines in emotional and academic well-being in their transitions to middle-level or junior high schools. This research helps to highlight the critical point that much of students' mental health involves the manner students make meaning of their school experiences in terms of how well their environment supports or undermines their fulfillment of basic psychological needs.

School environments also impact emotional distress to the extent that schools socialize adolescents in particular ways of making sense of their worlds. Both implicitly and explicitly, schools emphasize different ways of appraising the self and the purpose of school. Some environments can predispose children to think of their abilities as fixed and view their academic difficulties as unchanging personal deficits. Ample empirical evidence indicates that cognitive-motivational processes provide the vehicle by which school environments indulge students' learning and achievement-related behaviors (for a review, see Eccles, Wigfield, & Schiefele, 1998). The meaning adolescents derive form their school experiences instrumentally shape their beliefs about themselves as learners, about the content of what is learned, and about the goals of the learning process itself. Thus, adolescents' perceptions of school environments determine achievement-related beliefs, emotions and behavior. This important development views adolescents as active makers of meaning with social settings, rather than viewing adolescents as passive recipients of educational treatments. Aspects of school environments affect the emotional experiences of students directly through their fit or mismatch with basic psychological needs and indirectly through their impact on students' academic behavior and motivational beliefs. Adolescents who report frequent negative emotions tend to experience reduced academic functioning. For example, symptoms of depression, such as sadness, hopelessness, and loneliness, associate with lower achievement on standardized tests, lower teacher-rated grades, poorer peer relations (Roeser & Eccles, 1998). Likewise, adolescents who exhibit externalized distress, such as anger, frustration, and fears, also experience numerous school difficulties. Externalized distress relates to learning delays, poor achievement, social rejection, and aggressive behavior and misconduct in the classroom, and dropping out of school (Eccles, Lord, Roeser, Barber, & Jozefowicz, 1997). Thus, emotions of accomplishment, engagement and social relatedness all relate to school experiences.

Although research has identified key components of effective school environments, the current reality of schooling reveals that schools generally do not provide experiences that encourage adolescents to experience optimal functioning and develop competencies derived from their own initiatives. Schools provide only a limited context for adolescents to experience positive development. During schoolwork, for example, adolescents report high levels of boredom and report low intrinsic motivation to do school work. The primary reason for these findings is that adolescents in schools are operating in contexts that are other-directed; students engage in efforts under the control of incentives and structuring provided by adults (Larson, 2000). As students reach adolescence, schools stifle students' initiatives at times that they exhibit more ability to make their own decisions and control their actions. As a result, when adolescents reach their mid-teen years, they report a reduction in intrinsic motivation, a finding evidenced by declines in school grades (Eccles & Midgley, 1989). Schools currently provide little in the way of affective supports for their students, a point reinforced by Forman and Kalafat (1998) in their discussion of adolescents' reluctance to seek adults in the school setting to assist with even the most serious of problems. Their research highlights well how schools essentially fail to recognize and validate the importance of an appropriate climate for student growth and development. Schools that fail to do so unwittingly may be exacerbating risk for many of their students by failing to act upon the available evidence about the protective potential of the school environment (Doll & Lyon, 1998). Schools that fail to do so also fail to prevent more serious problems: Poor academic performance associates with a variety of negative behavioral and social outcomes (such as discipline problems, poor peer relations, drug use, psychological difficulties and delinquency). Despite the need, schools have yet to implement programs and services that enable students to become full participants in their own academic achievement and healthy development (Adelman & Taylor, 1998).

Although schools generally may not provide environments conducive to optimal functioning, schools can promote resilience and build capacities of students who otherwise follow the usual trajectories of risk. The existing research base provides empirical support for certain types of school-based resilience efforts. Research highlights the need to increase commitment to students existing in hazardous niches of multiple, chronic risk conditions. Effective approaches would incorporate simultaneous sources of support, including building upon the student's own coping mechanisms and those that deepen and strengthen the caretaking provided to the student. Taking this research seriously would certainly lead to considerable change in educational practices and the nature and functions of schooling.

THRIVING, EDUCATION AND THE LAW

Given the numerous difficulties presented to the legal system's efforts to protect students from violence and the more difficult task of fostering civic responsibility, efforts to harness the legal mandates to ensure that adolescents thrive certainly would seem illusory. Yet, current legal principles do not negate the possibility of harnessing the law to ensure the development of environments that would foster optimal adolescent development. Indeed, many legal mandates actually require the creation of programs that foster optimal development and many mandates support the creation of environments conducive to positive mental health.

CONSTITUTIONAL PARAMETERS

As the previous chapters reveal, parents historically controlled the extent and nature of their children's educations. That general rule, however, has gone through dramatic changes. Although parental rights retain some primacy, how educational issues are framed dictate the extent to which schools can offer services or create curricula designed to enhance adolescent development. When efforts to improve adolescents' emotional competences are framed in terms of educational issues and services, school officials have general control over the types of educations students receive, with the exception that parents retain the choice of removing their children from schools or even some curricular programs. When efforts are framed in terms medical issues and services, students gain increasing control over their medical decision making, although parents still retain considerable power to dictate the services their adolescents may receive.

Educational Services

School officials retain the general right to make curricular and administrative decisions. This important development reflects a move away from bestowing educational control to parents and a move away from recognizing students' own rights to their educational preferences. The Supreme Court allows significant limits on adolescents' rights and actually curtails schools' considerable discretion in their design and implementation of education programs. The major rule that emerges provides that schools may limit adolescents' right to information only to the extent that states properly inculcate and prepare adolescents for citizenship and full participation in a democratic society; school officials control school environments so long as they seek to create environments that reflect broader communal and societal values. The shift, and its supporting rationale, becomes perceptible through an analysis of three distinct lines of cases which profoundly impact efforts to rethink education programs.

The celebrated trilogy of parental rights cases provides the foundation for the first line of cases that address the extent to which schools can determine curricular needs. Through these decisions, the Supreme Court furnishes the basis for parents to control their children's education and be free from state intrusion. The first case, *Myer v. Nebraska* (1923), actually involved the right of teachers to pursue their profession. Yet, it is in *Myer* that the Court announced that parents had a right to "establish a home and bring up children" (p. 399) and that the state had impermissibly interfered with the parents' venerable right to control their children's education (p. 401). In the second case, *Pierce v. Society of Sisters* (1925), a lower court had struck down a state law that had declared it a misdemeanor for a parent or guardian to send a child between the ages of 8 and 16 to school other than the public school in the district where the child resided. The Court reaffirmed and gave parents the power to direct their children's education, so long as education was provided. In an oft-quoted statement in support of parental rights, the *Pierce* Court found that "the child is not the mere creature of the State; those who nurture him and direct his destiny have the right, coupled with a high duty, to recognize and prepare him for future obligations" (p. 535). Fifty years later, in *Wisconsin v. Yoder* (1972), the Court referred to *Pierce* as "a charter of the right of parents to direct the religious upbringing of their children" (p. 233) to find that the "primary role of parents in the upbringing of their children is now established beyond debate as an enduring American tradition" (p. 232). The *Yoder* Court upheld a challenge to a state law that required all children under the age of 16 to attend public or private school as it upheld the rights of parents to refuse to educate some children. As these cases strongly suggest, the parental right to control their children's educations has been well entrenched. Importantly, bestowing upon parents that right has two implicit outcomes: Firmly established parental rights minimize a school's inculcative function and diminish students' own right to determine their own upbringing when balanced against those of their parents.

The second line of decisions aims to support students' rights against efforts by school officials to control school environments. This line of cases reflects the Court's specific recognition of students' right to protection from governmental intrusion into students' right to engage in speech and right to protection from government-compelled speech. In the first case, *West Virginia State Board of Education v. Barnette* (1943), the Court used unusually powerful language to find "that no official, high or petty, can prescribe what shall be orthodox in politics, nationalism, religion, or other matters of opinion or force citizens to confess by word or act their faith therein" (p. 642). The Court found a school's requirement that all students salute the flag of the United States an unconstitutional exercise of governmental authority. In the following cases that also involved students' First Amendment rights, the Court further emphasized and reaffirmed its commitment to students' rights. In *Tinker v. Des Moines Independent Community School District* (1969), which involved a school's prohibition against students' wearing black arm bands to protest the Vietnam War, the Court struck down the ban as it found that students may not be confined to the expression of "officially approved" sentiments (p. 511). According to this approach, schools should encourage students to participate in the learning process. After these cases, commentators have described the Court's educational ideology as "discursive and analytical" where both teacher and student actively examine data (Gordon, 1984, p. 531) and as one that is "reciprocal rather than inculcative" (Senhauser, 1987, p. 956). The above cases contribute to the impression that students possess expansive educational rights. Yet, few other cases explicitly affirm students' rights to control educational environments, as reflected in recent cases that seemingly backtrack away from students' rights and tip the balance in favor of school administrators' right to control curricular decisions.

The third approach reflects a move toward according school officials increasing power in educational policy making. The approach actually has important roots in the parental-rights cases and largely dominates the Rehnquist Court's approach to educational rights. For example, when the *Pierce* Court had affirmed the rights of parents to control their children's educational development, the Court also had recognized the state's inter-est in regulating education and its inculcative functions. The Court had acknowledged the "power of the State reasonably to regulate all school-ing" and to require that "certain studies plainly essential to good citizen-ship must be taught, and nothing be taught which is essentially inimical to the public welfare" (*Pierce v. Society of Sisters*, 1925, p. 534). The more recent cases that aim to bestow upon school officials greater powers appeared more than half a decade after *Pierce* and quickly formed another foundational trilogy of cases. The first and transitional case, *Board of Education v. Pico* (1982), established the "right to receive information and ideas" in the context of school libraries (p. 867). As reviewed earlier, the Court upheld the removal of library books and highlighted that, in instances that limit youths' access to information, school boards have dis-cretion to remove books based on educationally relevant criteria but may not remove books based on partisan politics. That is, the school board would have acted unconstitutionally if mere politics would have been a substantial factor in removal. The Court construed the school board's rights as "vitally important 'in the preparation of individuals for partici-pation as citizens' and ... for 'inculcating fundamental values necessary to the maintenance of a democratic political system'" (p. 864). In curricular matters, the Court announced that school boards "might well defend their claim of absolute discretion" to transmit community values (p. 869). If the case left any doubt about the state's power to control the information youth receive, the next two cases firmly balanced the right to control information in the direction of school officials. In *Bethel School District v. Fraser* (1986), a 17-year-old senior delivered a sexually charged speech to nominate a fellow student for elective office (p. 687). The Court affirmed that students' constitutional rights in public school settings are more narrowly defined than those of adults in other settings (p. 682). That limitation in students' rights allowed school officials to curb forms of speech deemed threatening to others, disruptive and contrary to "shared values" (p. 683). Importantly, the Court reiterated its focus on community standards and the inculcative function of schools. According to the Supreme Court's interpretation of constitutional rights and obligations, public education must inculcate "fundamental values necessary to the maintenance of a democratic political system" (p. 681). Included in these values are tolerance of diverse and unpopular political and religious views that must be balanced against the interests of society in teaching the bounds of "socially appropriate behavior" (p. 681). The power of school authorities, acting as the inculcators of proper community values, was supported and developed further in *Hazelwood School District v. Kuhlmeier* (1988). In this instance, students alleged their free speech rights had been violated when their principal deleted two objectionable articles from their school paper. One article addressed issues of teen pregnancy and the other examined the impact of parental divorce on students. The *Hazelwood* Court upheld the authority of school officials to control the content of school-sponsored speech based upon "legitimate pedagogical concerns" (p. 273). The *Hazelwood* majority emphasized the role of schools as the primary vehicles for transmitting cultural values and their discretion in refusing to sponsor student speech that might be perceived as advocating conduct otherwise inconsistent with "the shared values of a civilized social order" (p. 272).

The most recent cases reveal that the Court approaches students' educational rights from two perspectives. One view reaffirms the authority of school officials to uphold the values of the community and another emphasizes the mission of the schools as the promotion of fundamental, democratic values. Thus, the Court accords the government considerable license to control public school classrooms in general and secular curriculum in particular in order to allow states, via schools, to fulfill their special responsibility to inculcate youth. Although the last three cases that deal directly with the power of school officials seems to be breaking new ground, it is important to note that the Supreme Court repeatedly has underscored the state's special responsibility in the social effort to transmit educational values that foster responsible citizenship. For example, the Court has emphasized that public education serves the "inculcat[ion] [of] fundamental values necessary to the maintenance of a democratic political system" (*Ambach v. Norwick*, 1979, pp. 76–77); that schools are a "principal instrument in awakening the child to cultural values, in preparing him for later professional training, and in helping him to adjust normally to his environment" (*Brown v. Board of Education*, 1954, p. 493); and that classrooms are a "market place of ideas" and "[t]he Nation's future depends upon leaders trained through wide exposure to [these ideas]" (*Keyishian v. Board of Regents*, 1967, p. 603). The Supreme Court's decisions emphasize the inculcative or indoctrinative nature of schooling for a given purpose; according to these decisions, public schools not only may but *should* "influence their students to adopt particular beliefs, attitudes, and values" (Mitchell, 1987, p. 700). Although the other series of cases recognized and fostered the socialization function of schooling, the current approach looks to socialization as a mechanism both to preserve community interests and preferences and to prepare students for citizenship in the larger society.

Therapeutic Services

The common law position regarding health care treatment for minors was that, until minors reached the age of majority, they lacked the legal authority to consent to their own health care (Shields & Johnson, 1992). The extent to which parents still retain considerable rights is exemplified by two situations involving potential conflicts between adolescents and their parents' rights: the provision of treatment over children's objections and efforts by adolescents to obtain treatment over parental objection (or without parental consent or notification).

The Court grants substantial parental authority over adolescents' medical decisions. Decisions that involve the fundamental right to liberty and freedom from confinement illustrate the point. In a 1979 ruling, *Parham v. J.R.*, (1979) the Court upheld a Georgia statute that allowed the admittance and commitment of minors to a mental institution. Under the challenged procedures, the minor had no right to notice, hearing, or counsel; and no legal right to challenge his or her involuntary confinement. Once the minor was observed, the facility could admit the minor "for such period and under such conditions as may be authorized by law" (p. 591). Rather than requiring formal hearings, the Court let stand the minimal procedures as it viewed sufficient protection of minors' rights through parents and third parties. Although the Court agreed that minors had a substantial and constitutionally protected liberty interest in not being confined unnecessarily, that interest was outweighed by the State's interest in avoiding "time-consuming procedural minuets" and the State's *"parens patriae* interest in helping parents care for the mental health of their children" in a manner that would not be "too onerous, too embarrassing, or too contentious" (p. 605). The Court also noted that the natural affinity of interest between parent and child, long recognized by law, properly allowed the "presumption that parents possess what a child lacks in maturity, experience, and capacity for judgment required for making life's difficult decisions" (p. 602). That natural affinity would lead parents to act in their children's best interests. The Court not only reviewed and applauded traditional understandings of the parent-child relationship but also wrote that "[t]he statist notion that governmental power should supersede parental authority in *all* cases because *some* parents abuse and neglect their children is repugnant to the American tradition" (p. 603). The Court's approach to the liberty interests of minors disregards and expressly declares irrelevant the choices and voices of children who would act contrary to their parents:

> We cannot assume that the result in *Meyer v. Nebraska* and *Pierce v. Society of Sisters* would have been different if the children there had announced a preference to learn only English or a preference to go to a public, rather than a church, school. The fact that a child may balk at hospitalization or complain about a parental refusal to provide cosmetic surgery does not diminish the parents' authority to decide what is best for the child. (pp. 603–604) (citations omitted)

The Court remains clearly concerned with the desire to reinforce the traditional understandings of the parent–child relationship.

Despite considerable respect for parental rights, the Court does not rest its decision conclusively on that view of family life. The Court still includes the extra protection of State officials and staff in adolescents' voluntary admission to mental institutions. The justification for reliance on those authorities, though, rests with an image of adolescents as essentially incompetent. The Court deemed minors incapable "even in adolescence" of making "sound judgements concerning many decisions, including their need for medical care or treatment" (p. 603). Although the Court suggested that the incapacity results in having parents make those judgments, the Court also used the incapacity to justify the exercise of *adult* authority. Adults, State officials and hospital staff actually serve two functions: they afford children the treatment similar to what their parents would *and* actually guard against parents who would not act in their children's interests. The mix of protection and autonomy reflects a move toward protection justified by parental authority, professional expertise, and important State interests. The Court recognizes a substantial proxy role for adults in making critical decisions on behalf of adolescents; adults are not only permitted, but obligated, to make judgments for adolescents. It does not matter whether adolescent's choices are subsumed by those of parents or by those of other adults.

The second situation involves adolescents' abilities to consent to their own health care. Early cases dealing with adolescents' reproductive rights illustrate the Court's concerns with parental control of adolescents and the control of both by the State. For example, in the mid 1960s and 1970s, the Court signaled its recognition of adolescents' right to autonomy and seemingly granted considerable power to adolescents. The Court first stressed the constitutional principle of adolescents' individual autonomy in *Cary v. Population Services Population International* (1977). In that case, the Court struck down a New York statute that prohibited the distribution of nonprescriptive contraceptives to minors under the age of 16 years. Equally signaling recognition of adolescents' autonomy was the early right to abortion case, *Bellotti v. Baird* (1979), in which the Court struck down a State statute that required parental consent for minors who sought an abortion. In the latter case, again, rather than granting adolescents complete autonomy, the state gains control. Although standing for ensuring adolescents' autonomy, the case has been interpreted as justifying three significant state interests that allow intrusion in minors' rights (1) protecting the unique vulnerability of children; (2) recognizing a child's diminished capacity to make intelligent decisions; and (3) facilitating the traditional parental role of child rearing (p. 640). Thus, the Court recognizes the state action requiring parental consent or involvement in important decisions of minors in order to protect its youth from adverse governmental action and from a child's own immaturity. These protections essentially involve three practical concerns. The first concern regards the minor's limited constitutional right to choose an abortion. The second issue relates to a state's interest in ensuring that the parents are involved in the decisions. The last consideration pertains to the parent's interest in participating and aiding in their child's growth, development, and physical and emotional well-being. To balance these potentially conflicting interests, the Court has developed a framework that attempts to reach a proper resolution for each minor who seeks an abortion. If states decide to require pregnant minors to obtain one or both parents' consent to an abortion, it must provide an alternative procedure where the authorization for the abortion may be obtained. In essence, the Court held that the state does not hold the authority to give a third party, a parent, veto power over a minor's fundamental right, which in this instance involved the limited right to *seek* an abortion. Importantly, only if the adolescents' interests at stake are deemed fundamental can states infringe on the parental right to control their children's access to health-related services.

FEDERAL LEGISLATION

The mandate for schools to become involved in the psychosocial, mental and social health of their students initially came from public laws 93-641 and 94-317, enacted by the federal government in the early 1970s. As a result, the primary and major focus of legislative activity derives from efforts to assist disabled students. The legislative history of IDEA indicates that a primary motive for its enactment was that students with disabilities often failed to receive educations. As a result, the IDEA required states to have a policy that "assures all children with disabilities the right to a free and appropriate public education" (Title 20 U.S.C., § 1412(1), 1998). States that failed to assure such educations would be denied federal financial educational assistance. The federal government required states to develop for each disabled child an "individualized educational program" that included a "specifically designed instruction to meet the unique needs of children with disabilities" (§ 1401(a)(20). IDEA requires that sates provide procedures for ensuing that children with disabilities are educated "to the maximum extent appropriate" with students who are not disabled (§ 1412(5)(b)).

Although much of the focus has been on emotionally disabled adolescents, federal legislative enactments also clearly impact thriving conditions. Most notably, for example *The Goals 2000: Educate America Act* (1994) provided impetus for changes in school based services and programs. *America 2000: An Education Strategy* outlined eight educational goals for the nation to aspire toward as we prepare for the 21st century. The national agenda for school reform provided a commitment to the socioemotional and physical health of all students, with prominent attention to mental health-related issues.

In addition to educational goals relating directly to emotional health, significant legislation, reviewed in the previous chapters, directly relates to providing students with educational environments conducive to positive social and emotional development. Most notably, anti-discrimination laws play an important role. Efforts to combat sex and racial discrimination, for example, seek to provide important opportunities for groups that previously were unable to enjoy important educational benefits and environments in which they could achieve goals. Likewise, efforts to redress economic concerns impact the extent to which schools will have the resources to offer effective educations and the extent to which students themselves could have the resources to take advantage of educational opportunities. Lastly, efforts to ensure religious freedom ensure that adolescents are able to hold and, in appropriate circumstances, express deep personal commitments and values.

Access to Mental Health Services

As we have seen, the common law position regarding health care treatment for minors was that, until minors reached the age of majority, they lacked the legal authority to consent to their own health care. Thus, any treatment rendered to a minor absent parental consent could subject the health care provider to legal actions for assault and battery. Two reasons justify parents' authority, as announced in the Supreme Court's guiding opinion, *Parham v. J.R.* (1979). This decision provides the broad parameters to resolve conflicts between parent and child regarding mental health treatment. In *Parham*, the Court noted how the broad parental authority rests on a presumption that parents possess what a child lacks in maturity, experience and judgment required for making life's difficult decisions. More important, historically it was recognized that natural bonds of affection lead parents to act in the best interests of their children. The general rule, then, holds that parental maturity and natural inclination to act in their children's best interests justifies granting parents legal control over their adolescents' access to medical services.

Despite that general rule, numerous exceptions allow minors to secure treatment without parental consent (for a review, see Levesque 2000a). Instances of emergency provide the first exception to the general rule: doctors could treat a child of any age, even in the absence of parental consent. Such cases imply the guardian's consent since delay would jeopardize the minor's health. In addition, emancipated minors need not obtain parental consent. The exception operates on the rationale that parents surrender their duties and minors are responsible for themselves. Although several states do not mention emancipation, it is important to note that the remaining states allow for access to medical services on the part of those who exhibit a degree of independence. For example, minors who are parents, married, in the military, or who live apart from their parents to consent to health care. A third exception which allows certain groups of minors may obtain medical treatment is through the "mature minor" exception. Minors eligible for the exception generally are able to understand the nature and importance of the medical steps which are characteristically not serious and complex. Note, however, that when medical procedures do become complex and the implications of the treatment arguably more serious, numerous states allow for a judicial by-pass for parental consent for specific medical services, such as abortion, and that alternative rests on the establishment of maturity. A fourth exception involves juvenile courts and child welfare agencies' power to provide youth access to medical care. The last major exception to the general rule that parents control adolescents' rights to consent to medical care derives from the specific problems or the specific services that are sought. Statutes typically concern themselves with two exceptions: pregnancy-related health services and treatment to deal with sexually transmitted and infectious diseases. Almost all states legislatively authorize minors to avoid parental consent to obtain medical treatment for venereal diseases or for sexually transmitted diseases.

The development of exceptions to the general rule that parents control their children's behaviors reflects remarkable progress to recognize the necessity of reaching adolescents. The sexually transmitted diseases exceptions are illustrative. Allowing minors' access to those services stems from a legislative recognition that society has a critical interest in facilitating and encouraging access to health services to reduce the spread of diseases among its citizens. These rules are justified by necessity, not by the actual maturity of minors or their inherent rights. As with the other aspects of the regulation of adolescents' lives, it remains to be determined whether the justifications for the rules reflect the reality of adolescent life and effectively deal with the apparent urgencies that contributed to legal reform.

Curricular and School-Related Services

Most states statutorily regulate some aspect of adolescents' mental health in school contexts. Their mandates, however, are remarkable for their diversity; programs reveal a wide range of curricula and services that differ in terms of aims, scope, implementation and content. Although some states may have more regulations than others, regulations all tend to be quite limited. The most frequent specifications, which come in the form of the need to address the needs of specific groups of students, illustrate the limitations. Thus, all states address the mental health needs of handicapped or disabled adolescents, some even single out for special services adolescents with severe emotional disturbances (e.g., Florida Statute, § 230.2317, 1999; Vermont Statutes Annotated, tit. 16, § 910, 2000). In addition, statutes affirm that schools could provide adolescents who have violated school rules (most notably rules regarding drugs and alcohol) with special services, including counseling, peer mediation, or other forms of intervention aimed at reducing their problem behavior (Delaware Code, Ch. 14 § 1605A, 1999; Maine Revised Statutes Annotated, 20 § 6606, 1999; New Jersey Statutes, § 18A:40A-11, 2000). Statutes also frequently address the mental health needs of adolescents identified as at risk for school failure; these statutes allow schools to provide special prevention services that frequently address emotional concerns (Arkansas

Statutes Annotated, § 6-5-601, 1999; Kansas Statutes Annotated, § 158.6451, 1999; Revised Statute of Missouri, § 166.260, 1999). Although the above statutes reveal important developments to address adolescents' mental health needs, three limitations emerge. First, the services are offered only to a small, targeted group of students. Second, the services tend to be reactive, and those that are not are less likely to be provided for through legislation. Third, except for disabled or handicapped adolescents, the services are phrased in a precatory manner, i.e., statutes tend to allow schools to offer services rather than mandating them.

Although the direct provision of services may be limited, it is important to highlight how statutes address mental health needs in other ways. Most notably, statutes provide for adolescents' mental health needs through curricular mandates. Most often, states require that schools provide students with some curriculum relating to health education (California Education Code, § 51220, 2000; Connecticut General Statutes, § 10-16b, 1999; Indiana Code Annotated, § 20-10.1-4-5, 2000; Iowa Code, § 256.11, 1999; Kansas Statutes Annotated, § 72-1101, 1999; Maine Revised Code Annotated, tit. 20, § 4723, 1999; Nevada Revised Statutes Annotated, § 389.018, 2000; North Dakota Century Code, § 15-41-24, 2000; Texas Education Code, § 28.002, 2000; Virginia Code Annotated, § 22.1-207, 2000). Although these curricular mandates are the most common, they actually deal mainly with physical health and the benefits that derive from a healthful lifestyle. Most statutes tend not to even define health education. Important exceptions to the failure to define health in a comprehensive manner do exist, with at least two states that take a very comprehensive view of health to include, for example, emotional development and the promotion of self-esteem or emotional health (Massachusetts Annotated Laws, ch. 69, § 1L, 2000; North Carolina General Statutes, § 115C-81, 1999). Rather than more explicitly defining health education as encompassing mental health, other states simply add separate curricular topics and programs that address mental health needs. Thus, Wisconsin encourages health education that builds self-esteem and personal responsibility (Wisconsin Statutes Annotated, § 118.019, 2000) and Alabama and Mississippi permit "wellness education" in addition to physical and health education (Alabama Code, § 16-6B-2, 2000; Mississippi Code Annotated, §37-13-21, 131, 2000). Most notably, though, many states encourage schools to initiate and conduct programs that, in addition to basic health concerns, would address family violence (Alaska Statutes, § 14.30.360, 2000), chemical abuse knowledge, prevention and/or intervention[1] and sexually transmitted diseases or sexuality education.[2] These curricular mandates highlight the significance legislatures attach to adolescents' mental health needs.

The above provisions certainly present important developments. Again, however, their limitations are important to highlight. Simply listing health education as a requirement for graduation generally leaves it narrowly defined and equated with physical health. Approaching health in this manner further fails to detail the nature of programs that would be mandated. As a result, these statutes' approach to health generally remains rather broad, vague and do not offer explicit guidance in terms of what instructors must teach. Likewise, approaching mental health needs by simply adding them to definitions of health reduces the chances that mental health needs will be addressed: statutes typically mandate health curriculum but only make optional the other curricular programs related to mental health needs, such as those dealing with drugs, violence, and sexuality. In addition, provisions for programs, even those that would most likely include mental health needs, tend to limit what can be taught which solidifies a focus on physical needs. For example, Louisiana allows for sexuality education but ignores mental health issues as it limits it to the study of human reproduction, pregnancy, childbirth, and venereal disease (Louisiana Revised Statutes Annotated, § 17:281, 2000). Again, provisions may seem expansive, but even the states that do address mental health issues through statutory mandates ultimately create limitations that run deep.

In addition to curricular mandates, state statutes sometimes do provide for health services. The most notable form of health service involves those provided through school-based health clinics. These clinics, however,

---

[1] These states include: Arizona Revised Statutes, § 15-712 (2000); California Education Code, § 51203 (2000); Connecticut General Statutes, § 10-19 (1999); Florida Statutes § 233.0612 (1999); Official Code of Georgia § 20-2-142 (2000); Idaho Code, § 33-1605 (2000); Louisiana Revised Statutes, 17:154 (2000); Maryland Education Code Annotated, § 7-411 (1999); Revised Statutes of Nebraska Annotated, § 79-712 (2000); New Jersey Statutes, § 18A:40A-2 (2000); New York Consolidated Laws Services, Education § 804 (1999); North Dakota Century Code, § 15-38-07 (2000); Pennsylvania Statutes, tit 24 § 15-1547 (1999); Rhode Island General Laws, § 16-21.2-4 (2000); Vermont Statutes Annotated, tit. 16, § 906 (2000); Revised Code of Washington, § 28A.170.080 (2000).

[2] These states include: Alabama Code, § 16-40-A-2 (2000); Arizona Revised Statutes, § 15-716 (2000); Arkansas Code Annotated, § 6-18-703 (2000); California Education Code, § 51553 (2000); Colorado Revised Statutes, § 22-25-101 (2000); Florida Statute, § 233.0612 (1999); Official Code of Georgia, § 20-2-143 (2000); Illinois Compiled Statues Annotated, ch 105, § 5/27-9.2 (2000); Iowa Code, § 256.11 (1999); Minnesota Statutes, § 121A.23 (2000); Michigan Statutes Annotated, § 15.41169 (1999); New Jersey Administrative Code, tit. 18A, §6:29-4.1 (2000); Oklahoma Statutes, tit. 70 § 11-103.3 (1999); Oregon Revised Statutes, § 336.455 (1997); Rhode Island General Law, §§ 16-22-17, 16-22-18 (2000); South Carolina Code Annotated, § 59-32-5 (1999); Tennessee Code Annotated, §§ 49-6-1005, 49-6-1301 (1999); Texas Education Code, § 28.004 (2000); Utah Code Annotated, § 53A-13-101 (2000); Virginia Code Annotated, § 22.1-207.1 (2000); Revised Code of Washington, § 28A.230.070 (2000); West Virginia Code, § 18-2-9(b) (2000).

tend to focus on the physical health needs of students, as exemplified by having nurses as the typical designated staff for health clinics and the absence of mentioning, for example, social workers (e.g., California Education Code, § 49426, 2000; Minnesota Statute, § 121A.21, 2000; Rhode Island General Laws, § 16-21-7, 2000; South Dakota Codified Laws, § 13-33A-1, 2000). Other statutes also provide for school health programs, but they do so in ways that do not necessarily address mental health needs, such as by simply delegating the nature of services to the Department of Education (Maryland Education Code Annotated, § 7-401, 1999; Mississippi Code Annotated, § 37-13-131, 2000; Revised Statutes of Nebraska Annotated, § 79-713, 2000). Statutes that do address issues beyond physical health needs focus on sexual activity and the statutory language typically involves highlighting the specific limits of the services clinics can offer by, for example, requiring parental consent in order to obtain services (Arkansas Statutes Annotated, § 6-18-703, 1999) and by limiting the psychological or mental health services to, for example, evaluation or consultation and the need to involve parents (Arkansas Statute Annotated, § 6-18-1005, 1999; Connecticut General Statutes, § 10-76v, 1999; Illinois Complied Statues Annotated, ch 105, 5/14-1.09.1, 2000; Texas Education Code, § 38.011, 2000).

Two additional points about the above statutory mandates deserve special emphasis. First, some states are notable for their absence of mandates that would control the state's approach to health, mental health, or other life-skills education. These states have no statute to regulate what could be labeled as ways that would guide the provision of services or creation of curricular materials that relate to adolescents' mental health. These states offer the least statutory protection since they do not mention what should or may be taught at all regarding adolescent mental health. Second, essentially no state explicitly provides for the rights of adolescents who seek services. Maryland provides one notable exception. Maryland law preserves the rights of student seeking to overcome drug abuse by making any statement they make to educators in their efforts to seek information to overcome any form of drug abuse "not admissible against the student in any proceeding" (Maryland Education Code Annotated, § 7-412, 1999). Importantly, other states focus on the rights of others and on essentially discouraging adolescents form seeking assistance; these statutes require reporting the use of alcohol or other controlled substances to authorities and protect those who make reports (Minnesota Statute, § 121A.29, 2000; New Jersey Statutes, § 18A:40A-12, 2000; Rhode Island General Laws, § 16-21-16, 2000).

Although problematic and, as argued below, in need of reform, diversity among state statutory mandates is significant for several reasons. For our purposes, the diversity reveals the relative failure of most states to address education that would directly address adolescents' mental health, even though states possess the authority to do so. The diversity also reveals challenges school systems face in their attempt to provide education: Schools must wrestle with the controversial and complex task of deciding what to teach and how to teach about mental health and provide environments conducive to mental health. Perhaps more importantly, though, the general failure amid some statutory mandates reveals that efforts to develop and actually enact statutes that could guide mental health programs at least are within the realm of possibility. States that guide the development of mental health programs through legislation indicate that all states may guide curricular matters regarding mental health education, that they may do so with broad statutory mandates, and that mandates also may provide explicitly for the provision of specific approaches and the delivery of services to adolescents. Given that states possess the authority to guide the actual implementation of policies impacting adolescents' mental health, it is important to consider the extent to which they also have the obligation to do so. Determining the nature of states' obligations rests on the ability to demonstrate the extent to which states have a compelling need and interest in certain forms of mental health education and services, and that level of necessity ensures that states have a concomitant right to design, implement, and impose a particular form of education on their citizens (cf., Levesque, 1998c).

CONCLUSION

Mental health research consistently finds that adolescents' negative mental health outcomes arise from their own risk behavior. These outcomes emerge from adolescents' delinquency, unsafe sexual activity, and other health-compromising behaviors; even the negative mental health outcomes resulting from victimization links to adolescents' own risk-taking. Although that may be the most robust and important finding, our analysis also reveals that adolescents' actions are far from self-determined and that negative outcomes are not necessarily self-inflicted. Community, family, peer, and school environments place adolescents in situations that lead to risk and problem behavior; and those same influences also provide potentially protective shields that help adolescents cope with negative outcomes and even allow adolescents to thrive. It is the promise of protective shields that lends so much significance to the role schools can play in fostering adolescents' mental health.

Recognizing the necessity of their important role in adolescents' emotional development, schools necessarily respond to students' mental health needs and do so in a diversity of ways. Most notably, schools provide clinics, links to services, skills development, general knowledge about mental health, and environments that themselves foster emotional responses. Although schools potentially impact mental health in numerous ways, current research reveals that schools do not necessarily take advantage of their influence on adolescent development and do not systematically address adolescents' mental health needs. Their failure continues despite research that documents important progress in recognizing that students need greater access to mental health services and to environments more conducive to positive mental health outcomes. That research now confirms that, with more consistent opportunities to receive information and gain skills, adolescents could be better empowered to make the necessary decisions to alleviate challenges to their mental health and also could be more empowered to limit adverse consequences of various risk-taking behaviors deemed inherent to their development. As expected, these opportunities would come not only from schools but also from links to other socializing institutions that would adopt and complement schools' efforts to profit from basic social science findings about the adolescent period.

Despite progress in identifying the nature of adolescents' needs and the ability to address those needs, the legal system has yet to respond effectively to further schools' efforts. Although some progress has been made to address adolescents' needs, the legal system pervasively fails to structure schools as environments that would enhance the vast majority of adolescents' mental health. Although the legal system typically does not respond in ways that would foster more effective school responses to adolescents' mental health needs, the legal system actually can permit schools to address those needs more effectively. We have seen how the legal system can guide the use of clinics, determine the availability and implementation of curricular programs, ensure that adolescents are exposed to appropriate knowledge and skill-building activities, delineate the boundaries of what schools can do, and channel school officials' and parents' actions with accepted rationales that balance their own needs with those of society and individual students. We also have seen how the legal system can help schools increase the role of parents in responding to mental health needs and, equally importantly, can help adolescents cope with troubled home and community environments. Likewise, we have now seen how adolescents can benefit most from services the legal system provides for them outside of schools when the legal system also ensures that schools provide adolescents with supportive environments that increase awareness about the nature of, need for, and access to those services.

Despite the legal system's ability to serve as an organizing force, it currently focuses on extremes and fails to structure school responses to normative challenges. The law typically focuses on extreme emotional disturbances and extreme problems adolescents would face (most notably, chemical dependency and life-threatening diseases). Even those mandates, though, remain fraught with limitations; states that statutorily address some of adolescents' problems tend to simply permit programs to exist rather than guide the development of programs and environments that would address adolescents' needs effectively. No legal mandate explicitly directs the ability of schools to help adolescents thrive. That vacuum necessarily relates to the somewhat chameleon-like qualities of optimal development. As we have seen, defining optimal development involves value judgments concerning the lifestyles and constellations of behaviors indicating thriving. In addition, the multidimensional nature of adolescence makes inappropriate the use of any single criterion of optimal development against which to judge all adolescents. Although what constitutes optimal functioning remains context embedded, we have seen how optimal functioning can be measured, described, taught, and its development monitored. The sources of optimal development are known and contribute to the development of principles identified as effective in fostering more positive mental health outcomes—e.g., effective environments address adolescents' needs, foster participation and inclusion in matters important to them, and help develop a sense of control and positive self-concept. These goals and principles, and the extent to which they must be fostered in different contexts, are precisely what provides schools with a potentially central role in fostering more positive mental health. Comprehensive programs and effective school environments can promote optimal functioning. How to integrate these principles into educational practice and subsequently into the indirect curriculum of schools remains to be determined; the next chapter explores possibilities guided by existing social science and law.

III

Fostering Adolescents

6

Ensuring the Promise of Education

The current reality of the legal regulation of schools and of trends in educational reform leads to the conclusion that we must rethink the law's approach to adolescents' schooling. The law pervasively fails to address the real and imagined problems facing adolescents, schools, and society. The ubiquitous failure to respond to the realities of adolescent development and adolescents' educational needs shatters two important myths about adolescents, their education, and the law. As we have seen in Chapter 2, the legal system always has sought to regulate adolescents' educations. These laws contradict popular perceptions that laws only now address schools' responses to problems associated with adolescent life. The previous three chapters challenge the even more popular perception that laws unduly stifle the discretion of educators. Rather than finding an over-regulation of schooling, a close look at existing legal mandates reveals that schools have very limited legal obligations to ensure students' safety, do not need to foster model citizens, and do not need to address the mental health needs of most of their students. Schools essentially have very little to worry about when they fail to educate students properly. Indeed, the law actually poses numerous obstacles for those who would want to invoke existing mandates to ensure that students receive more adequate educations.

The strikingly minimal requirements placed on schools present only part of the limitations of laws regulating schooling. What we know about the adolescent period suggests that laws that may appear effective actually may not respond to adolescents' realities. Even a cursory look at adolescents' high rates of behavioral and mental health problems and their apparent moral deficiencies establishes the failure of schools and the immense challenges schools face in responding to adolescents' realities. In addition, surprisingly few legislative mandates structure states' responses to education. Although the legal system does provide broad boundaries, it pervasively fails to structure schools' efforts to prevent violence, promote prosocial behavior and support adolescents' healthy emotional development. The current legal regulation of education, then, confirms how schools' responsibilities actually remain remarkably minimal. These requirements are likely to become even more minimal given recent legislative efforts to "deregulate" public schools.

This chapter continues the discussion that follows from having unveiled the myth that laws impose too many restrictions on schools' abilities to respond properly to students' developmental needs and to community concerns. The discussion envisions reforms that could respond to adolescents' problem behavior and foster healthy development by nurturing adolescents' opportunities to achieve healthy social integration and more positive mental health. These reforms require adopting a more expansive view of rights, one which views rights as both legal rights claims and as ways people treat one another in their everyday interactions. This view of rights, the following analysis suggests, better reflects the reality of adolescents' lives. Thus, although adolescents' formally recognized educational rights may be minimal, the nature of those rights, the extent to which they may be amplified, and the very reasons for schooling all serve as important and necessary starting points to chart paths toward reform. These starting points, and their implications, do not lead to the conclusion that more law stifles adolescents' educations. Instead, the analysis suggests that more law and respect for adolescents' basic rights must serve as the very foundation of adolescents' educations.

THE NEEDED LEGAL RESPONSE

The previous chapters revealed how, despite important limitations, legal responses to adolescents persistently reveal a concern for acting in adolescents' best interests, promoting healthy adolescent development, and fostering responsible citizenship. Indeed, these interests served as a dominant rationale for the establishment of public schools. Legal systems, though, have a peculiar way of addressing adolescents' concerns. Rather than serving as rationales to bestow more rights on adolescents and to develop institutional structures that respond to adolescents' needs, these concerns serve to bestow adults with control over the vast majority of adolescents' rights. This approach to ensuring adolescents' rights reflects the general belief that adult control furthers the interests of all of those involved: society, parents, and adolescents themselves. Given this belief, the legal system theoretically allows adults to control adolescents' rights to the extent that they foster and remain faithful to basic social interests. Adolescents' own interests still factor into the equation; but, they do not dictate outcomes. In educational arenas, the need to respect and foster community values provides the foundation for and limits to school officials' general right to dictate curricular matters. The extent to which students do have rights is determined by community values and the need to ensure that students receive educations deemed appropriate by local, state, and federal communities. Although those communities may not appropriately recognize and respond to adolescents' interests, society and its legal systems operate on the assumption that all share the common concern that adolescents act as, and mature into, responsible citizens able to engage in healthy relationships.

To ensure that all actually aim to realize the ideals of education, the legal system can better shape the role of education in adolescent life. As we have seen throughout the preceding chapters, adolescent development marked by model social dispositions and thriving emotional health requires that education allows adolescents to experience the realities of living in truly democratic communities, schools, families, and intimate relationships. Living democratically essentially entails adopting a propensity to respect others, acting to preserve others' interests, realizing that others' interests are inseparable from one's own, and thriving by engaging in habits that materialize those beliefs and dispositions. To ensure a move toward the development of curricular and extracurricular responses consistent with those values, the legal system can play a central role. The legal system can direct schools in ways that allow schools to create environments that engage students in understanding and practicing democracy's goals and ideals—conditions necessary for healthy adolescent development. The analyses undertaken in the previous chapters reveal that reaching these goals requires addressing four central issues.

ADOPT CLEAR SCHOOL POLICIES

Healthy adolescent development requires responsive and structured environments best achieved through the adoption of clear school policies. Although numerous rationales support the need for clear policies developed in light of adolescents' realities, research on school violence and prosocial development most readily reveals the need to adopt standards that address adolescents' concerns and special needs. Schools that foster violence tend not to address personal violence publicly and tend not to communicate a willingness or ability to respond. As confidence in school administrators and/or adults diminishes, informal social controls against violence weaken and lead to adolescents' choices to carry weapons to school, manage impressions by fighting or putting on a tough front, or retaliate against perceived transgressors. Likewise, schools that ignore adolescents' need to respond appropriately to injustices within or outside of schools do not foster prosocial behavior. Such schools fail to recognize students' need to move beyond their own individual interests by, for example, placing an emphasis on identifying with the common good. Schools that fail to enact effective policies also do not foster prosocial behavior when they fail to engage adolescents in decision making and in the construction of policies that would structure sources of social and emotional support. Schools best foster adolescent development when they formally recognize and respond to adolescents' developmental needs.

At the very least, the law can help ensure that schools recognize and respond to the need for the type of structured environments linked to positive adolescent development. The law can require the establishment of policies, guide educational experiences, and help develop environments conducive to following policies. Thus, the law can require schools to set clear policies to structure safe school environments and respond to disruptive forces. The law also can guide the development of curricular programs that foster prosocial behavior. The law also may help foster school climates that respond better to adolescents' psychological needs. These three potential roles may seem rather straightforward and obvious in light of the preceding chapters. Given that schools pervasively operate without policies, however, taking the proposals seriously would result in a radical shift in fostering adolescents' educational rights. States persistently lack clear policies to guide the social development of students and to create healthy school environments. Although poised to become a radical development, the effort would be neither unjustified nor unfeasible.

Given the pervasive failure to adopt clear and effective standards, developments in adolescents' educational rights must involve an attempt to develop policies that will foster adolescents' development and address societal concerns. The approach requires implementing clear policies supported and understood by students as measures that respond appropriately to pressing needs. Several examples of clear policies already exist. Hate crimes codes, sexual harassment policies, and numerous disciplinary policies already exist in many forms. Not only do clear examples already exist, social science research also suggests which policies would be most effective in addressing adolescents' needs. Effective policies enumerate improper conduct, educate students about policies, foster students' skills and abilities to tailor their conduct to responsible behavior, and effectively provide adolescents with access to redress both within schools and outside of them. Effective policies involve all who impact adolescents' schooling but especially include those most likely to be ignored—students themselves.

The identified need for policies suggests that existing codes, policies, and standards remain limited in three significant ways. First, the vast majority of states simply do not have comprehensive codes and do not require schools to enact them. The only consistent mandate requires that schools adopt policies for punishing students who fail to follow behavior codes. Second, states that do require the development of standards may not offer guidance on their development and not provide adequate resources to implement the policies properly. Thus, legislative mandates may require that schools make disciplinary codes known but they neither provide nor mandate courses or programs necessary for students and school personnel to ensure that students are educated in ways that would lead them to internalize and abide by standards. Third, many of the statutes that provide guidance fail to offer ways to hold schools accountable for failing to develop programs. As a result, students generally have little recourse when they have been harmed or when they have not been provided effective educational environments: schools simply can avoid liability except for the most egregious rights violations. In sum, students' rights simply are not developed enough so that schools could be held responsible for failing to recognize and respect those rights. Because of that failure, schools generally fail to address issues of violence, prosocial development, and positive mental health in a systematic and necessarily comprehensive manner. This failure leads to the second needed area of reform.

FOSTER SCHOOL ACCOUNTABILITY

A social environment that requires adolescents to be accountable for their actions (and, as much as practicable, those of others) must itself be held accountable. Schools provide no exception to this general rule and thus those that fail to provide a healthy environment should be held accountable. As we have seen in Chapter 3, victims of violence at school essentially have very little recourse when schools fail to protect them. Likewise, Chapter 4 emphasized how "victims" of a school's failure to educate them properly and ensure the development of socially responsible orientations cannot hold schools responsible for those deficiencies. Chapter 5 revealed that schools actually seek to avoid issues regarding mental health, actually contribute to adolescents' psychological distress, and only address this concern when students express serious emotional difficulties. Yet, schools still could be held more accountable for instituting clear standards for behavior in educational environments and in adolescents' relationships. Schools also could be held responsible for establishing a curriculum that fosters beliefs and behaviors consistent with such standards. This significant move envisions increasing schools' obligations to respond proactively. This would be an important development that moves away from current obligations that pervasively insulate schools from legal challenges.

In general, the legal system holds schools accountable through funding. This approach essentially involves three methods. The most innovative approach involves increasing competition among schools so that schools will engage in curricular reforms that will transform school environments. For example, school vouchers allow some students to go to schools of their parents' choice. By allowing such transfers, the belief is that schools will respond better to the needs of students and their parents. An alternative approach to holding schools accountable involves the traditional imposition of financial sanctions on schools that fail to address certain situations. For example, schools that do not comply with regulations that offer extra protections to disabled students in disciplinary matters could lose funding, and schools that fail to address sex discrimination could also be subject to sanctions. A third alternative involves traditional law suits against school officials and school districts. For example, school officials could be held responsible for failing to respond to harms students suffer while in school. These approaches all share commitment to adolescents' needs through structuring financial incentives, either to address adolescents' most minimal needs or to allow parents to determine the proper response to needs they perceive as important.

As currently applied, the above approaches remain unlikely to change school environments in ways that would foster adolescent development consistent with the values deemed necessary for democratic dispositions. School vouchers may increase competition and help transform some school environments. However, these efforts do not necessarily result in addressing students' social and psychological needs; those efforts also seemingly increase segregation, and fail to address the problems of those outside of schools, drop-outs (for a review, see Levesque, 1998c). Likewise, having schools lose their federal funding or having officials subject to lawsuits also seems inadequate. Current legal mandates offer school officials great deference and discretion that translate into the inability to hold schools liable. As a result of these standards, the measures schools take in response to alleged rights violations need not necessarily be effective; e.g., school personnel need not necessarily ensure the safety of students while they are in school (Fazal, 1999; Herman & Remley, 2000). Rather than providing true legal recourse and remedies for plaintiffs, the new standards provide exemptions for school districts in the event of violations. In fact, given the very high standards that must be met before the imposition of liabilities, it is improper to view the harms students suffer as rights violations. Legally, high standards mean that no rights were violated and that harms go unrecognized. From this view, the voucher system is equally pernicious—by essentially creating a legal vacuum, the voucher system operates without any obligation to recognize adolescents' needs and foster adolescents' own rights.

Given the current failures, the most reasonable alternative would be to have the legal system foster environments supportive of school accountability. This approach takes a much more programmatic view of rights; it views rights more as ways to structure environments so that they ensure the development of environments that increase rights-consciousness and internalization of mandates. These environments are largely self-enforcing; external environments (e.g., courts and legislatures) serve to ensure that the proper alternatives, boundaries, and appropriate issue resolution mechanisms are in place. Although not the subject of commentaries, this approach simply requires that schools make policies and standards known and actually integrated into school environments, rather than simply, at best, requiring the enactment of policies.

Schools could meet higher standards of accountability if the legal system helped ensure that effective policies became integrated, but not lost, into curricular and extra-curricular programs. In the context of addressing violence, for example, effective responses would require schools to (1) enhance awareness among students, teachers and school officials, (2) provide students with an adequate complaint or reporting mechanism, (3) take appropriate steps to react to reports of violence, and (4) provide individuals with skills to respond to actual and potential violence. Current laws focus only on listing the disciplinary actions that may arise from possible offenses. Although not yet instituted, similar policies could enhance schools' efforts to foster model social development. School policies that would effect more exemplary social attitudes and behaviors would (1) promote awareness of how to engage in prosocial behavior, (2) provide opportunities to engage in such activities and (3) actively support students and school personnel who exhibit model behavior. Current state statutes and federal mandates essentially ignore the need to foster prosocial behavior. Schools also could enact policies that address mental health concerns. They could (1) increase awareness of the nature of positive mental health, (2) provide environments conducive to seeking and benefitting from support, and (3) require a concerted effort to respond appropriately to students' needs and concerns. Current laws again pervasively fail to promote the type of environment that would contribute to positive mental health. Again, policies must address the central limitations of current responses: the failure to enhance awareness and failure to provide supportive environments conducive to internalizing values necessary for enhancing democratic life.

Although it would be important to turn to more innovative methods, traditional avenues of reform should not be ignored as they can be used to enhance schools' responses. Thus, school accountability simply could be increased by changing standards on which schools are held accountable. Statutes could ensure that school failures could result more readily in liability. For example and in terms of violence, instead of an extremely low standard of "actual notice," schools could be held accountable on a constructive notice standard; e.g., that specific school officials knew or should have known about the violence (not that they in fact knew), a standard already recommended by the Office for Civil rights for determining a school district's Title IX liability (Sexual Harassment Guidance, 1997). Alternatively, schools could be required to provide at least a minimal amount of response to problem environments, an approach that would require schools to demonstrate reasonable attempts to address violence as opposed to demonstrate lack of awareness about violence and conditions that foster it. The major goal is to foster supportive school environments. Using a similar standard may seem bizarre in the context of promoting mental health and prosocial behavior. Yet, the same principles may apply. Schools could be required to respond appropriately, which could include providing curricular credit for certain efforts, promoting discussion and exchange of information, supporting appropriate staff training, and ensuring that students have opportunities to engage in activities that foster certain basic interpersonal skills. Again, effective responses would recognize adolescents' developmental needs as worthy of response and would structure environments that foster healthy outcomes. The legal system can provide a supportive and awareness-enhancing mechanism by ensuring the development of enabling structures.

SUPPORT FAMILIAL OBLIGATIONS

Practical and legal concerns necessitate addressing the family's impact on adolescents' educational experiences. Families respond to adolescents' school experiences and place adolescents in situations that will evoke certain experiences. Without doubt, for example, families clearly play an important role in the production and support of delinquency, prosocial behavior and positive mental health. The significance of that role finds clear expression in law. The legal system generally grants parents the right *and* responsibility to control their children's educational experiences as well as their rights when involved in juvenile, mental health, and school systems. As we have seen, the power of parents remains so great that they may remove their children from public schools and educate them in alternative environments of their choice. The rights and necessary roles of parents certainly limit the potential reach and nature of school reform. Yet, neither parental rights nor their roles must remain immune from reform efforts to foster adolescent development in ways that could help achieve more positive outcomes.

The social sciences already reveal how families can contribute to the most effective developmental outcomes. As we repeatedly have seen, the combination of warm, structured child-rearing practices in parents with reasonably high expectations for competence strongly ties to success in multiple domains and to resilience among children at risk. In general, the more involvement, structure and autonomy granting opportunities adolescents receive from their parents, the more positively teens evaluate their own conduct, psychosocial development, and mental health (e.g., Gray & Steinberg, 1999). These democratic forms of parenting and family experiences provide adolescents with the qualities deemed most worth inculcating in individuals who would adopt democratic orientations to society and to their intimate relationships.

The social science understanding of family relationship styles contributing to the most effective development does not receive strong endorsement from current legal systems. Laws regulating family life and children's development assume that parents act to further their children's best interests. The current system, though, still allows for encouraging families to adopt orientations that would more likely foster healthy adolescent development. Most notably, the legal system allows for holding parents responsible when they fail to fulfill basic, minimal parental responsibilities. This approach finds clearest expression in efforts to hold parents responsible when their children have engaged in violence. When dealing with adolescent violence, the public threat is so great that it provides states with an appropriate rationale to intervene in families and to require parents to conduct themselves so as to reduce the risk that their children will engage in violence. Similar exceptions have been made with adolescents' access to medical and mental health services. Laws exempt the need for parental consent for many medical services, and those exceptions relate to the potential harm adolescents would endure or the burden their harms would place on society. Holding parents responsible in the educational context also is far from new; some states now punish parents,

by withholding welfare benefits, for their children's inadequate attendance or poor academic performance. When dealing with adolescents'
prosocial behavior, however, parents currently enjoy the most discretion.
Adolescents' inability to interact in prosocial manners typically remains
outside the purview of laws; parents even retain the right to raise sexist
and racist children, let alone the right to encourage children *not* to assist
others. Although the absence of prosocial behavior may not lead to deem-
ing parents irresponsible and to needing direct intervention, laws essentially do intervene to address these matters to the extent that they do hold
parents responsible for preventing violence and ensuring some level of
health—two factors linked to concern for others.

The search for statutes directly on point, however, runs the risk of
neglecting equally important and already existing statutes. Recall that the
law can serve as an organizing force that helps structure environments
conducive to fostering certain dispositions. In the context of families,
arguably the most important environment where the law may have a
direct impact involves family violence. The social sciences have established how family violence clearly increases the risk of victimization and
perpetration outside the home and impacts the extent to which adolescents will engage in prosocial behavior and experience positive mental
health. All states already have child abuse and neglect laws that could be
enforced more earnestly so that parents could be offered services and
destructive relationships could be severed. Even with exceptions that
allow for the most intrusive measures, however, existing laws regulating
family life would not address ways to foster positive mental health; these
laws focus on problems that already exist.

Although the law's reactionary focus frequently recurs in its
regulation of family life, the law still can support more innovative methods and "intervene" in families to bolster family supports and transform
social environments in which violent behaviors, antisocial attitudes,
and oppressive dispositions are learned or reinforced. The legal system
can serve to challenge attitudes that regularly generate, legitimize, and
reinforce negative outcomes. The legal system can support families and
engage in family building through community supports and partnerships
and can provide for parenting and family skills development programs.
Social commitment to these programs has yet to match and recognize the
extent to which even existing programs actually can powerfully impact
families at risk and help foster more positive adolescent development
(McCurdy & Jones, 2000).

It is important to emphasize how the suggestion made above takes a
rather different turn away from current approaches to fostering families'
positive roles in their children's education. The legal system historically

has sought to enhance the input of families in their children's educations. As a result, current efforts seek to link parents to schools, such as by requiring parental input in the establishment of certain health programs, notifying parents when their children are subject to certain disciplinary measures, enlisting the assistance of parents in determining the most appropriate placements for their disabled children and even giving parents the discretion to move their children to other schools. With the potential exception of disabled students, efforts to involve parents in the above manner have yet to yield expected outcomes. As we have seen, parental involvement remains abysmally low and parents who do get involved tend to represent a small minority's views. The effort highlighted above would seek to transform families themselves so that they resemble effective schools. Equally important, the efforts also mean that schools would transform themselves to develop positive, caring and productive relationships with families that may demonstrate behaviors and attitudes that differ from traditional expressions of support for their children's educations (e.g., parents that do not attend school activities, visit classrooms, and raise funds for school activities). Again, the effort focuses on enlisting the legal system to foster supportive socializing environments rather than simply permitting parental voice and allowing parents to get involved if they so desire. Efforts that address the nature of families, in addition to a focus on environments that lead to greater family involvement in their children's educations, would best allow for families to fulfill their obligations to their children, schools, and broader society.

LINK STUDENTS TO SERVICE-PROVIDING INSTITUTIONS

Schools and families persistently encounter difficulties in their efforts to provide supportive environments. Given those challenges, ensuring adolescents' healthy development means that adolescents must be provided with alternative ways to address their developmental needs. Adolescents' environments and experiences would be enhanced if schools were able to connect adolescents to service providing institutions, including service-provisions within schools. At a minimum, this approach to reform envisions providing adolescents with better access to juvenile justice, mental health, and legal systems. These efforts take three forms. They would (1) complement schools' and parents' roles, (2) provide adolescents with exits from failing families and school environments, and (3) ensure support for adolescents to exercise their rights to access services. These directions simply seek to benefit from what we know about effective service provision. Effective services emerge from environments that provide adolescents with basic knowledge about the services, skills to seek out services, and ways to maintain involvement in needed services. Legal mandates could help school systems and adolescents better exploit services in ways that would foster healthy adolescent development.

The legal system already has made immense progress in recognizing adolescents' rights in medical and mental health contexts. Most notably, numerous exceptions erode the general rule that parents control adolescents' access to these services. Although it would be important not to ignore the necessary role of parents, the legal system allows adolescents greater access when (1) the services are highly needed and (2) parents fail to recognize the need for the service or parents would hamper adolescents' access to assistance. This rule allows the law to protect the rights of responsible parents and of adolescents themselves. Although an important development, research consistently reveals that merely providing access to possible services remains inadequate and results in failed service delivery. The failures of policies currently regulating the adolescent mental health system, for example, mean that adolescents fail to seek formal needed support simply because they may be unaware of available opportunities for assistance, may rely on informal social networks, or, as we have seen, may define their adversities as normative, as requiring no intervention. Failing to offer support to actually get the needed services has the added negative effect of concealing the need for services, which results in viewing the services as unnecessary and, eventually, contributing to their demise.

The underutilization of formal support services indicates a possible role for the legal system. Most notably, a burden could be placed on school personnel to direct adolescents to support services. We already have seen how, in instances deemed important enough, schools already have an obligation to do so. Child abuse and neglect and children's disabilities provide the most readily legally recognized example. Current legal rules, however, typically allow school personnel to dispense with their limited obligations by alerting others to problems rather than alerting students to possible avenues of assistance. These approaches may be inadequate for addressing adolescents' mental health needs. As we have seen, the vast majority of students who actually seek mental health services do so to deal with family issues, especially parental drug abuse and violence. Although enlisting families could eventually benefit adolescents, assuming parental fitness may not be the most effective default. Although this approach may seem unavailable and legally problematic, the law already allows, with some exceptions, school personnel to link students with out-of-school services when schools do not or legally cannot offer the services themselves.

Similar patterns emerge from efforts to address violence. As in the mental health contexts, legal developments in this arena have been marked by immense progress. The legal system now has defined the contours of the rights of minors in the juvenile justice system and also has made provisions to ensure respect for those rights. Even those developments, however, remain limited. Most notably, the juvenile justice system remains highly reactive, and current trends seek to dismantle the system or at least remove its rehabilitative, preventative features. Second, the legal system essentially focuses solely on the rights of offenders. Only the last decade has witnessed some movement to ensure the rights of victims, as exemplified in efforts to address harassment in schools. Recognition of these two limitations provides fertile ground for developing reforms to address adolescents' needs.

In the context of victims' rights, adolescents clearly could benefit from adult guidance to help them address the violence they endure. Yet, research consistently reveals that adolescents remain reluctant to involve adults and that adults do not necessarily recognize the most frequent forms of violence perpetrated against adolescents. The currently ignored rate of adolescent relationship violence and harassment indicates well the undoubted failure of adults to protect adolescents. Equally illustrative, but now increasingly recognized as important to address, is the rampant bullying that occurs in schools. These failures suggest that adolescents would benefit from the right to obtain protection on their own behalf. Although it would seem that they already do have the right to access the legal system, the legal system essentially bars minors from seeking their own relief or simply does not recognize that their experiences warrant intervention. Likewise, the legal system currently does not support the construction of policies that would help adolescents recognize their victimization as something the legal system views as serious, does not provide adolescents with skills to seek assistance, and, in the end, fails to provide proper recourse for victims simply because they are minors unable to make legal claims. These failures support the proposition that legal reform must not only address schools and the environments they produce, it must also address the nature of the legal system.

In the context of offenders' rights, it is important to reorient perceptions of juvenile justice systems. Unlike the criminal justice system for adults, the juvenile justice system essentially developed as a therapeutic enterprise. Juvenile justice means ensuring adolescents' their rights by reintegrating them into their families, peer relationships, schools, and communities. The system merely serves as a source of services for adolescents identified as in need. From this perspective, reforms must take advantage of the manner policies leave considerable room for variations in efforts to hold adolescents accountable. Even though punishment may become the most dominant way to ensure accountability, effective punishment regimes place central concern on reintegration and the need to improve and preserve young offenders' future life chances (Levesque, 1996b). This is particularly important in the school context where the need to create policies and need to take infractions seriously may run the risk of cementing the juvenile justice system's response to adolescents in need by simply sanctioning rather than reintegrating them back into society. In the juvenile justice context, punishments for the sake of retribution can be tolerated only as last resorts and such punishment becomes suspicious when it compromises treatment and reintegration into families and communities and jeopardizes the long-term interests of the targeted offenders and victims (Levesque & Tomkins, 1996). This is the traditional reason for a separate legal system focusing on juveniles: juveniles (used interchangeably with children, minors and adolescents) are different from adults in that they are more susceptible to positive intervention and, because of cognitive and volitional developmental deficiencies, may be less culpable and thus more worthy of special treatment (e.g., Scott & Grisso, 1997). Addressing the rights and responsibilities of adolescent offenders reveals a need for change in juvenile justice services that mirror needed changes in educational services. Although juvenile justice reforms continue to engender much debate and many view the juvenile justice system as too lenient, even federal reports and evaluations of juvenile justice trends reveal that the juvenile justice systems reach effectiveness when they too adopt an educational approach, one that adapts to the risks and protective factors found in adolescents' environment, particularly by providing opportunities for children and youth, by addressing adolescents' victimization, and by providing more appropriate sanctions and treatment for delinquent adolescents (Coordinating Council on Juvenile Justice and Delinquency Prevention, 1996).

NECESSITY OF STATUTORY REFORM AND GUIDANCE

The diverse ways states guide the delivery of education provides room for considerable legal reforms. It is important to understand the need for statutory imperatives to catalyze efforts for change. Arguably, seven closely related rationales support the need to reconsider the current regulation of public schools and the benefits of statutory reform.

The presence of statutes creates and helps reinforce state education agency policy. This is significant for several reasons. Without a statute, program content or effectiveness abides by new and emergent streams of political capriciousness. Currently, just as they have historically, educational concerns remain within the purview of local politics and are determined largely by the personal relations among individual teachers, parents and local school officials (Emihovich & Herrington, 1997). Local discretion means that the provision of education that deals directly with values, responsible behavior, and controversial matters will vary greatly from area to area as teachers seek to cope with the wishes of parents in their particular schools. In addition to variations across districts, policies may change from year to year, depending upon who takes office and the desires of different parental groups. Perhaps more important than variations due to location and time is variation in the extent to which state education agencies will take no position and simply not address important components of education beyond the core curriculum. Non-curricular programs receive even less attention. Pupil services and health programs do not have high status in the educational hierarchy and in current health and education policy initiatives (Adelman & Taylor, 1998). Districts treat such activity, in policy and in practice, as desirable but not essential. Because they are not deemed essential, the programs and staff are marginalized. Planning programs, services, and delivery systems tend to be done on an ad hoc basis; interventions are referred to as auxiliary or support services rather than as necessary parts of general education. Statutory recognition could help determine the significance of the initiatives, relative to other school curricular concerns, and increase the likelihood of obtaining funding when scarce resources are allocated among competing goals.

In addition to setting state educational policy, statutory guidance also may assist in guiding curricular content and help ensure that effective strategies are taught. This is particularly important for topics that address controversial values and require students to adopt and practice beliefs some might find offensive. For example, several programs have been developed to combat coercive sexual activity. These programs have identified the need for comprehensive approaches, including the need to (1) use age-appropriate materials; (2) reduce risky behavior through abstinence, condom use, or avoiding drugs/alcohol which impair judgment; and (3) teach resistance skills to avoid peer pressure or unwanted sexual activity. Yet, few states require schools to address these issues (Levesque, 2000b). The significance of the failure to guide local decision makers is revealed by reviews that note how, when left to their own, education programs omit controversial topics related to sexual orientation, ignore matters related to sexual health, do not present general risk prevention information, and pervasively fail to discuss condom use (Levesque, 2000b). Relatedly, statutes help ensure more effective curriculum to the extent that they clarify administrators and teachers' roles. Failure to offer appropriate guides, for example, casts a shadow over class discussions and creates a tendency toward self-censorship. As a result, teachers fail to address overtly violent behavior and systemic violence, make false assumptions about adolescent development, and fail to realize that every student is an exception to general assumptions (Epp & Watkinson, 1997; Krueger, 1993). The failure is particularly prominent in the training of special education instructors who would benefit most from further training to reach audiences with different competencies (e.g., Foley & Dudzinski, 1995). Without mandates, schools do not implement effective programs.

Clearly delineated standards also are necessary to protect teachers and school personnel in ways that also protect adolescents' rights. This is particularly important when dealing with issues of violence and attempts to discuss potentially controversial topics. A public official has a defense of qualified immunity to a section 1983 action (actions which allow victims of rights violations to sue those who denied these rights) if she can show that her actions did not violate clearly established law. Thus, a student alleging a violation of rights has to overcome this defense in order to recover damages. In *Harlow v. Fitzgerald* (1982), the Supreme Court held that "government officials performing discretionary functions generally are shielded from liability for civil damages insofar as their conduct does not violate clearly established statutory or constitutional rights of which a reasonable person would have known" (p. 818). The remaining issue was to determine what "clearly established" meant. The Court elaborated on the definition in *Anderson v. Creighton* (1987). In that case, the Court held that "the right the official is alleged to have violated must have been 'clearly established' in a more particularized, and hence more relevant sense: [t]he contours of the right must be sufficiently clear that a reasonable official would understand that what he is doing violates that right" (p. 640). Thus, "the unlawfulness must be apparent" and not necessarily previously been held unlawful (p. 640). The Supreme Court's precedent reveals why policies are so important; statutory mandates could help determine what remains discretionary, which protects both school personnel and the rights of adolescents.

Support from statutory frameworks also would make the task of implementing programs less daunting. Five factors make such support an important consideration. First, school boards and state agency officials resist curriculum review and change when they face the risk of backlash (Emihovich & Herrington, 1997; Trudell, 1993). The fear of backlash ensures that officials act conservatively, which eventually increases the likelihood that students will voluntarily and involuntarily engage in practices adults and adolescents who are more knowledgeable generally would agree should not occur. Second, in addition to the nature of information, statutory guidance could make clear who would reveal the information. Considerable resistance, confusion and ambivalence surround issues of who should present certain subjects; statutes could help clarify whether teachers, public health physicians, or parents are the appropriate source of certain knowledge. Third, explicit guidance could help counter impediments to reform as it decisively pinpoints the over-riding legal interests and rights and as it offers a way to deliberate those considerations in program development. Researchers note that the failure of many school reforms largely rests on the failure to identify explicitly the rights of parents and those of their children, other students and schools (for a review, see Levesque, 1998c). Fourth, elected officials respond to majorities that elected them, which raises the concern for those who would offer less dominant viewpoints. Unrepresented, disadvantaged groups may be in need of most protection from the majority. As a result, the possibility arises that controversial topics may be suppressed which are valuable to society and adolescents. The proposal requires elected officials to respond to adolescents' concerns. Lastly, the approach addresses a critical part of the decline in "moral literacy," which stems from the trend in public schools to avoid controversial issues of community values and morality. Although schools may seek to cease acknowledging moral issues, they do not cease to teach morality. Schools simply become oblivious to the moral lessons and hidden curriculum they convey. This approach addresses that concern as it requires schools to confront issues that some may deem controversial.

State policies would also assist simply because national levels of policy making regarding adolescents' education still remain conspicuously reticent to respond. No federal statutory law or policy requires moral education or guides responses to violence. Federal guidance of mental health law remains limited; policies focus on cases involving disability and ignore conditions that stifle or foster positive mental health. In the context of many forms of education, the federal government explicitly adopts the position that it should not control the content (cf., Richards & Daley, 1994). Rather than dictating the content of education, federal statutes preclude the federal government from prescribing state and local curriculum standards: The Department of Education Organization Act, Section 103a; the Elementary and Secondary Education Act, Section 14512; Goals 2000, Section 319(b); and the General Education Provision Act, Section 438 (Levesque, 1998c). The federal government's removal from educational policy making renders even more critical the need for responses at state levels if students' educations are not to be left to the whim of local administrators who may not see the need for students' education for broader society.

The need for statutory assistance is particularly important given how current research generally fails to determine the effectiveness of existing programs and how many popular programs fail under close scrutiny. Well-delineated statutes would provide researchers with clear, measurable factors, such as rates of violence, delinquency, depression, and community involvement. By systematizing research, statutes could help ensure the development of more usable knowledge that allows policy makers to focus their attention on the areas of greatest need and those that contribute to failure. In addition, statutory guidance, by delineating the rights of all involved, would also help ensure that important interest groups are not ignored. Noticeably absent in the discourse relating to service provision in schools, for example, has been the inclusion of students, both as individuals and as peer groups, in decisions regarding school needs and interventions; even researchers have not included students in the emerging literature of the importance of consumer satisfaction and social validity in the selection of interventions (Bear, 1998). Likewise, the guidance could help support programs long enough to determine their effectiveness and factors that could ameliorate outcomes. This would help address a central reason for the failure to determine program effectiveness: statutory mandates could allow the programs to be systematically implemented long enough to sustain rigorous scientific analysis. Effective statutes would thus assure the foundation for much needed evaluative research.

Lastly, statutory guidance could help focus educational systems toward a more proactive, preventative, and enabling approach to adolescent development. Appropriate legislation can help ensure that schools remain faithful to their mission. As we have seen, schools necessarily exist to inculcate values, enhance mental health, and foster the development of productive citizens. The role statutes can play is particularly important and obvious in the context of dealing with violence. Statutes are more than practical tools to combat violence. The recognition reinforces that adolescents know they can be victims and assistance is available to them. As we have seen, to address violence in abusive and assaultive relationships, adolescents must first combat "normative confusion" and realize the destructiveness of their relationships. Legal recognition would do considerably more than help victims realize the devastating impact of the abusive behavior. Just as importantly, legal recognition would help combat fears that prevent adolescents from seeking assistance. The recognition also would do more than send proper messages to victims, and perpetrators also would receive a powerful message that the state disapproves. The disapproval could either lead to punishment or an offer of assistance to stop abusive behaviors. Beyond these important considerations, the legal recognition would indicate an important and necessary shift from defining victimization as a personal or relational problem to recognizing such behavior as a violent social problem and a broader human rights issue. Similar rationales apply to mental health and prosocial behavior. Rather than viewing these issues as simply individual concerns that hopefully will eventuate in positive outcomes, recognition of positive mental health and prosocial behavior as important social issues would help confirm society's obligation to assist adolescents and would help ensure adolescents' access to environments that can enable them, and society, to thrive.

RESPONDING TO POSSIBLE OBJECTIONS

Much distance exists between the current reality and potential for law to foster adolescents' educational rights and recognize adolescents' developmental needs. Important objections to the expansion of adolescents' educational rights remain potent enough to stifle the development of more comprehensive approaches to students' educational rights. Yet, the obstacles are not insurmountable. Indeed, the proposals rest on providing enabling structures that address obstacles. By focusing on basic democratic principles, confronting differences of opinion, and placing concern on basic societal and individual needs, the effort focused on ways to infiltrate and help shape the dominant discourse in educational reform. Focusing on guiding the development of responses to society's and adolescents' needs, though, results in the need to address two potential limits of that guidance: the extent to which state educational policy making may infringe on parental rights and the freedoms of private schools.

RESPECTING PARENTAL RIGHTS

The powerful role of parents and families in fostering environments conducive to appropriate education results in the law's tendency to leave much to families and a general hesitancy to not interfere in family matters. Parental rights, however, are far from absolute. The proposed policies still respect parental rights. The extent to which they do so requires separate analysis of three issues: the social image and nature of parental rights, the limitations placed on adolescents' rights, and the manner exceptions to parental rights indicate potential for rethinking the extent to which parents do control their children's rights.

The first critical concern involves the extent to which dealing with violence prevention, supporting prosocial behavior, and fostering positive mental health involves moral issues and the extent to which moral issues are viewed as needing to be taught in homes rather than in schools. Society tends to view morals as so important that their direction is best left to family discretion. This approach reflects the strongly ingrained tradition of parental responsibility for the upbringing of their children and assumption that parents are best able to determine and do what is best for their children. As a result, two approaches to dealing with morality in schools have gained dominance. One approach argues that parents should be given even greater rights to control the education of their children. In the alternative, others propose that education should remain morally neutral and that the law permits such moral neutrality. Both of these approaches remain problematic when considering adolescents' developmental needs in educational contexts.

The current image of parents' socializing role is problematic for four reasons. First, inculcation in schools does not violate legal principles as long as the values are transmitted in furtherance of a civilized social order and promotes democracy. Thus, schools do not inappropriately usurp the inculcative roles of parents. Counterposing the inculcative role of parents and noninculcative role of schools in a manner which is mutually exclusive and provides irreconcilable options simply creates a false dichotomy detrimental to adolescents and society. Schools may and do teach value preferences that serve inculcative functions essential to the formation of adolescent development. Second, we cannot depend on individual families to impart the values most necessary for life in a pluralistic democracy. Although families may emphasize tolerance and foster acceptance of difference, they also are likely to emphasize personal and localized concerns of the particular family unit and deemphasize the interests of social groups different from themselves. Such localism is not necessarily undesirable, so long as other institutions foster values necessary for civic behavior in a pluralistic society. Third, regardless of the cultural attachment to childhoods determined by parental caretaking, social scientists continue to document the influences and need of communal institutions (e.g., schools) and informal peer groupings in determining successful developmental outcomes. The significance of socialization outside of families is particularly important for adolescents. Although adolescents rely on families for important sources of support, for example, detaching from families places some adolescents in precarious positions. Providing adolescents with supportive environments simply would reflect the needs and the realities of adolescent life. Fourth, as venerable as parental rights may be, parents' rights clearly lose their legitimacy when society and adolescents are subjected to harm. The entire concept of compulsory education, deemed legitimate by society and formalized by law, means that parents retain the right to direct their children's educations, but the state may control that right and ultimately decide what is best for children. Our legal system of education under state control or supervision asserts that the state—rather than the parents—ultimately decide what is best for children. Society controls parental rights and responsibilities, regardless of the frequently evoked image of parental roles.

In addition to addressing perceptions of parental roles, the proposal must also address the realities of adolescents' rights. The proposal suggested that the legal system should allow for greater focus on adolescents' realities. This construction of adolescents' rights may lead to the false belief that focusing on students' own needs inappropriately infringes on the rights of parents and those acting as parents to determine the nature of adolescents' needs and to provide for those needs. The proposal, however, still necessarily leaves considerable discretion to school officials, teachers, parents and students in their ability to negotiate the control and content of education. In fact, it is this discretion that provides a basis of hope for reform. The discretion clearly allows for considering what is most problematically absent in educational reform: consideration of adolescents' self-determination. The needed support for self-determination, though, is not the type typically encountered in discussions of legal rights that focus on autonomy and autonomous decision making. For adolescents, in terms of both law and reality, self-determination is far from a solipsistic enterprise. Freedom to pursue self-determination is not the same as a blank license. It cannot be because of both legal mandates and the realities of what contributes to positive adolescent development. Most notably and in terms of law, constitutional norms impose important limits on adolescents' rights and constitutional theory of democratic governance seeks to enhance respect for individual differences but recognizes the need to participate in groups and community life. The practicalities of adolescent development also interject limits. Pedagogical effectiveness leading to optimal development derives from effective supports and boundaries. Students need opportunities to make real decisions and to be responsible for their consequences in order to develop an ability to make wise decisions and judge their results. The manner the law approaches parental rights and those acting as parents actually can help further the development of policies that address adolescents' needs.

The third concern involves how (rather than simply determining whether) the rights of parents may be infringed. We have seen how democratic principles appropriately may serve to guide the content and essential philosophy of education programs. Given that the very foundation of democracy rests on respect for diversity, tolerance, and restraint from compelling others to accept other's views, it remains to be determined the extent to which parents and their children can be compelled to participate in education programs based on democratic values. Several possibilities may determine the extent to which adolescents may opt-out, or be opted out, of programs or portions of programs. These variations deal with the extent to which parents, the state, and adolescents themselves may determine exposure to offensive materials.

Where school officials direct education toward making students full participatory members of society, and if education is a necessary part of education and children are members of society, then neither parents nor adolescents may object to the education. The argument would be that the perpetuation of ignorance in a given area is so crucial to the child's development that denying the education would not be in the adolescent's interests and would therefore be contrary to the adolescent's own rights and their parents' rights. Two prominent examples illustrate the nature and appropriateness of the claim. The first example involves rejection of the challenge that a public school's requirement that all students in grades 1–8 use a prescribed set of reading textbooks that were viewed as inconsistent with many of the plaintiffs' religious values. In the leading case, *Mozert v. Hawkins County Brd. of Educ.* (1987), the Court found "that the requirement that public school students study a basel reader series chosen by the school authorities does not create an unconstitutional burden under the Free Exercise Clause when the students are not required to affirm or deny a belief or engage or refrain from engaging in a practice prohibited by their religion" (p. 1070). The second example is even more directly on point in that the materials used to provide effective education were extremely controversial. In *Brown v. Hot, Sexy and Safer Productions* (1995), parents and students challenged compelled attendance to a sexually explicit AIDS and sex education program conducted at their public high school. In rejecting the claim, the Court noted that the parental right to control the education of their children does not extend to the "right to dictate individually what the schools teach their children" (p. 534). These cases reveal much more than support for school official power; they reveal the extent to which the legal system views education as a market for ideas and plays down how ideas impact development that could vary from a family's deeply held beliefs. Given appropriately articulated societal interests, schools can act paternalistically.

Although the paternalism of school officials may not be absolute, law still allows for several ways to affect similar outcomes without undue, coercive paternalism. For example, various opportunities permit parents and adolescents to opt-out of programs but those options could be curtailed. States may provide only strict conditions under which parents can keep their children out. For example, if parents propose that some aspects of the offered curriculum conflict with their beliefs, they may be allowed to opt out as long as they indicate how their child will receive some form of education that meets minimal criteria. Likewise, students may be provided the right to challenge their parents' decisions to withdraw them from selected aspects of education. This approach would be consistent with Supreme Court jurisprudence that provides adolescents with access to services that impact their private lives and mandates that alternatives be available for adolescents to obtain services, such as commonly done through the provision of judicial by-passes that examine the adolescent's needs and competence. Lastly, parents or their children could be allowed to opt-out only for certain aspects of education. The major example involves circumstances involving the availability of some medical services, services which may be deemed problematic to the extent that medical services typically are construed as under greater parental control. The general rule in instances in which school services are not construed as directly educational but more as services under direct parental control would be that students would not be compelled to avail themselves of those specific services but they still would have access to a socially supportive environment. That environment would allow students to acquire the knowledge necessary to make effective decisions and, admittedly more controversially, the environment would allow exposure to perspectives different from those of their parents.

REACHING PRIVATE SCHOOLS

Although states may provide adolescents with considerable protections if they remain in public schools, the protections are not as secure if parents exercise their right to educate their children outside of public school systems. State oversight and regulation of private schools, especially religious schools, remain minimal or non-existent. Indeed, private schools are essentially singled out of statutory mandates, and the Constitution prohibits states from using their funds to advance religion or otherwise become excessively entangled with religious schools. These issues are particularly important given the new trend toward creating charter schools rests largely on the belief that relieving schools from state and local regulations will allow them to experiment, innovate and better educate adolescents. Thus, for both religious and charter schools, law and policy generally aims to limit state intrusion and regulation—a tendency that directly challenges proposals that rely on increasing adolescents' legislated educational rights.

The failure of states to regulate private schools to any significant degree raises the question of whether states could do so if they wished. States have not attempted to regulate the content and nature of instructions in private schools to an extent that would set discernable precedents, and the Supreme Court has not set clear guidelines for halting states' intrusion into otherwise private matters. Yet, three points suggest that states still retain considerable power, if they choose to exercise it. First, state and federal courts consistently uphold state laws regulating state approval of private school teachers, instruction in core subjects, and reporting of attendance information. Importantly, the Supreme Court has refused to review these cases and thus approves at least of these minimal require-ments placed upon private schools through state regulation. Second, states may condition government financial assistance to private schools on their compliance with requirements that the states might not otherwise be constitutionally permitted to impose. The Supreme Court, for example, has upheld against First Amendment challenge Title IX's conditioning of federal financial assistance on compliance with the statute's provisions and found that "Congress is free to attach reasonable and unambiguous conditions to federal financial assistance that educational institutions are not obligated to accept" (*Grove City College v. Bell*, 1984, p. 575). Third, when the regulation connects to an important state interest relating to the children in these schools, the Supreme Court repeatedly has stressed that parents have no constitutional right to provide their children with a pri-vate school education unfettered by reasonable government regulation. Thus, if states can demonstrate the importance of its regulations for chil-dren's well-being and the societal interest in that result, Court precedent would find that the state not only has the power but the "high responsi-bility ... to impose reasonable regulations for the control and duration of basic education" (*Wisconsin v. Yoder*, 1972, p. 213).

In sum, so long as the programs are construed and construable as general education, school officials and the state maintain considerable control. For public schools, officials maintain control to the extent to which schools do not limit political and religious views or make partisan political and religious views the basis for education. As previously sug-gested, the analysis may lead to an uncomfortable outcome. The position allows for comprehensive discussions; but it does not allow for coercing onto objecting adolescents (whether objecting themselves or through their parents' objections) programs that may be construed as health services (e.g., although currently not even proposed in public schools, it is imagi-nable that some schools could provide needles to deal with dangers arising from drug use). For private schools, states could, at the very least, condition receipt of any financial aid a compliance with all important regulations presently applicable to public schools. State legislatures bear the full and only responsibility for setting and enforcing broad standards. As we have seen, an important part of those standards should include the development of education programs that respond to the needs of adolescents and those of a democratic society.

CONCLUSION

Despite the popular belief that society does not agree on what adolescents should do and be allowed to do in schools, societal ideals suggest agreed upon sets of moral beliefs, forms of thinking, and behaviors that schools must inculcate and tolerate in students. Schools can help foster many attributes deemed appropriate for all adolescents who live in a pluralistic, democratic society. Thus, schools can provide environments that are safe, help students deal effectively with violence, address deficiencies in prosocial behavior, and foster environments that allow adolescents to thrive. Rebutting the misperception that society disagrees too much about fundamental values is of enormous significance. The misbelief accounts for bestowing curricular control to local school officials and the parents who elect them. The rebuttal is even more significant because society actually does more than share broad values and aspirations deemed worth inculcating in the next generation. Society has the tools that could help schools foster the values, attitudes, and behaviors necessary for living in democratic, pluralistic, and civil communities.

To ensure the development of educational programs that reach effectiveness, research suggests that efforts must address four objectives. First, schools must acknowledge and address adolescents' needs, concerns and realities. Second, programs must give students information and experiences needed to become critical thinkers and responsible decision makers. Third, schools must create environments in which students and teachers share responsibility and decision making within a broad framework of what must be learned. Lastly, the entire curriculum must enshrine the values deemed worth instilling and must incorporate skills into students' everyday activities. The principles rest on the premise that, if society wants students to develop into citizens who can function peaceably in a diverse society, they should allow students to experience democracy in the classroom, schools, and communities and have their basic needs met in all their learning experiences. Given that schools already are in the business of inculcating students, fostering responsible citizenship values can and must be achieved by weaving them into various aspects of the curriculum and into a general pattern of school exhortations. To achieve full integration, the values must be woven at two critical levels: in students' interactions within schools and their interactions as students in the general community. Equipping students with the knowledge and ability to live in our civil society requires an educational environment that welcomes and addresses students' experiences.

Schools already undoubtedly recognize and seek to realize the above goals; but they fail to take adolescents' roles as seriously as research suggests they can. Theories of adolescent development now recognize the reciprocal nature of socialization which emphasizes the importance of students' cognition to make sense of the conflicting realities they experience. Previously, the belief was that the task of socialization involved the manner adults communicated what they knew to the next generation and that adolescents' internalized societal beliefs that were homogenous and marked by consensus. Society thus perpetuated itself through generations. That understanding of adolescents as passive recipients of coherent and cohesive adult wisdom no longer finds empirical support. Researchers now view adolescents as constructing self-concepts by reasoning, reflection and action, rather than simply internalizing experiences. Researchers also now recognize how society is far from based on a homogenous consensus with consistent messages. Adolescents must respond to social forces beyond their parents' control; a reality that requires society to provide adolescents with opportunities to shape not only their own destinies but their families, peer associations, schools, and broader communities. In addition to basic theories of adolescent development, it is important to emphasize the inherently active process of democracy. Democracy requires active engagement with others in a way that ensures that their claims are both heard and appropriately considered. The practice of democracy requires expressing one's views, listening to others' views, tolerating differences, acquiring skills to respond reasonably, seeking compromises, and acceding to legitimate majority views. Schools can allow students to confront and analyze diverse points of view and can support them as they experience challenging situations; schools can help students learn to engage in critical analysis and make choices about appropriate behavior. Research, then, reveals the need to provide students with opportunities to practice and develop certain habits and democracy requires the injection of student voice and promotion of student experimentation and inquiry in communal environments.

Given that available educational pedagogy and technology exists to enhance adolescents' development toward responsible behavior and given strong rationales for moving toward providing students with those tools, cause for failure must lie beyond pedagogical matters. The previous analyses propose that schools' failure to respond appropriately to societal demands and adolescents' realities reveals a fundamental failure of law. The legal and social reality in which adolescents and educational strategies find themselves hampers the development of effective programs and healthy adolescent development. The central problem that arises in the inculcation of values through schooling involves the manner the law generally fails to recognize the democratic challenges adolescents and schools face. The legal system remains generally indifferent to adolescents' need for and sense of autonomy, a posture largely determined by common law's failure to view minors as fully rational actors. The legal system continues to fail to prepare adolescents to seek the goals of pursuing truth, self-governance, and self-fulfillment. The extent to which students are unable to exercise responsible autonomy and self-control highlights the need for legal and educational reform. The apparent deficiencies in socialization also highlight the need to restructure society so that adolescents are socialized as democratic citizens rather than as a group that is neither needed nor welcomed in the economic, civil, and cultural tasks of continually renewing society.

Taken together, legal and social science scholarship examining adolescent development emphasizes well the need to focus on the ways adolescents serve as resources to their families, schools, communities and especially themselves. This perspective suggests that adolescents must be supported with the information, resources, and skills needed to work toward prosocial change in their own lives, in the adolescents' subculture and in broader society. Without doubt, the active agent in social change is participation by those who would benefit most by personal and societal reform. The suggestion made above and throughout the previous chapters proposes that adolescents must be differently socialized into the type of society and legal system in which they are expected to operate. Importantly, the analysis also suggests that the legal system and other major socializing institutions must accommodate for adolescents' peculiar needs consistent with democratic ideals. In addition, the analysis suggests that students can learn about, and actually practice, democratic lives. It is the numerous values necessary for democratic socialization that are important to inculcate, and such socialization involves the creation of environments that support and respect democratic living.

References

Adelman, H. S., & Taylor, L. (2000). Shaping the future of mental health in schools. *Psychology in the Schools, 37,* 49–60.

Adelman, H. S., & Taylor, L. (1998). Reframing mental health in schools and expanding school reform. *Educational Psychologist, 33,* 135–152.

Adelman, H. S., & Taylor, L. (1993a). School-based mental health: Toward a comprehensive approach. *Journal of Mental Health Administration, 20,* 32–45.

Adelman, H. S., & Taylor, L. (1993b). Mental health in schools: Moving forward. *School Psychology Review, 27,* 175–190.

Agostini v. Felton, 521 U.S. 203 (1997).

Aguilar, B., Sroufe, L. A., Egeland, B., & Carlson, E.(2000). Distinguishing the early-onset/persistent and adolescence-onset antisocial behavior types: From birth to 16 years. *Development & Psychopathology, 12,* 109–132.

Alabama Code, §§ 16-1-24.1(a); 16-40-A-2 (2000).

Alaska Statutes, §§ 14.20.030; 14.30.360 (2000).

Allen, J. P., Kuperminc, G., Philliber, S. & Herre, K. (1994). Programmatic prevention of adolescent problem behaviors: The role of autonomy relatedness, and volunteer service in the Teen Outreach Program. *American Journal of Community Psychology, 22,* 617–638.

Allensworth, D. D. (1993). Health education: State of the art, *Journal of School Health, 63,* 14–20.

Alsaker, F. D. (1995). Timing of puberty and reactions of puberty changes. In M. Rutter (Ed.), *Psychosocial disturbances in young people* (pp. 37–82). New York: Cambridge University Press.

Ambach v. Norwick, 441 U.S. 68 (1979).

Anderson, D. C. (1998). Curriculum, culture, and community: The challenge of school violence. In M. Tonry & M. H. Moore (Eds.) *Youth violence; Crime and justice: A review of research* (Vol. 24, pp. 317–364). Chicago, IL: University of Chicago Press.

Anderson v. Creighton, 483 U.S. 635 (1987).

Aneshensel, C. S., & Sucoff, C. A. (1996). The neighborhood context of adolescent mental health, *Journal of Health & Social Behavior, 37,* 293–310.

Anhalt, K., & Morris, T. L. (1998). Developmental and adjustment issues of gay, lesbian, and bisexual adolescents: A review of the empirical literature. *Clinical Child & Family Psychology Review, 1,* 215–230.

Arizona Revised Statutes, §§ 15-712; 15-716 (2000).

229

Arkansas Constitution, Art. 14, § 1 (2000).

Arkansas Code Annotated, § 6-18-703 (2000).

Arkansas Statutes Annotated, §§ 6-5-601; 6-18-703; 6-18-1005 (1999).

Arnett, J. (1992). Reckless behavior in adolescence: A developmental perspective. *Developmental Review, 12*, 339–373.

Arnett, J. J. (1999). Adolescent storm and stress, reconsidered. *American Psychologist, 54*, 317–326.

Arons, S. (1997). *Short route to chaos: Conscience, community, and the re-constitution of American schooling.* Amherst: University of Massachusetts Press.

Ashton, E., & Watson, B. (1998). Values education: A fresh look at procedural neutrality. *Educational Studies, 24*, 183–194.

Atkins, M. S., McKay, M. M., Arvanitis, P., London, L., Madison, S., Costigan, C., Haney, P., Zevenbergen, A., Hess, L., Bennett, D., & Webster, D. (1998). An ecological model for school-based mental health services for urban low-income aggressive children. *Journal of Behavioral Health Services and Research, 25*, 64–75.

Aurelia Davis v. Monroe County Board of Education, 862 F. Supp. 363 (M.D. GA, 1994).

Aurelia Davis v. Monroe County Board of Education, 119 S. Ct. 1661 (1999).

Balk, D. E. (1995). *Adolescent development: Early through late adolescence.* Pacific Grove, CA: Brooks/Cole.

Barber, B. R. (1992). *An aristocracy of everyone: The politics of education and the future of America.* New York: Ballantine.

Barker, L. A., & Adelman, H. S. (1994). Mental health and help-seeking among ethnic minority adolescents. *Journal of Adolescence, 17*, 251–263.

Baumrind, D. (1991). Effective parenting during the early adolescent transition. In P. E. Cowan & E. M. Hetherington (Eds.) *Advances in family research* (pp. 111–163). Hillsdale, NJ: Erlbaum.

Baumrind, D. (1996). The discipline controversy revisited. *Family Relations, 45*, 405–415.

Barksdale, B. (1981). *Brainpower for the Cold War: The Sputnik crisis and National Defense Education Act of 1958.* Westport, CT: Greenwood Press.

Beane, J. (1990). *Affect in the curriculum: Toward democracy, dignity, and diversity.* New York: Teachers College Press.

Bear, G. G. (1998). School discipline in the United States: Prevention, correction, and long-term social development. *School Psychology Review, 27*, 14–32.

Bearsley, C., & Cummins, R. A. (1999). No place called home: Life quality and purpose of homeless youths. *Journal of Social Distress & the Homeless, 8*, 207–226.

Bellotti v. Baird, 443 U.S. 622 (1979).

Bennett, W. (1993). *The book of virtues: A treasury of great moral stories.* New York: Simon & Schuster.

Bennett, W. J., DiIulio, J. J., Jr., & Walters, J. P. (1996). *Body count: Moral poverty and how to win America's war against crime and drugs.* New York: Simon & Schuster.

Bethel School District No. 403 v. Fraser, 478 U.S. 675 (1986).

Bereiter, C. (1973). *Must we educate.* Englewood Cliffs, NJ: Prentice-Hall.

Berkowitz, M. W., & Grych, J. H., (1998). Fostering goodness: Teaching parents to facilitate children's moral development. *Journal of Moral Education, 27*, 371–392.

Berndt, T. J. (1999). Friends' influence on students' adjustment to school. *Educational Psychologist, 34*, 15–28.

Berndt, T. J., Hawkins, J. A., & Jiao, Z. (1999). Influence of friends and friendship on adjustment to junior high school. *Merrill-Palmer Quarterly, 45*, 13–41.

Berube, Maurice R. (1994). *American school reform: Progressive, equity, and excellence movements, 1883–1993.* Westport, CT: Praeger.

Blasi, A. (1995). Moral understanding and moral personality: The process of moral integration. In W. Kurtines & J. L. Gerwirtz (Eds.) *Moral development: An introduction* (Vol. 1, pp. 229–253). Needham Heights, MA: Allyn and Bacon.

Bledstein, B. J. (1976). *The culture of professionalism: The middle class and the development of higher education in America.* New York: Norton.

Blyth, D., & Leffert, N. (1995). Communities as contexts for adolescent research. *Journal of Adolescent Research, 10,* 64–87.

Board of Education, Island Trees v. Pico, 457 U.S. 853 (1982).

Board of Education v. Pico, 457 U.S. 853 (1982).

Bogos, P. M. (1997). "Expelled. No Excuses. No Exceptions."—Michigan's zero-tolerance policy in response to school violence: M.C.L.A. Section 380.1311. *University of Detroit Mercy Law Review, 74,* 357–387.

Botvin, G. J., & Tortu, S. (1988). Preventing adolescent substance abuse through life skills training. In R. H. Price, E. L. Cowen, R. P. Lorion, & J. Ramos-McKay (Eds.) *Fourteen ounces of prevention: A casebook for practitioners* (pp. 98–110). Washington, DC: American Psychological Association.

Botvin, G. J. (1995). Principles of prevention. In R. H. Coombs & D. Ziedonis (Eds.) *Handbook on drug abuse prevention: A comprehensive strategy to prevent the abuse of alcohol and other drugs* (pp. 19–44). Boston: Allyn and Bacon.

Botvin, G. J., Baker, E., Dusenbury, L., Botvin, E. M., & Diaz, T. (1995). Long-term follow-up results of a randomized drug abuse prevention trial in a white middle-class population. *Journal of the American Medical Association, 273,* 1106–1112.

Bourgois, P. I. (1995). *In search of respect: Selling crack in El Barrio.* New York: Cambridge University Press.

Bowker, L. (Ed.) (1997). *Masculinities and violence.* Thousand Oaks, CA: Sage.

Bremner, R. H. (Ed.) (1970). *Children and youth in America: A documentary history, Vol. I: 1600–1865.* Cambridge, MA: Harvard University Press.

Brendgen, M., Vitaro, F., & Bukowski, W. M. (2000). Deviant friends and early adolescents' emotional and behavioral adjustment. *Journal of Research on Adolescence, 10,* 173–189.

Brenner, N. D., Simon, T. R., Krug, E. C., & Lowry, R. (1999). Recent trends in violence-related behaviors among high school students in the United States. *Journal of the American Medical Association, 282,* 440–446.

Brophy, J. E. (1996). *Teaching problem students.* New York: Guilford.

Broterton, D. C. (1996). The contradictions of suppression: Notes from a study of approaches to gangs in three public high schools. *Urban Review, 28,* 95–117.

Bowes, J. M., Chalmers, D., & Flanagan, C. (1997). Children's involvement in household work: Views of adolescents in sex countries. *Family Matters: Australian Journal of Family Studies, 46,* 26–30.

Brown, B. B. (1990) Peer groups. In S. S. Feldman & G. R. Elliott (Eds.) *At the threshold: The developing adolescent* (pp. 171–196). Cambridge, MA: Harvard University Press.

Brown, B. B. (1996). Visibility, vulnerability, development, and context: Ingredients for a fuller understanding of peer rejection in adolescence. *Journal of Early Adolescence, 16,* 27–36.

Brown v. Board of Education, 347 U.S. 483 (1954).

Brown v. Hot, Sexy and Safer Productions Inc., 68 F.3d 525 (1st Cir. 1995), cert. denied, 64 U.S.L.W. 3591 (U.S. Mar. 4. 1996) (No. 1158).

Boyes, M. C., & Allen, S. G. (1993). Styles of parent-child interaction and moral reasoning in adolescence. *Merrill-Palmer Quarterly, 39,* 551–570.

Boyte, H. C. (1991). Community service and service education. *Phi Delta Kappan, 72,* 765–767.

Bryant, T. J. (1998). The death knell for school expulsion: The 1997 Amendments to the Individuals With Disabilities Education Act. *American University Law Review, 47,* 487–555.

Bryk, A. S., Lee, V. E., & Holland, P. B., (1993). *Catholic schools and common good*. Cambridge, MA: Harvard University Press.

Burton, L. M., Obeidallah, D. A., & Allison, K. (1996). Ethnographic insights on social context and adolescent development among inner-city African-American teens. In R. Jessor, A. Colby & R. A. Shweder (Eds.) *Ethnography and human development: Context and meaning in social inquiry* (pp. 395–418). Chicago: University of Chicago Press.

Button, H. W., & Provenzo, E. E., Jr. (1983). *History of education and culture in America*. New York: Allyn and Bacon.

Butts, R. F. (1978). *Public education in the United States: From revolution to reform*. New York: Holt, Rinehart & Winston.

Bybee, R. W., & Gee, E. G. (1982). *Violence, values, and justice in the schools*. Boston: Allyn and Bacon.

California Constitution, Arts. 9,1; 9,5 (2000).

California Education Code, §§ 32228.1-32234; 49426, 51203; 51220; 51553 (2000).

Callahan, R. E. (1962). *Education and the cult of efficiency*. Chicago: University of Chicago Press.

Canterbury, R. J., McGarvey, E. L., Sheldon-Keller, A. E., Waite, D., Reams, P., & Koopman, C. (1995). Prevalence of HIV-related risk behaviors and STDs among incarcerated adolescents. *Journal of Adolescent Health, 17*, 173–177.

Carlson, C., Paavola, J., & Talley, R. (1995). Historical, current, and future models of schools as health care delivery settings. *School Psychology Quarterly, 10*, 184–202.

Cary v. Population Services Population International, 431 U.S. 678 (1977).

Cedar Rapids Community School District v. Garret F., 526 U.S. 66 (1999).

Centers for Disease Control (1998). *Leading causes of mortality and morbidity and contributing behaviors in the United States*. http://ww.cdc.gov.nccdphp/dash/ahsumm/ ussumm.htm.

Chamberlain, P., & Moore, K. J. (1998). Models of community treatment for serious offenders. In J. Crane (Ed.) *Social programs that really work* (pp. 258–276). Princeton, NJ: Russell Sage.

Chapin, J. R. (1998). Is service learning a good idea? Data from the National Longitudinal Study of 1998. *Social Studies, 89*, 205–212.

Chernoff, R., Combs-Orme, T., Risley-Curtiss, C., & Heisler, A. (1994). Assessing the health status of children entering foster care. *Pediatrics, 93*, 504–601.

Chubb, J. E. & Moe, T. M. (1990). *Politics, markets and American schools*. Washington, DC: The Brookings Institution.

Clement, P. F. (1997). *Growing pains: Children in the Industrial Age, 1850–1915*. New York: Twayne Publishers.

Cloud, R. C.(1997). Federal, state, and local responses to school violence. *Education Law Reporter, 120*, 877–894.

Cnaan, R. A., Wineburg, R. J., & Boddie, S. C. (1999). *The newer deal: Social work and religion in partnership*. New York: Columbia University Press.

Cocozza, J. J., & Skowyra, K. (2000). Youth with mental health disorders: Issues and emerging responses. *Juvenile Justice, 7*, 3–13.

Code of Alabama, §§ 16-8-1; 16-6B-2 (2000).

Cohen, J. H., Weiss, H. B., Mulvey, E. P., & Dearwater, S. R. (1994). A primer on school violence prevention, *Journal of School Health, 64*, 309–313.

Cohen, P., & Cohen, J. (1996). *Life values and adolescent mental health*. Mahwah, NJ: Erlbaum.

Cohen, S. S. (1974). *A history of colonial education; 1607–1776, Studies in the history of American education*. New York: Wiley.

Cohen, S. (1999). *Challenging orthodoxies: Toward a new cultural history of education*. New York: Peter Lang.

Cohen, S. (1983). The mental hygiene movement, the development of personality and the school: The medicalization of American education. *History of Education Quarterly, 23*, 123–149.

Colby, A., & Damon, W. (1995). The development of extraordinary moral commitment. In M. Killen & D. Hart (Eds.) *Morality in everyday life: Developmental perspectives* (pp. 342–370). New York: Cambridge University Press.

Coleman, J. (1961). *The adolescent society.* NY: Free Press.

Coll, C. G., Crnic, K., Lamberty, G., Wasik, B. H., Jenkins, R. G., Vasquez, H., & McAdoo, H. P. (1996). An integrative model for the study of developmental competencies in minority children. *Child Development, 67,* 1891–1914.

Collins, W. A., Maccoby, E. E., Steinberg, L., Hetherington, E. M., & Bornstein, M. H. (2000). Contemporary research on parenting: The case for nature and nurture. *American Psychologist, 55,* 218–232.

Colorado, Revised Statutes, § 22-25-101 (2000).

Conger, K. J., Conger, R. D., & Scaramella, L. V. (1997). Parents, siblings, psychological control, and adolescent adjustment. *Journal of Adolescent Research, 12,* 113–138.

Connecticut Constitution, Art. 8, 1 (2000).

Connecticut General Statutes, §§ 10-76b et seq.; 10-16b; 10-19 (1999).

Connonlly, S. D., Paikoff, R. L., & Buchanana, C. M. (1996). Puberty: The interplay of biological and psychosocial processes in adolescence. In G. R. Adams & R. Montemayor (Eds.) *Psychosocial development during adolescence* (Vol. 8, pp. 259–299). Thousand Oaks, CA: Sage.

Conoley, J. C., & Conoley, C. W. (1991). Collaboration for child adjustment: Issues for school- and clinic-based child psychologists. *Journal of Consulting and Clinical Psychology, 59,* 821–829.

Cook, P. J., & Laub, J. H. (1998). The unprecedented epidemic in youth violence. In M. Tonry & M. H. Moore (Eds.) *Youth violence; Crime and justice: A review of research* (Vol. 24, pp. 27–64). Chicago, IL: University of Chicago Press.

Combating Council on Juvenile Justice and Delinquency Prevention (1996). *Combating violence and delinquency: The national juvenile justice action plan.* Washington, DC: Department of Justice, Office of Juvenile Justice Delinquency Prevention.

Corbett, G. F. (1999). Special education, equal protection and education finance: Does the Individuals with Disabilities Education Act violate a general education student's fundamental right to education? *Boston College Law Review, 40,* 633–672.

Cremin, L. A. (1970). *American education: The colonial experience, 1607–1783.* NY: Harper & Row.

Cremin, L. A. (1961). *The transformation of the school: Progressivism in American education, 1876–1957.* New York: Knopf.

Csikszentmihalyi, Mihaly, & Rathunde, Kevin (1993). The measurement of flow in everyday life: toward a theory of emergent motivation. In Janis E. Jacobs (Ed.) *Developmental perspectives on motivation* (pp. 57–97). Lincoln, NE: University of Nebraska Press.

Cuban, L. (1984). *How teachers taught: Constancy and change in American classrooms 1890–1980.* White Plains, New York: Longman.

Cuban, L. (1990). Reforming again, again, and again. *Educational Researcher, 19 (Jan.–Feb.),* 3–13.

Damon, W., & Colby, A. (1996). Education and moral commitment. *Journal of Moral Education, 25,* 31–37.

Davidson, P. & Youniss, J. (1991). Which comes first, morality or identity? In W. Kurtines & J. L. Gerwirtz (Eds.) *Handbook of moral development and behavior* (Vol. 1, pp. 105–121). Hillsdale, NJ: Erlbaum.

Davis, A. F. (1967). *Spearheads for reform: The social settlements and the progressive movement, 1890–1914.* New York: Oxford University Press.

Davis v. Monroe County Bd. of Educ., 120 F. 3d 1390, 1401 (11th Cir. 1997) (en banc).

Delaware Code, Ch. 14 § 1605A (1999).

DelFattore, J. (1992). *What Johnny shouldn't read: Textbook censorship in America*. New Haven: Yale University Press.

D'Emidio-Caston, M., & Brown, J. H. (1998). The other side of the story: Student narratives on the California Drug, Alcohol, and Tobacco Education Programs. *Evaluation Review, 22*, 95–117.

Demos, J. (1986). *Past, present and personal: The family and the life course in American history*. New York: Oxford University Press.

DeRoche, E. F., & Williams, M. M. (1998). *Educating hearts and minds: A comprehensive character education framework*. Thousand Oaks, CA : Corwin Press.

DeShaney v. Winnabago County Department of Social Services, 489 U.S. 189 (1989).

Devine, J. (1995). Can metal detectors replace the panopticon? *Cultural Anthropology, 10*, 171–195.

Dewey, J. (1899/1990). *The school and society*. Chicago, IL: University of Chicago Press.

Dewey, J. (1916). *Democracy and education: An introduction to the philosophy of education*. New York: Macmillan.

Dillon, J. B. (1879). *Oddities of colonial legislation in America, as applied the public lands, primitive education, religion, morals, Indians, etc., etc.* Indianapolis, IN: Robert Douglas Publishers.

D'Imperio, R. L., Dubow, E. F., & Ippolito, M. F. (2000). Resilient and stress-affected adolescents in an urban setting. *Journal of Clinical Child Psychology, 29*, 129–142.

Dishion T. J., McCord J., & Poulin, F. (1999). When Interventions harm: Peer groups and problem behavior. *American Psychologist, 54*, 755–764.

Dodge, K. A. (1991). The structure and function of reactive and protective aggression. In D. J. Pepler & K. H. Rubin (Eds.) *The development and treatment of childhood aggression* (pp. 211–218). Hillsdale, NJ: Erlbaum.

Doll, B., & Lyon, M. A. (1998). Risk and resilience: Implications for the delivery of educational and mental health services in schools. *School Psychology Review, 27*, 348–363.

D. R. v. Middle Bucks Area Vocational Technical School, 972 F.2d 1364, 1371–75 (3rd Cir. 1992) cert. denied 113 S.Ct. 1045 (1993).

Dryfoos, J. G. (1994). *Full-service schools*. San Francisco: Jossey-Bass.

Dryfoos, J. G. (1995). Full service schools: Revolution or fad? *Journal of Research on Adolescence, 5*, 147–172.

Duncan, B. J. (1997). Character education: Reclaiming the social. *Educational Theory, 47*, 119–131.

Duchnowski, A. J. (1994). Innovative service models: Education. *Journal of Clinical Child Psychology, 23*, 13–18.

Dupre, Anne P. (1996). Should students have constitutional rights? Keeping order in public schools. *George Washington Law Review, 65*, 49–105.

Durlak, J. A. (1997). Primary prevention programs in schools. *Advances in Clinical Child Psychology, 19*, 283–318.

Durlak, J. A. (1995). *School-based prevention programs for children and adolescents*. Thousand Oaks, CA: Sage.

Durlak, J. A., & Wells, A. M. (1998). Evaluation of indicated preventive intervention (secondary prevention) mental health programs for children and adolescents. *American Journal of Community Psychology, 26*, 775–802.

Dwyer, J. G. (1998). *Religious schools v. children's rights*. Ithaca, NY: Cornell University Press.

Easterlin, R. A., & Crimmins, E. M. (1991). Private materialism, personal self-fulfillment, family life, and public interest: the nature, effects, and causes of recent changes in the values of American youth. *Public Opinion Quarterly, 55*, 499–533.

Eccles, J. S., Lord, S. E., Roeser, R. W., Barber, B. L., & Jozefowicz, D. M. H. (1997). The association of school transitions in early adolescence with developmental trajectories through high school. In J. Schulenberg, J. Maggs & K. Hurrelmann (Eds.) *Health risks and developmental transitions during adolescence* (pp. 283–320). New York: Cambridge University Press.

Eccles, J. S., Midgley, C., Wigfield, A., Buchanan, C. M., Reuman, D., Flanagan, C., & MacIver, D. (1993). Development during adolescence: The impact of stage-environment fit on young adolescents' experiences in schools and families. *American Psychologist*, 48, 90–101.

Eccles, J. S., Wigfield, A., & Schiefele, U. (1998). Motivation to succeed. In W. Damon (Series Ed.) & N. Eisenberg (Vol. Ed.) *Handbook of child psychology: Vol. 3. Social, emotional, and personality development* (5th ed., pp. 1017–1095). New York: Wiley.

Eccles, J. S., & Midgley, C. (1989). Stage-environment fit: Developmentally appropriate class-rooms for young adolescents. In C. Ames & R. Ames (Eds.) *Research on motivation in education: Vol. 3. Goals and cognitions* (pp. 13–44). NY: Academic Press.

Eccles, J., Barber, B., Jozefowicz, D., Malenchuk, O., & Vida, M. (1999). Self-evaluations of competence, task values, and self-esteem. In N. G. Johnson, M. C. Roberts & J. Worell (Eds.) *Beyond appearance: A new look at adolescent girls* (pp. 53–83). Washington, DC: American Psychological Association.

Edwards v. Aguillard, 482 U.S. 578 (1987).

Eisenberg, N. (1992). *The caring child*. Cambridge, MA: Harvard University Press.

Eisenberg, N., & Fabes, R. A., (1991). Prosocial behavior and empathy: A multimethod developmental perspective. In M. S. Clark (Ed.) *Prosocial behavior* (pp. 34–61). Newbury Park, CA: Sage.

Eisenberg, N., & Fabes, R. A. (1998). Prosocial development. In W. Damon (Series Ed.) & N. Eisenberg (Vol. Ed.) *Handbook of child psychology, Vol. 3: Social, emotional, and personality development* (5th ed., pp. 701–778). Newbury Park, CA: Sage.

Elliott, D. S., Hamburg, B. A., & Williams, K. R. (1998). Violence in American schools: An overview. In D. S. Elliott, B. A. Hamburg & K. R. Williams (Eds.) *Violence in American schools* (pp. 3–28). New York: Cambridge University Press.

Elbedour, S., Center, B. A., Maruyama, G. M., & Assor, A. (1997). Physical and psychological maltreatment in schools. *School Psychology International*, 18, 201–215.

Emihovich, C., & Herrington, C. D. (1997). *Sex, kids, and politics: Health services in school*. New York: Teachers College Press.

Empey, L. T. (1979). The social construction of childhood and juvenile justice. In L. T. Empey (Ed.) *The future of childhood and juvenile justice* (pp. 1–34). Charlottesville: University of Virginia Press.

Engel v. Vitale, 370 U.S. 421 (1962).

Ennett, S. T., & Bauman, K. E. (1996). Adolescent social networks: School, demographic and longitudinal considerations. *Journal of Adolescent Research*, 11, 194–215.

Ennis, C. D. (1996). When avoiding confrontation leads to avoiding content: Disruptive students' impact on curriculum. *Journal of Curriculum & Supervision*, 11, 145–162.

Epp, J. R., & Watkinson, A. M. (Eds.) (1997). *Systemic violence in education: Promise broken*. Albany: State University of New York.

Epperson v. Arkansas, 393 U.S. 97 (1963).

Erikson, E. (1968). *Identity: Youth and crisis*. New York: Norton.

Esbensen, F.-A., & Osgood, D. W. (1999). Gang resistance education and training (GREAT): Results from the national evaluation. *Journal of Research in Crime & Delinquency*, 36, 194–225.

Estelle v. Gamble, 429 U.S. 97 (1976).

Evans, J. M. (1992). Let our parents run: Removing the judicial barriers for parental governance of local schools. *Hastings Constitutional Law Quarterly*, 19, 963–1008.

Fabes, R. A., Carlo, G., Kupanoff, K., & Laible, D. (1999). Early adolescence and prosocial/ moral behavior I: The role of individual processes. *Journal of Early Adolescence, 19*, 5–16.

Farrell, B. G. (1999). *Family: The making of an idea, an institution, and a controversy in American culture.* Boulder, CO: Westview Press.

Farrington v. Tokushige, 273 U.S. 284 (1927).

Fasick, F. A. (1994). "On the 'Invention' of Adolescence." *Journal of Early Adolescence, 14*, 6–23.

Fassinger, R. E. (1996). Adolescence options and optimizations. *Counseling Psychologist, 24*, 491–498.

Fazal, F. (1999). Is actual notice an actual remedy? A critique of *Gebser v. Lago Vista Independent School District. Houston Law Review, 36*, 1033–1091.

Fendrich, J. (1993). *Ideal citizens.* Albany: State University of New York Press.

Feld, B. C. (1999). *Bad kids: Race and the transformation of the juvenile court.* New York: Oxford University Press.

Feldman, S. S., & Weinberger, D. A. (1994). Self-restraint as a mediator of family influences on boy's delinquent behavior: A longitudinal study. *Child Development, 65*, 195–211.

Fergusson, D. M., & Horwood, J. L. (1996). The role of adolescent peer affiliations in the continuity between childhood behavioral adjustment and juvenile offending. *Journal of Abnormal Child Psychology, 24*, 205–221.

Fine, M. (1991). *Framing dropouts: Notes on the politics of an urban public high school.* Albany: State University of New York Press.

Finn-Stevenson, M., & Zigler, E. F. (1999). *Schools of the 21st century: Linking child care and education.* Boulder, CO: Westview Press.

Flacks, R. (1988). *Making history: The American left and the American mind.* New York: Columbia University Press.

Flaherty, L. T., Weist, M. D., & Warner, B. S. (1996). School-based mental health services in the United States: History, current models and needs. *Community Mental Health Journal, 32*, 341–352.

Flanagan, C., & Galay, L. (1995). Reframing the meaning of "political" in research with adolescents. *Perspectives on Political Science, 24*, 31–41.

Flanagan, C. A., Bowes, J. M., Jonsson, B., Csapo, B., & Sheblanova, E. (1998). Ties that bind: Correlates of adolescents' civic commitments in seven countries. *Journal of Social Issues, 54*, 457–475.

Flanders, J. (1925). *Legislative control of the elementary curriculum.* New York: Teachers College.

Fletcher, A. C., Elder, G. H., Jr., & Mekos, D. (1999). Parental influences on adolescent involvement in community activities. *Journal of Research on Adolescence, 10*, 29–48.

Florida Statutes, §§ 231.02(1); 232.27(j); 233.0612; 230.2317 (1999).

Foley, R. M., & Dudzinski, M. (1995). Human sexuality education: Are special educators prepared to meet the educational needs of disabled youth? *Journal of Sex Education and Therapy, 21*, 182–191.

Forman, S. G., & Kalafat, J. (1998). Substance abuse and suicide: Promoting resilience against self-destructive behavior in youth. *School Psychology Review, 27*, 398–406.

Franklin v. Gwinette County Public Schools, 503 U.S. 60 (1992).

Freedman, M. (1993). *The kindness of strangers: Adult mentors, urban youth, and the new voluntarism.* San Francisco: Jossey-Bass

Friedenberg, E. S. (1962). *The vanishing adolescent.* New York: Dell.

Friedenberg, E. S. (1965). *Coming of age in America: Growth and acquiescence.* New York: Random House.

Gager, P. J., & Elias, M. J. (1997). Implementation of prevention programs in high-risk environments: Application of the resiliency paradigm. *American Journal of Orthopsyhiatry, 67*, 363–373.

Galenson, D. (1981). *White servitude in colonial America: An economic analysis.* Cambridge, MA. Cambridge University Press.

Garmezy, N. (1991). Children in poverty: Resilience despite risk. *Psychiatry, 56*, 127–136.

Garmezy, N., Matsen, A. S., & Tellegen, A. (1984). Studies of stress-resistant children: A building block for developmental psychopathology. *Child Development, 55*, 97–111.

Gebser et al. v. Lago Vista Independent School District, No. 96-1866, 524 U.S. 274 (1998).

Georgia Code Annotated, § 20-2-1885 (1999).

Gildrie, R. P. (1994). *The profane, the civil and the godly: The reformation of manners in orthodox New England, 1649–1749.* University Park: Pennsylvania State University Press.

Glanz, K., Lewis, F. M., & Rimer, B. K. (Eds.) (1997). *Health behavior and health education: Theory, research and practice* (2nd ed). San Francisco: Jossey-Bass.

Glennon, T. (1993). Disabling ambiguities: Confronting barriers to the education of students with emotional disabilities. *Tennessee Law Review, 60*, 295–364.

Goals 2000: Educate America Act—Safe Schools (1994). Public Law 103–227, 108 Stat. §§ 204 et seq. (1994).

Goldstein, A. P., Palumbo, J., Striepling, S., & Voutsinas, A. M. (1995). *Break it up.* Champaign, IL: Research Press.

Goldstein, A. P., & Conoley, J. C. (1997). Student aggression: Current status. In A. P. Goldstein & J. Close Conoley (Eds.) *School violence intervention: A practical handbook* (pp. 3–19). New York: Guilford Press.

Goodlad, J. I., Soder, R., & Sirotnik, K. A. (Eds.) (1990). *The moral dimensions of teaching.* San Francisco: Jossey-Bass.

Goodmark, L. (1997). Can poverty lawyers play well with others? *Georgetown Journal on Fighting Poverty, 4*, 243–270.

Gordon, R. M. (1984). Freedom of expression and values inculcation in the public school curriculum. *Journal of Law & Education, 13*, 523–579.

Goss v. Lopez, 491 U.S. 565 (1975).

Gottfredson, D. (1997). School-based crime prevention. In L. W. Sherman, D. Gottfredson, D. MacKenzie, J. Eck, P. Reuter & S. Bushway (Eds.) *Preventing crime: What works, what doesn't, and what's promising* (Ch. 5, pp. 1–74). Washington, DC: U.S. Department of Justice, Office of Justice Programs.

Gottfredson, G. D., & Gottfredson, D. C. (1985). *Victimization in schools.* New York: Plenum.

Graber, J. A., Brooks-Gunn, J., & Warren, M. P. (1995). The antecedents of menarcheal age: Heredity, family environment, and stressful life events. *Child Development, 66*, 346–359.

Graff, H. J. (1985). Early adolescence in Antebellum America: The remaking of growing up. *Journal of Early Adolescence, 5*, 411–427.

Gray, M. J., & Steinberg, L. (1999). Unpacking authoritative parenting: Reassessing a multidimensional construct. *Journal of Marriage and the Family, 61*, 574–587.

Gregory, J. F. (1997). Three strikes and they're out: African American boys and American schools' responses to misbehavior. *International Journal of Adolescence & Youth, 7*, 25–34.

Greer, C., & Kohl, H. (Eds.) (1995). *A call to character.* New York: HarperCollins.

Greven, P. J. (1977). *The Protestant temperament: Patterns of child-rearing, religious experience and the self in early America.* New York: New American Library.

Groeschel, R. W. (1998). Discipline and the disabled student: The IDEA reauthorization responds. *Wisconsin Law Review, 1998*, 1085–1132.

Grolnick, W. S., Deci, E. L., & Ryan, R. M. (1997). Internalization within the family. In J. E. Grusec & L. Kuczynski (Eds.) *Parenting and children's internalization of values: A handbook of contemporary theory* (pp. 135–161). New York: Wiley.

Grossberg, M. (1985). *Governing the hearth: Law and the family in nineteenth-century America.* Chapel Hill: University of North Carolina Press.

Grove City College v. Bell, 465 U.S. 555 (1984).

Grusec, J. E., & Goodnow, J. J. (1994). Impact of parental discipline methods on the child's internalization of values: A reconceptualization of current points of view. *Developmental Psychology, 30*, 4–19.

Guerra, N. G., Nucci, L., & Huesmann, L. R. l (1994). Moral cognition and childhood aggression. In L. R. Huessmann (Ed.), *Aggressive behaviors: Current perspectives* (pp. 13–32). New York: Plenum.

Gun Free Schools Act of 1994, 20 U.S.C. 8921 (1994).

Gutmann, A. (1999). *Democratic education.* Princeton, NJ: Princeton University Press.

Hafen, B. C. (1993). Schools as intellectual and moral associations. *Bringham Young University Law Review, 1993*, 605–621.

Hall, G. S. (1904). *Adolescence: Its psychology and its relations to anthropology, sociology, sex, crime, religion, and education.* New York, New York: Appleton.

Hamovitch, B. A. (1996). Socialization without voice: An ideology of hope for at-risk students *Teachers College Record, 98*, 286–306.

Harlow v. Fitzgerald, 457 U.S. 800 (1982).

Harris, K. M. (1999). The health status and risk behaviors of adolescents in immigrant families. In D. J. Hernandez (Ed.) *Children of Immigrants: Health, adjustment, and public assistance* (pp. 286–347). Washington, DC: National Academy Press.

Hart, D., Atkins, R., & Ford, D. (1998). Urban America as a context for the development of moral identity in adolescence. *Journal of Social Issues, 54*, 513–530.

Hart, D., & Fegley, S. (1995). Prosocial behavior and caring in adolescence: Relations to self-understanding and social judgment. *Child Development, 66*, 1346–1359.

Hart, D., Yates, M., Fegley, S., & Wilson, G. (1995). Moral commitment in inner-city adolescents. In M. Killen & D. Hart (Eds.) *Morality in everyday life: Developmental perspectives* (pp. 317–341). New York: Cambridge University Press.

Hattie, J., Marsh, H. W., Neill, J. T., & Richards, G. E. (1997). Adventure education and outward bound: Out-of-class experiences that make a lasting difference. *Review of Educational Research, 67*, 43–87.

Hawes, Joseph (1991). *The children's rights movement: A history of advocacy and protection.* Boston: Twayne.

Hawkins, J. D., Farrington, D. P., & Catalano, R. F. (1998). Reducing violence through schools. In D. S. Elliott, B. A. Hamburg & K. R. Williams (Eds.) *Violence in American schools* (pp. 188–216). NY: Cambridge University Press.

Hawkins, J. D., Herrenkohl, T., Farrington, D. P., Brewer, D., Catalano, R. F., & Harachi, T. W. (1998). A review of predictors of youth violence. In R. Loeber & D. P. Farrington (Eds.) *Serious and violent juvenile offenders: Risk factors and successful interventions* (pp. 106–146). Thousand Oaks, CA: Sage.

Hay, D. F., Castle, J., Stimson, C. A., & Davies, L. (1995). The social construction of character in toddlerhood. In M. Killen & D. Hart (Eds.) *Morality in everyday life: Developmental perspectives* (pp. 23–51). New York: Cambridge University Press.

Hazelwood School District v. Kuhlmeier. 484 U.S. 260 (1988).

Heater, D. B. (1990). *Citizenship: The civic ideal in world history, politics and education.* New York: Longman.

Heaviside, S., Rowand, C., Williams, C., & Farris, E. (1998). *Violence and discipline problems in U.S. public schools: 1996–97.* Washington, DC: National Center for Education Statistics.

Heise, M. (1994). Goals 2000: Educate America Act: The federalization and legalization of educational policy. *Fordham Law Review, 63*, 345–381.

Hektner, J. M. (1997). *Exploring optimal personality development: A longitudinal study of adolescents.* Dissertation Abstracts International: Section B: The Sciences & Engineering, Vol. 57(11–B), 7249.

Helwig, C. C. (1995). Adolescents' and young adults' conceptions of civil liberties: Freedom of speech and religion. *Child Development, 66,* 152–166.

Henggeler, S. W. (1994). A consensus: Conclusions of the APA Task Force Report on Innovative Models of Mental Health Services for Children, Adolescents, and Their Families. *Journal of Clinical Child Psychology, 60,* 953–961.

Henggeler, S. W., Schoenwald, S. K., Boruin, C. M., Eowland, M. D., & Cunningham, P. B. (1998). *Multisystemic treatment of antisocial behavior in children and adolescents.* New York: Guilford.

Herman, M. A., & Remley, T. P., Jr. (2000). Guns, violence, and schools: The results of school violence: Litigation against educators and students shedding more constitutional rights at the school house gate. *Loyola Law Review, 46,* 389–439.

Higginson, J. G. (1999). Defining, excusing, and justifying deviance: Teen mothers' accounts for statutory rape. *Symbolic Interaction, 22,* 25–36.

Hofstadter, R. (1995). *The age of reform: From Bryan to F.D.R.* New York: Knopf.

Honig, B. (1985). *Last chance for our children: How you can help save our schools.* Reading, MA: Addison-Wesley.

Honig v. Doe, 848 U.S. 305 (1988).

J. C. & Hawkins, D. J. (1998). Prevention of youth violence. In M. Tonry (Ed.) *Youth violence; crime and justice: An annual review of research* (Vol. 20, pp. 263–315). Chicago, IL: University of Chicago Press.

Huizinga, D., & Jakob-Chien, C. (1998). The contemporaneous co-occurrence of serious and violent offending and other problem behaviors. In R. Loeber & D. P. Farrington (Eds.) *Serious and violent juvenile offenders: Risk factors and successful interventions* (pp. 47–67). Thousand Oaks, CA: Sage.

Hunter, J. D. (1991). *Culture wars: The struggle to define America.* New York: Basic Books.

Hyman, I. A., & Snook, P. A. (1999). *Dangerous schools: What we can do about the physical and emotional abuse of our children.* San Francisco: Jossey-Bass.

Hyman, I. A., Weiler, E., Perone, D., Romano, L., Britton, G., & Shanock, A. (1997). Victims and victimizers: The two faces of school violence. In A. P. Goldstein & J. C. Conoley (Eds.) *School violence intervention: A practical handbook* (pp. 426–459). New York: Guilford.

Idaho Code, § 33–1605 (2000)

Illinois Compiled Statutes Annotated, tit. 105, §§ 5/14-1.09.1; 5/27-9.2; 5/27-23.4 (2000).

In re Gault, 387 U.S. 1 (1967).

Indiana Code Annotated, § 20-10.1-4-4.5 (2000).

Individuals with Disabilities Education Act Amendments, 20 U.S.C. §§ 1400–1500 (Supp. III 1998).

Ingraham v. Wright, 430 U.S. 651 (1977).

Iowa Code, §§ 256.11; 256.18 (1999).

Janssens, J. M. A. M., & Gerris, J. R. M. (1992). Child rearing, empathy and prosocial development. In J. M. A. M. Janssens & J. R. M. Gerris (Eds.) *Child rearing: Influence on prosocial and moral development* (pp. 57–75). Amsterdam: Swets & Zeitlinger.

Jenson, J. M., & Howard, M. O. (Eds.) (1999). *Youth violence: Current research and recent practice innovations.* Washington, DC: National Association of Social Work Press.

Jepson, L., Juszczak, L., & Fisher, M. (1998). Mental health care in a high school based health service. *Adolescence, 33,* 1–15.

Johnson, H. B. (1991). *Sleepwalking through history: America in the Reagan years.* NY: Norton.

Johnson, M. K. , Beebe, T., Mortimer, J. T., & Snyder, M. (1998). Volunteerism in adolescence: A process perspective. *Journal of Adolescent Research, 8,* 309–332.

Johnston, N. M. (1999). The Chicago public schools and its violent students: How can the law protect teachers? *DePaul Law Review, 48,* 907–948.

Juszczak, L., Fisher, M., Lear, J. G., & Freidman, S. B. (1995). Back to school: Training opportunities in school-based health centers. *Journal of Developmental and Behavioral Pediatrics, 16*, 101–104.

Kaestle, C. (1983). *Pillars of the republic: Common schools and American society: 1780–1860.* New York: Hill and Wang.

Kahne, J., & Westheimer, J. (1996). In the service of what? The politics of service learning. *Phi Delta Kappan, 74*, 593–99.

Kansas Statutes Annotated, §§ 72-1101; 158.6451 (1999).

Katz, M. (1968). *The irony of early school reform: Educational innovation in mid-nineteenth century Massachusetts.* Boston: Beacon.

Kazdin, A. E. (1995). *Conduct disorders in childhood and adolescence* (2nd ed.). Newbury Park, CA: Sage.

Kelleher, K. J., Taylor, J. L., & Rickert, V. I. (1992). Mental health services for rural children and adolescents. *Clinical Psychology Review, 12*, 841–852.

Keller, S. (1998). Something to lose: The black community's hard choices about educational choice. *Journal of Legislation, 24*, 67–98.

Kelley, B. T., Huizinga, D., Thornberry, T. P., & Loeber, R. (1997). *Epidemiology of serious violence.* Washington, DC: Office of Juvenile Justice and Delinquency Prevention.

Kentucky Constitution, 183 (2000).

Kentucky Revised Statutes, §158.440 (1999).

Kerr, M., & Stattin, H. (2000). What parents know, how they know it, and several forms of adolescent adjustment: Further support for a reinterpretation of monitoring. *Developmental Psychology, 36*, 366–380.

Kessler, R. C., Foster, C. L., Saunders, W. B., & Stang, P. E. (1995). Social consequences of psychiatric disorders, I: Educational attainment. *American Journal of Psychiatry, 152*, 1026–1032.

Keyishian v. Board of Regents, 385, U.S. 598 (1967).

Kinney, D. (1993) From nerds to normals: The recovery of identity among adolescents from middle school to high school. *Sociology of Education, 66*, 21–40.

Kirkpatrick, W. (1992). *Why Johnny can't tell right from wrong: Moral illiteracy and the case for character education.* New York : Simon & Schuster.

Kirschenbaum, H. (1977). *Advanced value clarification.* La Jolla, CA: University Associates.

Knitzer, J. (1993). Children's mental health policy: Challenging the future. *Journal of Emotional and Behavioral Disorders, 1*, 8–16.

Kowaleski-Jones, L. (2000). Staying out of trouble: Community resources and problem behavior among high-risk adolescents. *Journal of Marriage & the Family, 62*, 449–464.

Kett, J. F. (1977). *Rites of passage: Adolescence in America 1790 to the present.* New York: Basic Books.

Kliebard, H. M. (1985). Psychology … the teacher's Blackstone: G. Stanley Hall and the effort to build a developmental curriculum for youth. *Journal of Early Adolescence, 5*, 467–478.

Kohlberg, L. (1985). The just community approach to moral education in theory and practice. In M. Berkowitz & F. Oser (Eds.) *Moral education: Theory and application* (pp. 27–88). Hillsdale, NJ: Lawrence Erlbaum.

Kraft, R. J. (1996). Service learning. *Education & Urban Society, 28*, 131–150.

Kronenfeld, J. J. (2000). *Schools and the health of children: Protecting our future.* Thousand Oaks, CA: Sage.

Krueger, M. M. (1993). Everyone is an exception: Assumptions to avoid in the sex education classroom. *Phi Delta Kappan, 74*, 569–572.

Lab, S. P., & Clark, R. D. (1996). *Discipline, control, and school crime: Identifying effective intervention strategies.* Final report of the National Institute of Justice, under grant no. 93-IJ-CX-0034. Washington, DC: U.S. Department of Justice, National Institute of Justice.

Lamb's Chapel v. Center Moriches Union Free School District, 113 S. Ct. 2141(1993).

Lapsley, D. K., Enright, R. D., & Serline, R. C. (1985). Toward a theoretical perspective on the legislation of adolescence. *Journal of Early Adolescence, 5*, 441–466

Larson, R. W. (2000). Toward a psychology of positive youth development. *American Psychologist, 55*, 170–183.

Larson, R., & Richards, M. H. (1991). Daily companionship in late childhood and early adolescence: Changing developmental contexts. *Child Development, 62*, 284–300.

Larson, R., & Richards, M. H. (1994). *Divergent realities: The emotional lives of mothers, fathers, and adolescents.* New York: Basic Books.

Laub, J. H., & Lauritsen, J. L. (1993). Violent criminal behavior over the life course: A review of the longitudinal and comparative research. *Violence and Victims, 8*, 235–252.

Lau v. Nichols, 414 U.S. 563 (1974).

Laursen, B., Coy, K. C., & Collins, W. A. (1998). Reconsidering changes in parent-child conflict across adolescence: A meta-analysis. *Child Development, 69*, 817–832.

Lawrence, R. A. (1998). *School crime and juvenile justice.* New York: Oxford University Press.

Lear, J. G., Gleicher, H. B., St. Germaine, A., & Porter, P. J. (1991). Reorganizing health care for adolescents: The experience of the school-based adolescent health care program. *Journal of Adolescent Health, 12*, 450–458.

Lee v. Weisman, 112 S. Ct. 2649 (1992).

Leming, J. S. (2001). Integrating a structured ethical reflection curriculum into high school community service experiences: Impact on students' sociomoral development. *Adolescence, 36*, 33–45.

Lerner, R. A. (1995). *American youth in crisis: Challenges and options for programs and policies.* Thousand Oaks, CA: Sage.

Leventhal, T., & Brooks-Gunn, J. (2000). The neighborhoods they live in: The effects of neighborhood residence on child and adolescent outcomes. *Psychological Bulletin, 126*, 309–337.

Levesque, R. J. R. (1994). The internationalization of children's human rights: Too radical for American adolescents? *Connecticut Journal of International Law, 9*, 237–293.

Levesque, R. J. R. (1996a). Is there still a place for violent youth in juvenile justice? *Aggressive and Violent Behavior, 1*, 69–79.

Levesque, R. J. R. (1996b). Future visions of juvenile justice: Lessons from international and comparative law. *Creighton Law Review, 29*, 1563–1585.

Levesque, R. J. R. (1998a). The politics of schooling and adolescent life. *New York University Review of Law & Social Change, 24*, 635–653.

Levesque, R. J. R. (1998b). Emotional maltreatment in adolescents' everyday lives: Furthering sociolegal reforms and social service provisions. *Behavioral Sciences and the Law, 16*, 237–263.

Levesque, R. J. R. (1998c). Educating American youth: Lessons from children's human rights law. *Journal of Law and Education, 27*, 173–209.

Levesque, R. J. R. (2000a). *Adolescents, sex, and the law: Preparing adolescents for responsible citizenship.* Washington, DC: American Psychological Association.

Levesque, R. J. R. (2000b). Sexuality education: What adolescents' educational rights require. *Psychology, Public Policy & the Law, 4*, 953–988.

Levesque, R. J. R., & Tomkins, A. J. (1995). Revisioning juvenile justice: Implications of the new child protection movement. *Journal of Urban and Contemporary Law, 48*, 87–116.

Lewinsohn, P. M., Hops, H., Roberts, R. E., Seeley, J. R., & Andrews, J. A. (1993). Adolescent psychopathology: I. Prevalence and incidence of depression and other DSM-III-R disorders in high school students. *Journal of Abnormal Psychology, 102*, 133–144.

Liberman, M. (1993). *Public education: An autopsy.* Cambridge, MA: Harvard University Press.

Lipsey, M. W., & Derzon, J. H.(1998). Predictors of serious delinquency in adolescence and early adulthood: A synthesis of longitudinal research. In R. Loeber & D. P. Farrington (Eds.)

Serious and violent juvenile offenders: Risk factors and successful interventions (pp. 86–105). Thousand Oaks, CA: Sage.

Lochman, J. E., & Dodge, K. A. (1994). Social-cognitive processes of severely violent, moderately aggressive, and nonaggressive boys. *Journal of Consulting and Clinical Psychology, 62*, 366–374.

Lockwood, D. (1997). *Violence among middle school and high school students: Analysis and implications for prevention, Research in Brief.* Washington, DC: U.S. Department of Justice, National Institute of Justice.

Loeber, R., & Hay, D. F. (1997). Key issues in the development of aggression and violence from childhood to early adulthood. *Annual Review of Psychology, 48*, 371–410.

Loeber, R., Keenan, K., & Zhang, Q. (1997). Boys' experimentation and persistence in developmental pathways toward serious delinquency. *Journal of Child and Family Studies, 6*, 321–357.

Loeber, R., & Stouthamer-Loeber, M. (1998). Development of juvenile aggression and violence: Some common Misconceptions and controversies. *American Psychologist, 53*, 242–259.

Louisiana Revised Statutes, Tit. 17 §§ 154; 281; 286 (2000).

Loveless, T. (1997). The structure of public confidence in education. *American Journal of Education, 105*, 127–159.

Lubick, G. M. (1999). *The evolution of educational theory in the United States.* Westport, CT: Praeger.

Luthar, S., & Zigler, E. (1991). Vulnerability and competence: A review of research on resilience in childhood. *American Journal of Orthopsychiatry, 61*, 6–22.

Macchiarola, F. J., Lipsky, D., & Gartner, A. (1996). The judicial system & equality in schooling. *Fordham Urban Law Journal, 22*, 567–601.

Macleod, D. I. (1998). *The age of the child: Children in America, 1890–1920.* New York: Twayne Publishers.

Madsen, D. (1974). *Early national education: 1776–1830.* New York: Wiley.

Maguin, E., & Loeber, R. (1996). Academic performance and delinquency. In M. Tonry (Ed.) *Youth violence; Crime and justice: An annual review of research* (Vol. 20, pp. 145–264). Chicago, IL: University of Chicago Press.

Maine Revised Statutes Annotated, tit. 20 §§ 6606; 4723 (1999).

Masten, A. S., & Coatsworth, J. D. (1998). The development of competence in favorable and unfavorable environments: Lessons form research on successful children. *American Psychologist, 53*, 205–220.

Males, M. (1996). *The scapegoat generation: America's war on adolescents.* Monroe, ME: Common Courage Press.

Maryland Constitution, Art. VIII, 8 (2000).

Maryland Education Code Annotated, §§ 7-401; 7-411; 7-412 (1999).

Massachusetts Annotated Laws, ch. 69, § 1L (2000).

Massachusetts Constitution, pt. 2, ch. 5, 2 (2000).

Mayer, M. J., & Leone, P. E. (1999). A structural analysis of school violence and disruption: Implications for creating safer schools. *Education & Treatment of Children, 22*, 333–356.

McAdam, D. (1988). *Freedom summer.* New York: Oxford University Press.

McClellan, B. E. (1999). *Moral education in America: Schools and the shaping of character from colonial times to the present.* New York: Teachers College Press.

McClintock, M., & Herdt, G. (1996). Rethinking puberty: The development of sexual attraction. *Psychological Sciences, 5*, 178–183.

McCurdy, K., & Jones, E. D. (2000). *Supporting families: Lessons from the field.* Thousand Oaks. CA: Sage Publications.

McGrath, D. J., & Kuriloff, P. J. (1999). 'They're going to tear the doors of this place': Upper-middle-class parent school involvement and the educational opportunities of other people's children. *Educational Policy, 13*, 603–629.

McLatchie, R. (1997). Psychological adjustment and school performance in immigrant children. *Journal of Psychological Practice, 3*, 34–46.

McLoyd, V. C. (1998). Socioeconomic disadvantage and child development. *American Psychologist, 53*, 185–204.

McLoyd, V. C., & Steinberg, L. (Eds.) (1998). *Studying minority adolescents: Conceptual, methodological, and theoretical issues.* Mahwah, NJ: Erlbaum.

Melvin, D. H. II, (1995). The desegregation of children with disabilities. *DePaul Law Review, 44*, 599–671.

Merelman, R. M. (1985). Revitalizing political socialization. In R. Herrmann (Ed.) *Political psychology* (pp. 279–319). San Francisco: Jossey-Bass.

Mintz, S., & Kellogg, S. (1988). *Domestic revolutions: A social history of American family life.* New York: Free Press.

Michigan Statutes Annotated, §§ 15.4005; 15.41169 (1999).

Minden, S. D. (1995). The constitutionality of mandatory community service programs in public schools. *Southern California Law Review, 68*, 1391–1416.

Minnesota Constitution, Art. XIII, 1 (2000).

Minnesota Statutes, §§ 120A.03 ; 121A.21; 121A.29; 121A.23; 120B.22 (2000).

Minow, M. (1999). Reforming school reform. *Fordham Law Review, 68*, 257–289.

Mississippi Code Annotated, §§; 37-3-83; 37-13-21; 37-13-131 (2000).

Mitchell v. Helms, 530 U.S. 793 (2000).

Moffitt, T. E. (1993). Adolescence-limited and life-course-persistent antisocial behavior: A developmental taxonomy. *Psychological Review, 100*, 674–701.

Moore, K. P., & Sandholtz, J. H. (1999). Designing successful service learning projects for urban schools. *Urban Education, 34*, 480–499.

Moore, K. A, & Glei, D. (1995). Taking the plunge: An examination of positive youth development. *Journal of Adolescent Research, 10*, 15–40.

Motes, P. S., Melton, G., Simmons, W. E. W., & Pumariega, A. (1999). Ecologically oriented school-based mental health services: Implications for service system reform. *Psychology in the Schools, 36*, 391–401.

Mozert v. Hawkins Country Board of Education, 827 F.2d 1058 (6th Cir. 1987), cert. denied, 484 U.S. 1066 (1988).

Myer v. Nebraska, 262 U.S. 390 (1923).

Myhra, Alison G. (1999). No shoes, no shirt, no education: Dress codes and freedom of expression behind the postmodern schoolhouse gates. *Seton Hall Constitutional Law Journal, 9*, 337–400.

Natasi, B. K., Varies, K., Bernstein, R., & Pluymert, K. (1998). Mental health programming and the role of school psychologists. *School Psychology Review, 27*, 217–233.

National School Boards Association (1993). *Violence in the schools: 'Iow America's school boards are safeguarding our children.* Alexandria, VA: National School Boards Association.

Nevada Revised Statutes Annotated, §§ 389.018; 391.312 (2000).

New Hampshire Revised Statutes Annotated §§ 186-C et seq., (2000)

New Jersey Constitution, Art. VIII, 4 (2000).

New Jersey Statutes, tit. 18A: §§ 40A-2; 40A-11; 40A-12; 6:29-4.1(2000).

New Jersey v. T. L. O, 469 U.S. 325 (1985).

New Mexico Statutes Annotated, § 22-10-22 (2000).

New York Consolidated Laws Services, Education § 804 (1999).

Noguera, P. H. (1995). Preventing and producing violence: A critical analysis of responses to school violence. *Harvard Educational Review, 65*, 189–212.

Nolan, J. L. Jr., (1998). *The therapeutic state: Justifying government at century's end*. New York: New York University Press.

North Carolina Constitution, Arts. IX, 1; IX, 2(1) (2000).

North Carolina General Statutes, §§ 115C-81; 115C-81(e1)(7)-(8); 115C-81 (a4); 115C-105.45 (1999).

North Dakota Constitution, Arts. VIII, 1; VIII, 2 (2000).

North Dakota Century Code, §§ 15-38-07; 15-41-24 (2000).

Office of Technology Assessment (1991). *Adolescent health*. Congress of the United States, Washington, DC: Government Printing Office.

Official Code of Georgia, §§ 20-2-142; 20-2-143 (2000).

Ogbu, J. I. (1981). Origins of human competence: A cultural-ecological perspective. *Child Development, 52*, 413–429.

Ohio Revised Code Annotated, §§ 3313.66; 3313.663(A); 3319.41 (2000).

O'Keefe, J. M. (1997). Children and community service: Character education in action. *Journal of Education, 179*, 47–62.

Oklahoma Statutes, tit. 70 § 11-103.3 (1999).

O'Neill, W. L. (1971). *Coming apart: An informal history of America in the 1960s*. NY: Quadrangle Books.

Oregon Revised Statutes, § 336.455 (1997).

Orr, D., & Ingersoll, G. (1995). The contribution of level of cognitive complexity and pubertal timing to behavioral risk in young adolescents. *Pediatrics, 95*, 528–533.

Paglia, A., & Room, R. (1999). Preventing substance use problems among youth: A literature review and recommendations. *Journal of Primary Prevention, 20*, 3–50.

Parham v. J. R., 442 U.S. 584 (1979).

Parker, W. C. (1996). "Advanced" ideas about democracy: Toward a pluralist conception of citizen education. *Teachers College Record, 98*, 104–125.

Parker, W. C., & Zumeta, W. (1999). Toward and aristocracy of everyone: Policy study in the high school curriculum. *Theory and Research in Social Education, 27*, 9–44.

Parks, C. P. (1995). Gang behavior in the schools: Reality or myth. *Educational Psychology Review, 7*, 41–68.

Pearson, F. S., & Jackson, T. (1991). Fear of school-related predatory crime. *Sociology and Social Research, 75*, 117–125.

Pedersen, D. M. (1998). A homemade switchblade knife and a bent fork: Judicial place setting and student discipline. *Creighton Law Review, 31*, 1053–1105.

Pellegrini, A. D., Bartini, M., & Brooks, F. (1999). School bullies, victims, and aggressive victims: Factors relating to group affiliation and victimization in early adolescence. *Journal of Educational Psychology, 91*, 216–224.

Pennsylvania Constitution, Art. 3, 14 (2000).

Pennsylvania Statutes, tit 24 § 15-1547 (1999).

Petersen, A. C., Compas, B. E., Brooks-Gunn, J., Stemmler, M., Ey, S., & Grant, K. E. (1993). Depression in adolescence. *American Psychologist, 48*, 155–168.

Petersen, G. J., Pietrzak, D., & Speaker, K. M. (1998). The enemy within: A national study on school violence and prevention. *Urban Education, 33*, 331–359.

Perkinson, H. J. (1995). *The imperfect panacea: American faith in education*. New York: McGraw-Hill

Pfeiffer, S. I., & Reddy, L. A. (1998). School-based mental health programs in the United States: Present Status and a blueprint for the future. *School Psychology Review, 27*, 84–96.

Pianta, R. C., & Walsh, D. J. (1998). Applying the construct of resilience in schools: Cautions for a developmental systems perspective. *School Psychology Review, 27*, 407–419.

Pierce v. Society of Sisters, 268 U.S. 510 (1925).

Platt, A. (1977). *The child savers: The invention of delinquency (2d ed.)*. Chicago, IL: University of Chicago Press.

Plyler v. Doe, 457 U.S. 202 (1982).

Porter, G., Epp, L., & Bryan, S. (2000). Collaboration among school mental health professionals: A Necessity, not a luxury. *Professional School Counseling, 3,* 315–323.

Prawat, R. S. (2000). The two faces of Deweyan Pragmatism: Induction and social constructionism. *Teachers College Record, 102,* 805–840.

Pulliam, J. D., & Van Patten, J. (1999). *History of education in America (7th ed.)*. Upper Saddle River, NJ: Merrill.

Purpel, D. E. (1999). *Moral outrage in education*. New York: Peter Lang.

Pyle, J. J. (1997). Socrates, the schools, and civility: The continuing war between inculcation and inquiry. *Journal of Law and Education, 26,* 65–89.

Quinn, J. (1999). Where need meets opportunity: Youth development programs for early teens. *Future of Children, 9 (Fall),* 96–116.

Rachelson, A. D. (1997). Expelling students who claim to be disabled: Escaping the Individuals With Disabilities Education Act's "stay-put" provisions. *Michigan Law & Policy Review, 2,* 127–158.

Radke-Yarrow, M., & Brown, E. (1993). Resilience and vulnerability in children of multiple risk families. *Development and Psychopathology, 5,* 581–592.

Ramey, C. T., & Ramey, S. L. (1998). Early intervention and early experience. *American Psychologist, 53,* 109–120.

Raskoff, S. A., & Sundeen, R. A. (1999). Community service programs in high schools. *Law & Contemporary Problems, 62,* 73–111.

Ravitch, D. (1985). *The schools we deserve*. New York: Basic Books.

Ravitch, D. (1974). *The great school wars*. New York: Basic Books.

Ravitch, D., & Viteritti, J. (1996). A new vision for city schools. *Public Interest, 122,* 3–16.

Reed, R. R. (1996). Education and the state constitutions: Alternatives for suspended and expelled students. *Cornell Law Review, 81,* 582–622.

Rehabilitation Act of 1973, Section 504, 29 U.S.C. § 701 (Supp. 1994).

Resnick, M. D.,Bearman, P. S., Blum, R. W., Bauman, K. E., Harris, K. M., Jones, J., Tabor, J., Beuhring, T., Sieving, R. E., Shew, M., Ireland, M., Bearinger, L., & Udry, J. R. (1997). Protecting adolescents form harm: Findings from the National Longitudinal Study on Adolescent Health. *Journal of the American Medical Association, 278,* 823–832.

Revised Code of Washington, §§ 28A.170.080; 28A.230.070; 28A.300.270 (2000).

Revised Statutes Missouri, §§ 167.171 (4); 166.260; 161.650 (1999).

Revised Statutes of Nebraska Annotated, §§79-267; 79-713; § 79-712; 79-809 (2000).

Rhode Island General Laws, §§ 16-2-17(a); 16-12-3; 16-21-16; 16-21.2-4; 16-21-7, 16-22-17, 16-22-18 (2000).

Richards, C. L., & Daley, D. (1994). Politics and policy: Driving forces behind sex education in the United States. In J. C. Drolet & K. Clark (Eds). *The sexuality education challenge: Promoting healthy sexuality in young people* (pp. 47–68). Santa Cruz, CA: ETR Associates.

Richards, M. H., & Larson, R. (1993). Pubertal development and the daily subjective states of young adolescents. *Journal of Research on Adolescence, 3,* 145–169.

Rigby, K. (2000). Effects of peer victimization in schools and perceived social support on adolescent well-being. *Journal of Adolescence, 23,* 57–68.

Roberts, M. C. (Ed.) (1996). *Model programs in child and family mental health*. Mahwah, NJ: Erlbaum.

Roeser, R. W., & Eccles, J. S. (1998). Adolescents' perceptions of middle school: Relation to longitudinal changes in academic and psychological adjustment. *Journal of Research on Adolescence, 8,* 123–158.

Roeser, R. W., Eccles, J. S., & Strobel, K. R. (1998). Linking the study of schooling and mental health: Selected issues and empirical illustrations at the level of the individual. *Educational Psychologist, 33*, 153–176.

Rosenberger v. Rector and Visitors of University of Virginia, 115 S.Ct. 2510 (1995).

Rosenthal, B. S. (1998). Non-school correlates of dropout: An integrative review of the literature. *Children and Youth Services Review, 20*, 413–433.

Rotheram-Borus, M. J. (1988). Assertiveness training with children. In R. H. Price, E. L. Cowen, R. P. Lorion & J. Ramos-McKay (Eds.) *Fourteen ounces of prevention: A casebook for practitioners* (pp. 83–97). Washington, DC: American Psychological Association.

Rothman, D. J. (1980). *Conscience and convenience: The asylum and its alternative in progressive America.* Boston: Little, Brown.

Root, S. C. (1997). School-based service: A review of research for teacher educators. In J. A. Erickson & J. Anderson (Eds.) *Learning with the community: Concepts and models for service learning in teacher education* (pp. 42–52). Washington, DC: American Association for Higher Education.

Rutter, M. (1987). Psychosocial resilience and protective mechanisms. *American Journal of Orthopsychiatry, 37*, 317–331.

Rutter, M., Giller, H., & Hagell, A. (1998). *Antisocial behavior by young people.* New York: Cambridge University Press.

Ryan, J. E. (1999). Schools, race, and money. *Yale Law Journal, 109*, 249–316.

Ryan, R. M. (1993). Agency organization: Intrinsic motivation, autonomy, and the self in psychological development. *The Nebraska Symposium on Motivation, 40*, 1–56.

Ryan, R. M., & Deci, E. L. (2000). Self-determination theory and the facilitation of intrinsic motivation, social development, and well-being. *American Psychologist, 55*, 68–78.

Safe Schools Act of 1994, 20 U.S.C. 5961 (1994).

Salomone, R. C. (2000). *Visions of schooling: Conscience, community and common education.* New Haven, CT: Yale University Press.

Sampson, R. J., & Lauritsen, J. L. (1993). Violent victimization and offending: Individual-, situational- and community-level risk factors. In A. J. Reiss, Jr., & J. A. Roth (Eds.) *Understanding and preventing violence. Vol. 3: Social Influences* (pp. 1–114). Washington, DC: National Academy Press.

Samples, F., & Aber, L. (1998). Evaluations of school-based violence prevention programs. In D. S. Elliott, B. A. Hamburg, & K. R. Williams (Eds). *Violence in American schools: A new perspective* (pp. 217–252). New York: Cambridge University Press.

San Antonio Independent School District v. Rodrigues, 411 U.S. 1 (1973).

Santa Fe Independent School District v. Doe, 530 U.S. 290 (2000).

Santelli, J., Vernon, M., Lowry, R., Osorio, J., DuShaw, M., Lancaster, M. S, Pham, N., Song, E., Ginn, E., & Kolbe, L. J. (1998). Managed care, school health programs, and adolescent health services: Opportunities for health promotion. *Journal of School Health, 68*, 434–441.

Sarason, S. (1995). *Parental involvement and the political principle: Why the existing governance structure of schools should be abolished.* San Francisco: Jossey-Bass.

Scales, P. C. (1999). Reducing risks and developing assets: essential actions for promoting adolescent health. *Journal of School Health, 69*, 113–119.

Scales, P. C., Blyth, D. A., Berkas, T. H., & Kielsmeier, J. C. (2000). The effects of service-learning on middle school students' social responsibility and academic success. *Journal of Early Adolescence, 20*, 332–358.

Schneider, B., & Stevenson, D. (1999). *The ambitious generation: America's teenagers, motivated but directionless.* New Haven, CT: Yale University Press.

Schneider, D. M.(1968). *American kinship: A cultural account.* Englewood Cliffs, NJ: Prentice Hall.

Schonert-Reichl, K. A. (1999). Relations of per acceptance, friendship adjustment, and social behavior to moral reasoning during early adolescence. *Journal of Early Adolescence, 19,* 249–279.

School Dist. of Abington Tp., Pa. v. Schempp, 374 U.S. 203 (1963).

Schulenberg, J., Maggs, J., & Hurrelmann K. (Eds.) (1997). *Health risks and developmental transitions during adolescence.* New York: Cambridge University Press.

Scott, E. S., Reppucci, N. D. & Woolard, J. L. (1995). Evaluating adolescent decision making in legal contexts. *Law & Human Behavior, 19,* 221–244,

Scott, E. S., & Grisso, T. (1997). The evolution of adolescence: A developmental perspective on juvenile justice reform. *Journal of Criminal Law & Criminology, 88,* 137–189.

Seidman, E., & French, S. E. (1997). Normative transitions to urban schools during adolescence: The optimal timing and nature of preventive interventions. In H. J. Walberg, O. Reyes, & R. P. Weissberg (Eds.) *Children and youth: Interdisciplinary perspectives* (pp.166–189). Thousand Oaks, CA: Sage.

Seligman, M. E. P., & Csikszentmihalyi, M. (2000). Positive psychology: An introduction. *American Psychologist, 55,* 5–14.

Serow, R. C. (1983). *Schooling for social diversity: An analysis of policy and practice.* New York: Teachers College Press.

Seybolt, R. F. (1969). *Apprenticeship and apprenticeship education in colonial New England and New York, American education: Its men, ideas, and institutions.* New York: Arno Press.

Shedler, J., & Block, J. (1990). Adolescent drug use and psychological health: A longitudinal inquiry. *American Psychologist, 45,* 612–630.

Sheley, J. F., McGee, Z. T., & Wright, J. D. (1995). *Weapon related victimization in selected inner-city high school samples (NCJ-151526).* Rockville, MD: National Criminal Justice Reference Service.

Shields, J. M., & Johnson, J. M. (1992). Collision between law and ethics: Consent for treatment with adolescents. *Bulletin of the American Academy of Psychiatry & Law, 20,* 309–323.

Singer, S. I. (1996). *Recriminalizing delinquency: Violent juvenile crime and juvenile justice reform.* New York: Cambridge University Press.

Skiba, R. J. & Peterson, R. L. (2000). School discipline at a crossroads: From zero tolerance to early response. *Exceptional Children, 66,* 335–346.

Smith, C., & Thornberry, T. P. (1995). The relationship between childhood maltreatment and adolescent involvement in delinquency. *Criminology, 33,* 451–477.

Smith, K. B., & Meier, K. J. (1995). *The case against school choice: Politics, markets, and fools.* Armonk, NY: M.E. Sharpe

Smith, D. S., & Hindus, M. S. (1975). Premarital pregnancy in America 1640–1971: An overview and interpretation. *Journal of Interdisciplinary History, 4,* 537–570.

Snyder, H. N. (1998). Serious, violent and chronic juvenile offenders: An assessment of the extent and trends in officially-recognized serious criminal behavior in a delinquent population. In R. Loeber & D. P. Farrington (Eds.) *Serious and violent juvenile offenders: Risk factors and successful interventions* (pp. 428–444). Thousand Oaks, CA: Sage.

Snyder, H. N., & Sickmund, M. (1995). *Juvenile offenders and victims: A national report.* Office of Juvenile Justice and Delinquency Prevention. National Center for Juvenile Justice. August.

Sousa, C. A. (1999). Teen dating violence: The hidden epidemic. *Family & Conciliation Courts Review, 37,* 356–374.

South Carolina Code Annotated, §§ 59-32-5 (1999).

South Dakota Codified Laws, §§ 13-32-3; 13-33A-1 (2000).

Speicher, B. (1994). Family patterns of moral judgment during adolescence and early adulthood. *Developmental Psychology, 30,* 624–632.

Spergel, I. A. (1995). *The youth gang problem: A community approach.* New York: Oxford University Press.

Spivack, G., & Shure, M. B. (1974). *Social adjustment of young children: A cognitive approach to solving real-life problems.* San Francisco: Jossey-Bass.

Spring, J. (1997). *The American school: 1642-1996* (4th ed.). New York: McGraw Hill.

Stein, N. (1999). *Classrooms & courtrooms: Facing sexual harassment in K-12 schools.* New York: Teachers College Press.

Steinberg, L. (1990). Autonomy, conflict, and harmony in the family: In S. Feldman & G. Elliott (Eds.) *At the threshold: The developing adolescent* (pp. 255–276). Cambridge, MA: Harvard University Press.

Steinberg, L. (1996). *Beyond the classroom: Why school reform has failed and what parents need to do.* NY: Simon & Schuster.

Steinberg, L. (1999). *Adolescence* (5th ed.). Boston: McGraw Hill.

Steinberg, L., & Cauffman, E. (1996). Maturity and judgment in adolescence: Psychosocial factors in adolescent decision making. *Law and Human Behavior, 20,* 249–272.

Stern, S. B., Smith, C. A., & Jan, S. J. (1999). Urban families and adolescent mental health. *Social Work Research, 23,* 15–28.

Strasburger, V. C. (1997). "Sex, drugs, rock'n roll" and the media: Are the media responsible for adolescent behavior? *Adolescent Medicine: State of the Art Reviews, 8,* 403–414.

Stone, F. M. & Boundy, K. B. (1994). School violence: The need for a meaningful response. *Clearinghouse Review, 28,* 453–465.

Striegel-Moore, R. H., & Cachelin, F. M. (1999). Body image concerns and disordered eating in adolescent girls: Risk and protective factors. In N. G. Johnson, M. C. Roberts & J. Worell (Eds.) *Beyond appearance: A new look at adolescent girls* (pp. 85–108). Washington, DC: American Psychological Association.

Sugarman, S. D. (1991). Using private schools to promote public values. *University of Chicago Legal Forum, 1991,* 171–210.

Sutton, J. R. (1988). *Stubborn children: Controlling delinquency in the United States.* Berkeley: University of California Press.

Swenson, K. (2000). School finance reform litigation: Why are some state supreme courts activist and others restrained? *Albany Law Review, 63,* 1147–1182.

Tappan, M. B. (1998). Moral education in the zone of proximal development. *Journal of Moral Education, 27,* 141–161.

Tedeschi, J., & Felson, R. B. (1994). *Violence, aggression and coercive actions.* Washington, DC: American Psychological Association.

Teitelbaum, L. E., & Harris, L. J. (1977). Some historical perspectives on the governmental regulation of children and parents. In L. E. Teitlbaum & A. R. Gough (Eds.) *Beyond control: Status offenders in the juvenile court* (pp. 1–44). Cambridge, MA: Ballinger.

Tennessee Code Annotated §§ 49-1-214; 49-6-1005, 49-6-1007; 49-6-1301; 49-6-3401; 49-6-4203 (1999).

Texas Education Code, § 4.001; 21.101(d); 28.002; § 28.004; 37.007; 37.001(e); 37.001(d)(3); 38.011(2000).

Thomas, C. W., & Bishop, D. M. (1984). The effect of formal and informal sanctions on delinquency: A longitudinal comparison of labeling and deterrence theories. *Journal of Criminal Law & Criminology, 75,* 1222–1245.

Thornberry, T. P., Krohn, M. D., Lizotte, A. J., & Chard-Wierschem, D. (1993). The role of juvenile gangs in facilitating delinquent behavior. *Journal of Research in Crime and Delinquency, 30,* 55–87.

Tinker v. Des Moines Independent Community School District, 393 U.S. 503 (1969).

Title VI of the Civil Rights Act of 1964, 42 U.S.C. § 2000d (Supp. 1994).

Title IX of the Education Amendments of 1972, 20 U.S.C. § 1681 (a) (Supp. 1994).

Title IX., Pub. L. No. 92–318, 86 Stat. 235 (1999).

Title 42, U.S.C. § 1983 (1998).

Thorpe, F. N. (1909). *The federal and state constitutions, colonial charters, and other organic laws of the states, territories, and colonies now and heretofore forming the United States of America.* Washington, DC: Government Printing Office.

Tobler, N. S., & Stratton, H. H. (1997). Effectiveness of school-based drug prevention programs: A meta-analysis of the research. *Journal of Primary Prevention, 18,* 71–128.

Tones, K., & Tilford, S. (1994). *Health education: Effectiveness, efficiency and equity* (2nd ed.). London: Chapman & Hall.

Tonry, M. (1999). Rethinking unthinkable punishment policies in America. *UCLA Law Review, 46,* 1751–1791.

Torney-Purta, J. (1990). Youth in relation to social institutions. In S. Feldman & G. Elliott (Eds.) *At the threshold: The developing adolescent* (pp. 457–478). Cambridge, MA: Harvard University Press.

Townsend, B. L. (2000). The disproportionate discipline of African American learners: Reducing school suspensions and expulsions. *Exceptional Children, 66,* 381–391.

Trevarthen, C. (1993). The function of emotions in early infant communication and development. In J. Nadel & L. Camainoi (Eds.) *New perspectives in early communicative development* (pp. 48–81). London: Routledge.

Troen, S. K. (1985). Technological development and adolescence: The early twentieth century. *Journal of Early Adolescence, 5,* 429–439.

Trudell, B. K. (1985). The first organized campaign for school sex education: A source of critical questions about current efforts. *Journal of Sex Education and Therapy, 11,* 10–16.

Tyack, D., & Hansot, E. (1982). *Managers of virtue.* New York: Basic Books.

Tyack, D. (1976). Ways of seeing: An essay on the history of compulsory schooling. *Harvard Educational Review, 46,* 355–389.

Tyack, D., James, T., & Benovot, A. (1987). *Law and the shaping of public education, 1785–1954.* Madison: University of Wisconsin Press.

Ungar, M. T. (2000). The myth of peer pressure. *Adolescence, 35,* 167–180.

United States v. Lopez, 514 U.S. 549 (1995).

Urban, W. L., & Wagoner, J. L., Jr. (1996). *American education: A history.* New York: McGraw Hill.

Utah Administrative Regulations, 277-105-5C (1995).

Utah Code Annotated, §§ 53A-11-904 ;53A-13-101; 53A-13-101(4); 53A-13-101.2 (2000).

Utman, C. H. (1997). Performance effects of motivational state: A meta-analysis. *Personality and Social Psychology Review, 1,* 170–182.

Verba, S., Schlozman, K. L., & Brady, H. E. (1995). *Voice and equality: Civic voluntarism in American politics.* Cambridge, MA: Harvard University Press.

Verchick, R. R. (1991). Engaging the spectrum: Civic virtue and the protection of student voice in school-sponsored forums. *John Marshall Law Review, 24,* 339–391.

Veronia School District v. Acton, 515 U.S. 646 (1995).

Vermont Statutes Annotated, tit. 16 §§ 906; 910 (2000).

Vigil, J. D. (1999). Streets and schools: How educators can help Chicano marginalized gang youth. *Harvard Educational Review, 69,* 270–288.

Virginia Code Annotated §§ 22.1-207; 22.1-207.1; 22.1-278; 22.1-279.3 (2000).

Virginia Constitution, Arts. I, § 15; VIII, § 1 (2000).

Wade, R. C. (1997). Community service learning and social studies curriculum: Challenges to effective practice. *The Social Studies, 88,* 197–202.

Wade, R. C., & Saxe, D. W. (1996). Community service learning in the social studies: Historical roots, empirical evidence, critical issues. *Theory & Research in Social Education, 24,* 331–359.

Walker, L., & Taylor, J. (1991). Family interaction and the development of moral reasoning. *Child Development, 62,* 264–283.

Walkerdine, V. (1981). On the regulation of speaking and silence: Subjectivity, class, and gender in contemporary schooling. In C. Steedman, C. Urwin, & V. Walkerdine (Eds.) *Language, gender, and childhood* (pp. 203–241). Boston: Routledge and Kegan Paul.

Wall, H. M. (1990). *Fierce communion: Family and community in early America.* Cambridge, MA: Harvard University Press.

Wallace, J. M., Jr., & Forman, T. A. (1998). Religion's role in promoting health and reducing risk among American youth. *Health Education & Behavior, 25,* 721–742.

Walton v. Alexander, 20 F.3d 1350 (5th Cir. 1994).

Warman, D. M., & Cohen, R. (2000). Stability of aggressive behaviors and children's peer relationships. *Aggressive Behavior, 26,* 277–290.

Warner, B. S., Weist, M. D., & Krulak, A. (1999). Risk factors for school violence. *Urban Education, 34,* 52–68.

Washington Constitution, Art. IX, 2 (2000).

Weist, Mark D. (1997). Expanded school mental health services: A national movement in progress. In T. J. Ollendick & R. J. Prinz (Eds.) *Advances in clinical child psychology* (Vol. 19, pp. 319–352). New York: Plenum.

Weisz, J. E., Weiss, B., & Donenberg, G. R. (1992). The lab versus the clinic. *American Psychologist, 47,* 1578–1595.

Weiner, B. (1995). *Inferences of responsibility: A foundation for a theory of social conduct.* New York: Guilford.

Welsh, W. N., Greene, J. R., & Jenkins, P. H. (1999). School disorder: The influence of individual, institutional, and community factors. *Criminology, 37,* 73–115.

Welsh, W. N., Jenkins, P. H., & Greene, J. R. with Caron, D., Hoffman, E., Kurtz, E., Perone, D., & Stokes, R. (1996). *Building a culture and climate of safety in public schools in Philadelphia: School based management and violence reduction.* Final report to the National Institute of Justice, under award no. 93-IJ-CX-0038. Washington, DC: U.S. Department of Justice, National Institute of Justice.

West Virginia Code, § 18-2-7b; 18-2-9(b) (2000).

West Virginia State Board of Education v. Barnette, 319 U.S. 624 (1943).

Werthamer-Larsson, L. (1994). Methodological issues in school-based services research. *Journal of Clinical Child Psychology, 23,* 121–132.

Wyoming Statute Annotated §§ 21-2-205, 21-4-306 (2000).

Wiebe, R. H. (1967). *The search for order, 1877–1920.* New York: Hill and Wang.

Williams, C., & Bybee, J. (1994). What do children feel guilty about? Developmental and gender differences. *Developmental Psychology, 30,* 617–623.

Wilson, D., Rodrigue, J. R., & Taylor, W. C. (Eds.) (1997). *Health promoting and health compromising behaviors among minority adolescents.* Washington, DC: American Psychological Association.

Wilson, J. Q., & Petersilia, J. (1995). *Crime.* San Francisco, CA: Institute for Contemporary Studies Press.

Wilson, J., & Musick, M. (1999). The effects of volunteering on the volunteer. *Law & Contemporary Problems, 62,* 141–168.

Wisconsin Constitution, Art. 10, 3 (2000).

Wisconsin Statutes Annotated, § 118.019 (2000).

Wisconsin v. Yoder, 406 U.S. 205 (1972).

Wood v. Strickland, 420 U.S. 308 (1975).

Woodhouse, Barbara B. (1992). "Who owns the child?": *Meyer* and *Pierce* and the child as property. *William and Mary Law Review, 33,* 995–1122.

Yates, M., & Youniss, J. (1996). A developmental perspective on community service. *Social Development*, 5, 85 111.

Yoshikawa, H. (1994). Prevention as cumulative protection: Effects of early family support and educaiton on chronic delinquency and its risks. *Psychological Bulletin*, 115, 28–54.

Youniss, J., McLellan, J. A., & Yates, M. (1997). What we know about engendering civic identity. *American Behavioral Scientist*, 40, 620–631.

Youniss, J., & Smollar, J. (1985). *Adolescent relations with mothers, fathers, and friends*. Chicago: University of Chicago Press.

Youniss, J., & Yates, M. (1999). Youth service and moral-civic identity: A case for everyday morality. *Educational Psychology Review*, 11, 361–376.

Youniss, J., & Yates, M. (1997). *Community service and social responsibility in youth*. Chicago, IL: University of Chicago Press.

Youngberg v. Romeo, 457 U.S. 307 (1982).

Zelizer, V. A. (1985). *Pricing the priceless child: The changing social value of children*. New York: Free Press.

Zimring, F. E., & Hawkins, G. (1995). *Incapacitation: Penal confinement and the restraint of crime*. New York: Oxford University Press.

Index